· ESTONIA ·

Westview Series on the Post-Soviet Republics
Alexander J. Motyl, Series Editor

· ESTONIA ·
Return to Independence

REIN TAAGEPERA

Published in cooperation with
The Harriman Institute

WESTVIEW PRESS
Boulder · San Francisco · Oxford

Westview Series on the Post-Soviet Republics

Chapter 4 is largely condensed from Romuald Misiunas and Rein Taagepera, *The Baltic States: Years of Dependence 1940–1980* (Berkeley: University of California Press), copyright © 1983 by Romuald Misiunas and Rein Taagepera. Reprinted with permission of University of California Press.

Published in 1993 in the United States of America by Westview Press, Inc., 5500 Central Ave-nue, Boulder, Colorado 80301-2877, and in the United Kingdom by Westview Press, 36 Lonsdale Road, Summertown, Oxford OX2 7EW

Library of Congress Cataloging-in-Publication Data
Taagepera, Rein.
  Estonia : return to independence / Rein Taagepera.
    p.   cm. — (Westview series on the post-Soviet republics)
  Includes bibliographical references (p.   ) and index.
  ISBN 0-8133-1199-3 (hard). — ISBN 0-8133-1703-7 (pbk.)
    1. Estonia—History.   I. Title.   II. Series.
DK503.54.T33   1993
947'.41—dc20   92-21376
                                                                              CIP

Printed and bound in the United States of America

The paper used in this publication meets the requirements of the American National Standard for Permanence of Paper for Printed Library Materials Z39.48-1984.

10   9   8   7   6   5   4   3

· Contents ·

Illustrations
and Tables

· Preface ·

The past and the present are intertwined. History cannot be written "as it actually took place." One has to weigh and select, and this means that one inevitably uses filters. Historians who pretend to be neutral merely are saying they have never seriously questioned their biases. Facing our biases does not abolish them, but this is the only way to try to attenuate the effect of filters. What are some of my filters?

There is the filter of a boy of eight hiding in the rye while some village buildings were burning and Soviet troops lined his parents against a wall (they escaped)—and who soon after heard that people he knew had vanished in the antioccupation reaction on trumped-up charges. There is also the filter of a teenager sensing the incongruity of his being part of the French colonial society in Morocco while Russians were colonizing his homeland. Further, there is the Ph.D. physicist trained to ask "But is another explanation possible, and how do you get the precise data needed to tell the difference?" And so on.

Another set of filters made itself felt in September 1991 as Estonia finally regained its independence. One year earlier, when I proposed to Westview Press the title *Estonia: Return to Independence*, it was an informed act of faith; it still was so in July 1991 as I was completing the draft manuscript. Then, sticking to travel plans made far in advance, I arrived in Estonia on 25 August 1991—five days after Estonia's proclamation of immediate independence, adopted in the midst of a messy coup in Moscow. Two weeks later, fifty countries, including the United States and, finally, the USSR, had recognized Estonia's return to independence. I found myself chairing the first public meeting of a brand new People's Center Party and was elected to the Estonian Constitutional Assembly—its only member to reside in the Western Hemisphere. These were heady days. Obligingly, reality had adjusted itself to my book title. But what about the filter?

When I read my draft in light of Estonia's regained independence, many events as far back as 1938 suddenly looked different; their interpretation and relative importance had changed. I also faced a different readership. One deep bias we all share is a liking for the status quo, provided it does not affect us negatively in a direct way. Except for improving our own situation, we wish the rest of the world to remain comfortably unchanged. I remember a colleague patiently trying to persuade me in May 1991 of the economic inadvisability and, indeed, impossibility of Estonia's independence—and happily congratulating me on that same independence in September. He had not reversed his position. He remained a staunch proponent of the status quo in faraway places. It was the status quo that had shifted, and Estonia's independence now was part of it.

Thus, apart from my own biases, I had to adjust to a changed attitude on the part of prospective readers. In July 1991, the title *Estonia: Return to Independence* was disquietingly anti–status quo and had to be defended against all sorts of objections. In 1993, it is likely to be a comfortingly pro–status quo statement (unless catastrophic reversals take place). Accordingly, the average reader's reception of even the nineteenth-century history of Estonia would be different.

Mikhail Gorbachev's abdication and the formal end of the USSR in December 1991 again changed the status quo and hence our perception of the past. My criticism of Gorbachev in Chapters 6 and 7, written while his tanks still threatened Estonia, might sound in 1993 as if I was whipping a dead horse. And when the United States recognized the independence of Kazakhstan in December 1991, less than four months after recognizing the Estonian resumption of independence, the tireless Estonian efforts toward that goal during the preceding years looked less crucial than they did in September 1991.

Thus, history cannot be *perceived* as it actually unfolded, because perception belongs to the present. Inescapably, as we interpret and reinterpret past events in light of what followed, the past and the present become intertwined.

* * *

An earlier book I coauthored on the Baltic states (Misiunas and Taagepera 1983) was called "encyclopedic" by one critic, and he had a point. The subject matter was so wide-ranging and novel that the essential facts crowded out the evaluation of them. Because of the existence of that previous book, the narrower geographic scope of the present one, and Toivo Raun's recent and thoroughly documented *Estonia and the Estonians* (1991a), I have been able to take a different approach this time. I often ask: "What is the overall meaning of this mass of facts?" and give my answer for the reader to accept, reject, or hold in abeyance. As for details, I refer to earlier books, especially for pre-1980 history. The second half of the present book deals with the events and issues of the last ten years, the events that led Estonia from a totally silenced colony to recovery of its independence, and more detail is given for this period. The bibliography includes works on all periods of history but especially those published since 1982 in English.

I do not believe that dryness in language adds to the scholarly quality of a book or that the pronoun "I" should be banned. I have by now written all too many articles, especially on electoral systems worldwide, to show that I am no stranger to traditional scholarly style. Here, I have chosen a more personal style, one that retains ample emphasis on scholarship yet will be accessible to a variety of readers.

Translation of names of organizations always presents problems. When it precedes a noun, the term *Eesti* could mean either ethnically Estonian or territorially "of Estonia," whereas *Eestimaa* has only the latter meaning. To maintain the distinction, I have translated *Eesti* as "Estonian" and *Eestimaa* as "of Estonia" when these terms precede a noun in a post-1980 name. All translations of passages and poems from Estonian are mine, unless otherwise indicated.

I thank Küllo Arjakas, Karl Aun, Peet Kask, Evald Laasi, Vello Pettai, and especially Toivo Raun for valuable comments on the manuscript. Chapter 4 (1945–1980) is largely condensed from Romuald Misiunas and Rein Taagepera, *The Baltic States: Years of Dependence 1940–1980,* copyright © 1983 Romuald Misiunas and Rein Taagepera. I am using this material with the kind permission of the University of California Press.

Most of the photographs in the book are by Kalju Suur; three are by Heldur Napp, Mart Niklus, and T. Hellam; and several are reproduced from *Meie Maa* (1955–1957) and *Eesti Vabariik 1918–1940* (1968), published by Eesti Kirjanike Kooperatiiv (EKK) (Estonian Writers Cooperative) in Lund, Sweden. All these are used by permission. One photo by an unknown photographer was handed to me in 1987 by two students who tried to make the situation in Estonia 1987 known to the world, and one comes from *Tartu* (1960), Eesti Riiklik Kirjastus (ERK) (Estonian State Publishers). I thank them all.

Rein Taagepera

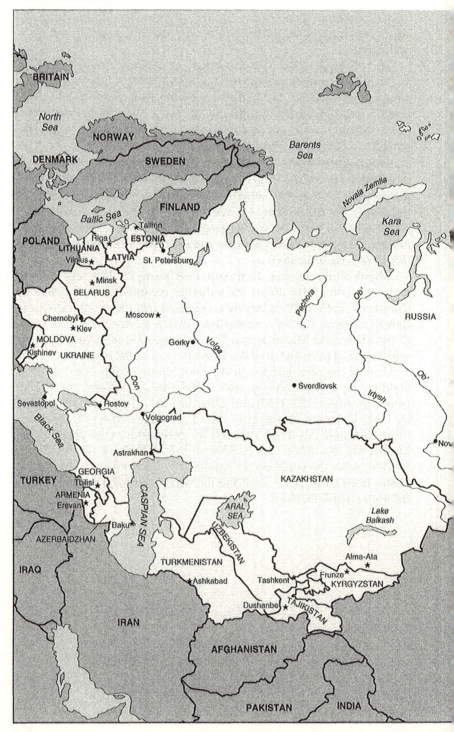

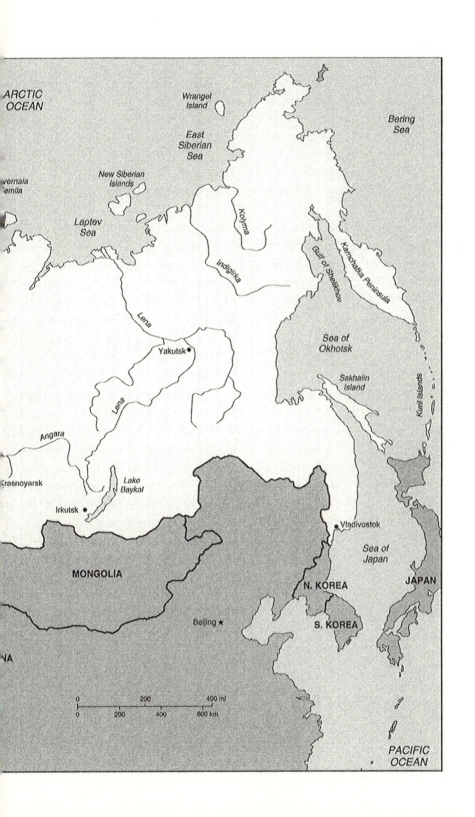

ARCTIC
OCEAN

Wrangel
Island

Bering
Sea

East
Siberian
Sea

vernaia
emila

New Siberian
Islands

Kolyma

Laptev
Sea

Indigirka

Gulf of Shelikhov

Kamchatka Peninsula

Lena

Yakutsk

Sea of
Okhotsk

Sakhalin
Island

Kuril Islands

Lena

Angara

Lake
Baykal

Krasnoyarsk

Irkutsk

Vladivostok

Sea of
Japan

JAPAN

MONGOLIA

N. KOREA

Beijing ★

S. KOREA

NA

0   200   400 ml
0   200   400   600 km

PACIFIC
OCEAN

· ESTONIA ·

· ONE ·

Estonia's Role
in the World

Estonia exists. That much is by now certain for the informed observer. Some may have had doubts in the early 1980s, but only if they restricted themselves to the political aspect. As a nation with a definite cultural-linguistic self-identity, Estonia always continued to exist, despite a long period of political submergence.

Does it matter? The world would not collapse if Estonia ceased to exist. Come to think of it, the world would not collapse either if Russia ceased to exist, since it has survived the demise of Sumeria and the Incan Empire. But it would be a different world. How would the world be different without Estonia?

I shall begin with Estonia's unique pioneering in two aspects of human relations: successful practice of peaceful methods during intense political struggle and implementation of cultural autonomy for ethnolinguistic minorities. Next, I will indicate how Estonia's small size is not just a liability but also an asset. Finally, the country's geographical destiny as a bridge between Western and Eastern Europe will be outlined, and some of Estonia's cultural-scientific contributions will be indicated.[1]

A LABORATORY OF PEACEFUL METHODS
OF POLITICAL STRUGGLE

In 1991, Estonia regained independence, after four years of intense political struggle and without a single politically motivated death or even (to the best of my knowledge) hospitalization. Twentieth-century Europe has seen several other bloodless political separations: Norway from Sweden in 1905, Iceland from Denmark in 1944, and Malta from Britain in 1964. But Estonia separated from the Soviet Union under more adverse circumstances. Given the large number of recent Russian colonists understandably reluctant to give up their language and housing privileges, Estonia had a population mix similar to that in Algeria in the late 1950s, which had

1

Estonia's Geopolitical Location, 1990s

led to a very nasty struggle. To turn an Algeria-like amalgam of groups into a Norway-like outcome must be considered a triumph deserving of a Nobel peace prize!

This achievement reflects favorably not only on Estonians but also on the Russian colonists and the Soviet occupation garrisons, because in a tense situation it takes only one violent party to have bloodshed (as occurred with Soviet "insecurity" forces in neighboring Lithuania and Latvia). In part, Estonia was lucky; Soviet insecurity troops simply gunned down unarmed Latvians and Lithuanians, no questions asked. But it is a type of luck that would be inconceivable in much of Europe, from Northern Ireland to Southern Ossetia. It seems that in much of the world, the cultural reflex is to shoot first and negotiate later, and Estonia's own past offers examples of such violence—all the more the reason to ask how Estonia kept its struggle peaceful this time.

What is it in the Estonian culture that kept Estonia away from violence? When and how did it develop, under which circumstances, and how was it transmitted to the Russian colonists? How was it conveyed to Soviet troops, including the tank crews rushed in from Russia on the very day of Estonia's resumption of independence (20 August 1991), that there was no hurry to start shooting immediately? What were the networks of communication among the Estonian government, the local Soviet military commanders, and the colonist leaders who repeatedly considered proclaiming a secessionist colonial enclave? And in terms of political culture, why did the occasionally bloody fights between Estonian and Russian youth gangs that occurred during the period of colonization subside in the late 1980s, when the rising political tension could have supplied those who ached for a fight with a patriotic veneer?

The answers to such questions need a special sociological and micropolitical research project. Chapters 5 through 7 of this book supply some background materials and reinforce the message that such questions are of worldwide interest. By the time this volume is read, Estonia's luck may have run out and blood may have been spilled in some unpredictable circumstances. Such a development would not undo the record, however: that a small country reachieved independence through a very intense yet peaceful four-year political struggle. To delay violence is the first step toward avoiding it.

A MODEL CULTURAL AUTONOMY FOR MINORITIES

The prospect of continued nonviolence in Estonian ethnic politics is reinforced by Estonia's exemplary handling of ethnolinguistic minorities during its previous period of independence (1918–1940), discussed in Chapter 3. Concentrated minority populations made use of the usual local government and taxation mechanisms, but even those who were dispersed could do so through nonterritorial cultural autonomy. The latter implemented certain proposals made by Otto Bauer and Karl Renner regarding Austria-Hungary, though these came too late to solve the nationalities problems of that empire. To quote Arend Lijphart's *Democracies* (1984:183–184), a worldwide analysis of democratic institutions and practices:

> The first practical application of the Bauer-Renner proposals occurred in Estonia in 1925. Cultural minorities of a given minimum size were given the right to establish their own schools and cultural institutions, governed by elected councils with legislative and taxing powers. The jurisdiction of these cultural councils was defined in terms of membership in a cultural community regardless of geographical residence. The Russian and Swedish minorities did not set up such cultural councils, mainly because they were geographically concentrated and could therefore use local self-governmental institutions. However, the more scattered German and Jewish minorities

did make use of the opportunity of the new law, and their cultural councils soon proved successful.

Estonia's seems to be the only successful attempt to apply such "corporate federalism," and thus it is of worldwide importance for solving ethnic tensions. Why was it successful in Estonia, and why only in Estonia?

In fall 1991, cultural autonomy legislation similar to that of 1925 was winding its way through the Estonian parliament, but the country's ethnic composition had changed dramatically. Germans and Swedes had returned to their ancestral lands during World War II, and many of those Jews who escaped the German occupation had emigrated in the 1970s and 1980s. The Russian component had increased from 8 percent to over 30 percent, and Ukrainians and Belarusians had become significant minorities. How would cultural autonomy fare under these new conditions? Even if it failed (which I do not expect), we would learn more about the conditions under which nonterritorial cultural autonomy can succeed. Estonia continues to be a laboratory of international importance for peaceful and fair interactions between majority and ethnic minority populations.

I hasten to say that Estonians are not flawless—if they were, their solutions would be irrelevant to the rest of this world. Estonians have their share of intolerance, racism, hatred, envy, emotionalism, opportunism, and anger. But their successes in bloodless political struggle and cultural autonomy for minorities have come despite such tendencies, sometimes even as a conscious counteraction to what has been said to be a wolf in every human (and I apologize to the wolves for this blatant speciesism!).

THE IMPORTANCE OF BEING THE SMALLEST

Estonia is the world's smallest continental nation-state with its own distinct language and a fully developed modern culture based on this language. These features warrant some explanation before I indicate why smallness is of interest.

Estonia has a population of one million Estonians and half a million recent colonists and an area of close to 50,000 square kilometers. One-fifth of the member states of the United Nations are less populous than Estonia, and one-fourth have a smaller area. In this sense, Estonia is not among the tiniest independent countries. However, many of the least populous countries do not have a distinct national language, and those that do have not achieved a fully developed modern culture based on that language. One can read Miguel Cervantes or Yasunari Kawabata, consult a nine-volume encyclopedia, go to the opera, or study quantum mechanics—all using the Estonian language. Such richness of activity is available in only one other language spoken by a mere million or fewer people: Icelandic.

Much larger than Estonia in geographical area, Iceland has developed a modern culture on the basis of only a quarter million speakers of Icelandic—a process aided by the island's being sheltered by hundreds of kilometers of sea all around it. Estonia has been anything but sheltered, as illustrated during its long history by invasions and foreign rules originating from the east, the south, and the west.

Why has the Estonian language succeeded when all other languages with so few speakers have not, except the insular Icelandic? One reason is that Estonia too is quasi-insular. To the north, it faces the Gulf of Finland; to the west the Baltic Sea separates it from Sweden; to the east most of its border with Russia is Lake Peipsi, one of the largest in Europe. Only to the south does Estonia lack a clear geographical border, but there it faces Latvia, which is only slightly larger than Estonia. However, Estonia lacks mountains, another geographical feature that helps shelter peoples. Moreover, the surrounding bodies of water are so narrow that they have served as roadways as much as barriers. Nevertheless, a map of Europe reveals many equally isolated corners where a small language area could have survived and developed but did not.

Thus, we have to consider the language itself.[2] Estonian belongs to the Finno-Ugric family of languages, which once were spoken throughout the area ranging from the Volga River to the Arctic Ocean and from the Ural Mountains to the Baltic Sea. They survive in Hungary, Finland, Estonia, and, precariously, near the Volga (Mordvin, Mari, Udmurt, Komi). In the western half of the former Finnic realm, several Finnic languages are still spoken by some hundred thousand people, but only Finnish and Estonian, both in quasi-insular surroundings,[3] have developed into modern all-purpose languages. Most languages in Europe belong to the Indo-European language family, and the drastically different grammar and basic vocabulary of the Finnic languages certainly made a gradual absorption more difficult; it also hindered the ability of Finnic populations to access new ideas and technologies useful for survival.

A third factor intervened. Both Finland and Estonia were at the border of the Catholic/Protestant and the Orthodox branches of Christianity. Although the resulting wars and conquests brought hardships, they also helped build up a separate identity. Actually, the religion factor was somewhat interrelated with the two others: Geography and language contributed to fixing the religious borders. (The extent to which these observations also apply to Latvia and Lithuania is discussed in the next chapter.)

In sum, Estonia became the smallest continental language area in the world to break through to modern culture because a small quasi-insular area (1) had a language very different from that of most of its neighbors, (2) was geographically and politically isolated from its linguistic kinfolk, and (3) was strategically set so that its peculiarities could fix a major religious-cultural border at that location and thus reinforce its distinct identity. In terms of geographical and linguistic isolation, the Welsh, the Bretons, and the Basques come close, but they are not located near a cultural border zone.

To all these objective reasons (or rationalizations) one must add random luck (although Estonia's history often looks pretty unlucky) and/or some special resilience. Whereas the Finns' self-characterization includes the largely positive *sisu* (resilience, guts), the Estonians' *jonn* (grit) has multiple connotations ranging from persistence and endurance to obstinacy, stubbornness, self-will, willfulness, caprice, and spite (Saagpakk 1982:192). Less appreciated by the Estonians themselves than by outsiders, this potentially divisive characteristic is compensated for by a remarkable ability to cooperate under some conditions.

"National character" is a murky field of inquiry that has no easy answers, but some quality in Estonians has enabled them to survive and develop with an extremely small population, though their numbers have not grown but have remained at that precarious size. Compared with some other equally small modernizing nations of a hundred years ago, Estonians have remained at one million, while Slovaks and Albanians have multiplied to several million. As the world population grew from one to five billion, the Estonians had zero population growth, partly through foreign-induced losses but mainly because of a low birthrate. Perhaps a world that emulates Estonia's low birthrate would be a gentler world.

Let us now consider the importance of being the smallest nation-state. Besides being worth an entry in the record books and offering intellectual interest, a country of borderline size is a useful case to scholars and policymakers when the question arises of whether modernization in a given area is better carried out through developing a local premodern language or making its speakers shift to another language. Estonia's emergence during the nineteenth century (see Chapter 2) supplies some basis for estimating under what conditions peasant languages are worth developing.

Both options—developing such a language or learning an already developed one—represent investments, though very different ones. Losing one's cultural roots, as anchored in language and folklore, can be traumatic, especially in the midst of radical economic change. Yet adhering to a local language can impede contacts with the world permanently, although the disadvantage has been reduced, somewhat paradoxically, by the worldwide shift to English. In many areas of the world, several foreign languages were required in the early 1900s—German and Russian, and preferably also English and French, in the case of Estonia—but only two languages would be needed in the future: the local and English.[4] Estonia's history suggests that under certain conditions even a language spoken by only a million people can be used as a vehicle of modernization.

A BRIDGE BETWEEN WESTERN AND EASTERN EUROPE

Europe has always been more than its Atlantic seacoast. Its composers include Liszt, Sibelius, and Tchaikovsky. Its science includes Mendeleyev's periodic table, Bolyai's geometry, and the astronomy of Copernicus. Europe extends all the way to the Urals. But this Europe has repeatedly been split into East and West—in 395, in 1054, and again in 1945. Along with many other nations, Estonia straddles this intra-European fault line. Estonia uses the Latin script and shares in the Protestant values, but has been ruled from the East for several centuries. It has been a military and a cultural battlefield, an advanced defense position, or a *cordon sanitaire* of one or the other half of Europe. But it has also been a bridge.

Being a bridge will be a major role for Estonia and its neighbors as the two halves of Europe begin to merge. A glance at a map may suggest that Estonia, Latvia, and even Lithuania might be marginal to this healing of Europe compared with Poland, Hungary, Belarus, or Ukraine. However, the northern location of the Baltic states is compensated for by their maritime connections and population mix. A successful bridge nation needs a spirit of dignified accommodation and an understanding of both sides of Europe. Estonia and its neighbors may qualify. They may evolve into a Baltic bridge in the new downtown of Europe.[5]

ESTONIA'S CONTRIBUTION TO WORLD CULTURE

Smallness in area and population is no absolute barrier to cultural greatness—witness Athens—and Estonia's contribution to world culture should be considered. The outcome is honorable mention but hardly any first prizes.

The first cultural figure of some renown emanating from Estonia was the Spanish court painter Michel Sittow, also known as Miguel Sittoz (1469–1525). Tartu University was founded four years earlier than Harvard, but it was soon closed for a century. During this period, the only semimajor addition to Estonians who affected the world was a former serf who briefly led the Russian army against Napoleon under the name of General Johann von Michelson (1735–1807).

In the nineteenth century, Estonia began to contribute to world science, although the people involved did not identify themselves as Estonians. The world's first measurement of the distance of a fixed star was carried

The main building of Tartu University, built 1803–1809, still serves its original educational purpose. F. Schlater's lithograph 1852. Reproduced from *Tartu* (1960), Eesti Riiklik Kirjastus.

out at Tartu University (1837) by Friedrich G. W. Struve (1793–1864). Scientists born in Estonia included Karl Ernst von Baer (1792–1876), founder of embryology, Karl Claus (1796–1864), who discovered the element ruthenium; and Heinrich F. Emil Lenz (1804–1856), the originator of the Lenz rule of electromagnetic induction. Tartu University graduate Wilhelm Ostwald (1853–1932) won the Nobel chemistry prize in 1909.

Twentieth century major Estonian-born scientists include neurosurgeon Ludvig Puusepp (1875–1942), astronomers Ernst Öpik (1893–1988) and Jüri Toomre (b. 1940); and Lauri Vaska (b. 1925), the inventor of the Vaska compound in organic chemistry. In literary studies, Juri Lotman (b. 1922) of Tartu University is internationally known for his work in semiotics and structuralism. The music of Eduard Tubin (1905–1982) and Arvo Pärt (b. 1935) has lately received worldwide exposure (see Ashby 1987), and Neeme Järvi (b. 1937) has conducted symphony orchestras on several continents.

The period of Soviet occupation was not conducive to full development of talent. All too often, merely adequate performance was praised and true originality was spurned, and interaction with the world at large was severely restricted. Pärt and Järvi were forced to leave to the West in 1979 (see Järvi 1987). To what extent Estonia's contribution to world culture will expand under conditions of independence remains to be seen. Increased participation will depend largely on whether the country's general cultural atmosphere can be purged of the provincial mix of smugness and hesitancy and can promote a demanding self-confidence.

As of now, Estonia's most visible role in the world is pioneering in various types of social relations: peaceful methods of political struggle, cultural autonomy, the implications of smallness, and East-West relations.

NOTES

1. For basic information on Estonia, a thorough and up-to-date source is *The Baltic States: A Reference Book*, Tallinn/Riga/Vilnius: Estonian, Latvian, and Lithuanian Encyclopedia Publishers, 1991. This 266-page book has various statistics and overviews of geography, history, culture, and politics. It also has a telephone directory for government agencies, tourist attractions, businesses, media, and so on, and short biographies and addresses of some 1,500 Baltic public figures. The five-page phrase section helps, incidentally, to give one an idea of the differences among the Estonian, Latvian, and Lithuanian languages.

2. An overview of the Estonian language is given in the Introduction of Paul F. Saagpakk's 1,200-page *Estonian-English Dictionary* (1982).

3. A north Finnish folksong talks of Finland as "Finn-island" (*Suomensaari*).

4. This subject was the topic of the first article I succeeded in publishing in Soviet-occupied Estonia: Rein Taagepera, "Eesti-vene-inglise keelekolmnurk" [Estonian-Russian-English language triangle], *Vikerkaar*, June 1988, 86–87; in Russian, "Estonsko-russko-angliiskii treugol'nik," *Raduga*, June 1988, 61–63.

5. Rein Taagepera, "The Baltic Bridge," in *The Baltic States: A Reference Book* (1991), 6–7.

TWO

From Prehistory
to World War I

As the heavy shield of the last Ice Age receded, around 9000 B.C., Estonia was partly submerged. Relieved of its burden, the ground began to rise. It still does, slowly changing into connecting peninsulas what used to appear as isolated islands on ancient maps.[1]

The ice scraped deep parallel furrows into the ground and leveled the hills. The highest point in Estonia, Suur Munamägi (Great Egg Mountain) reaches only 318 meters (about 1,000 feet) above sea level. I first visited it in 1989. If it weren't for the observation tower, I would have walked down the other side, waiting for the hill to begin. I annoyed my companions Marju and Peeter by saying so, but they got even as we reached the top of the tower: the view was eerie. Columns of fog rose from the woods toward the somber sky. The clouds briefly parted, just in the right direction, and there was the faraway town of Võru basking in full sunshine. Then it was gone. "Now you understand how those folk tales came about, of cities engulfed by lakes," Marju said.

PREHISTORY

The first known human settlements, in the valley of the Pärnu River, date back to 7500 B.C. Little is known about this "Kunda culture," named after another prehistoric settlement on the northern coast. These ancient people may have contributed a few dozen words to the Estonian language (Jaanits et al. 1982:53), such as *mägi* (hill) and *mets* (forest). Around 3500 B.C., new people must have entered the area, because the style of tools and utensils changed. In particular, pottery now was decorated by pressing a comblike tool against fresh clay. Spread out from the Ural Mountains to the Baltic, the bearers of the "comb-ceramic culture" most likely spoke Finno-Ugric languages. They presumably assimilated the Kunda people.[2]

This must have been the last time a new population took over in Estonia, because all later changes in culture have been gradual. Subsequent

Historical Features of Estonia to the 1980s

Suur Munamägi, the highest point in Estonia. Photo O. Haidak, around 1935, *Meie Maa* IV (1957), Eesti Kirjanike Kooperatiiv. Reprinted with permission.

millennia brought conquests and appreciable mixing, but all later comers eventually melted into the resident population. The continuity in culture suggests that the language also must have remained basically the same; thus, the comb-ceramic people must have spoken a Finnic language ancestral to the present Estonian and Finnish.

For one to understand the frame of mind of present-day Estonians, these prehistoric considerations are important. The Estonians live on ancestral grounds where their language can be traced back for perhaps 5,000 years. When they talk of hills and forests, they may even use the only words used for those features ever since humans arrived in Estonia. Their sense of permanence contrasts with the present-time orientation of a melting pot such as the United States. Compared with Estonians, even most other European people are relative newcomers to their lands. This is not a value judgment regarding the proper mix of orientation toward the present and the past. For better or for worse, Estonians have a sense of their permanence in Estonia. The emphasis is on language rather than race. Those newcomers who learn Estonian will fit in; those who don't remain aliens.

The next wave of immigration into Estonia came around 2000 B.C. by people who decorated their pots by impressing a multistranded cord and who used stone axes shaped vaguely like boats. They most likely spoke a Baltic language ancestral to the present Lithuanian and Latvian. The carriers of the boat-ax culture entered the area of the present-day Baltic states from the southwest, and some traveled through Finland all the way to the Arctic Ocean. The two cultures mixed and fused. The Finnic language prevailed in Finland and Estonia, the Baltic language in Lithuania and Latvia. In Latvia the process was slowest: Latgale (eastern Latvia) lost its Finnic character only after A.D. 500, and some Finnic Livonian villages held out in northern Kurzeme (Courland, western Latvia) until World War II.

The last major immigration wave into the area, that of eastern Slavic tribes (around A.D. 500), stopped short of Estonia. These ancestors of Russians gradually assimilated Finnic peoples further east, such as the Votes, who lived southwest of St. Petersburg, and the Vepsians and Karelians, whose languages still survive in the Karelian Republic and south of it. The linguistic borders around Estonia by A.D. 1000 remained largely the same until the twentieth century.

Estonia received immigrants, mainly from the south, but it also sent them north, over the Gulf of Finland. Much of present-day Finland was inhabited by Samis (Lapps) who spoke a language distantly related to the Finnic language in Estonia. During the first millennium A.D., immigrants from Estonia and Karelia began to fuse and form the present-day Finns. The Samis were pushed ever further toward the Arctic Ocean during the second millennium A.D.

Agriculture started to complement hunting, fishing, and food gathering in Estonia by 1500 B.C., but progress was slow in these northern climes. By 500 B.C., Estonia began to shift from the stone and bone age to the iron age, largely bypassing the bronze age because the metal is not native to the Baltic region. By A.D. 1000, Estonia had become an important transit station on the Viking trade route to Russia and Byzantium, and its economy began to catch up with that of central Europe. A preurban trading center formed on the site of the future city of Tallinn.

INDEPENDENT ESTONIA, A.D. 1200

By 1200, Estonia had a population of at least 150,000, compared with some 700,000 in Sweden and less than 100,000 in Finland. Population density was 3 persons per square kilometer, compared with less than 2 in Sweden but 7 in Poland, 12 in Denmark, and over 20 in Germany (based on data in McEvedy and Jones 1978).

The basic socioeconomic unit was the farm, consisting of an extended family and, for wealthier families, servants and non-Estonian slaves (obtained as booty in raids). Farms were bunched into villages loosely governed by village elders. The society was clearly male-dominated, with occasional polygamy. Freemen were basically equal, and there was no nobility in the usual sense of the term.[3]

The predominant religion was a cult of ancestors and animism; every grove, lake, and house had a guardian spirit. Gods formed a rather rudimentary pantheon, even compared with those of Latvians and Lithuanians, and grain and animals were sacrificed to them. The practice of both cremation and burial suggested a variety of beliefs. There were no full-time priests and no written tradition.

Politically, Estonia paralleled the structure of its gods and spirits: nonhierarchical. It remained more fragmented than Lithuania but was more organized than Finland, in line with the decreasing population densities toward the north. Estonia consisted of eight major and several minor federations of even smaller entities. These smaller entities (*kihelkond*) functioned as the basic units of defense for a group of villages, maintaining one or several strongholds that served as a place of refuge for people and cattle in case of hostile raids that usually (but not always) came from outside the Estonian language area. A *kihelkond* elder probably was not an inheritable position, although some families likely had a tradition of leadership. These elders had little institutionalized or coercive power and depended on persuading the freemen about their common interest. The major federations (*maakond*) were units within which mutual raiding did not occur; they served as mobilization bases for raids, usually outside the Estonian language area. The elder of a *maakond* was presumably selected by the *kihelkond* elders for an undefined period. Most of the *maakond* elders may have met once a year for talks, but no countrywide leader was selected.

Among the neighboring peoples, the Scandinavians and the Russians had more organized kingdoms and principalities, and the Lithuanians were on the point of developing them. The Latvian pattern was similar to the Estonian structure. Because the larger-scale organization depended on making use of brute force against one's own people, the Estonian-Latvian pattern was more egalitarian and less despotic. In the long run, it was also less efficient in self-defense.

Up to 1200, the Estonians more than held their own. Why the Scandinavian Vikings largely bypassed Estonia in their adventures and state building in Russia is unclear. The Ukrainian-centered Kievan Rus' state established a garrison in an Estonian fortress, but only for some thirty years.[4] As the Viking era subsided because of Christianity and the broader aims of the Scandinavian kings, the Baltic Sea was taken over by the Estonians, Curonians (western Latvians), and Karelians, whose raids reached as far as Denmark. In 1187, raiders from the eastern side of the Baltic burned Sigtuna, the royal capital of Sweden. The same year, Saladin pushed the Crusaders out of Jerusalem, a faraway event that was to have more of an impact on Estonia than was the sack of Sigtuna.

Why Christianization Bypassed Estonia

When Russia was Christianized around 1000, the eastern coast of the Baltic sea, from Lithuania to Finland, remained the last non-Christian region in Europe west of the Volga River. Being thus out of synchronization with their neighbors' conversion had major negative consequences for these people, and the causes are worth elucidation.

My overview of prehistory has focused on languages, because these form the basis of modern national identity in the Baltic area, where religion and other identifiers play a secondary role (except in Lithuania). Language is a means of communication; the converse of this obvious statement is that lack of a common language impedes communication. The Estonian elders may have met once a year with each other but not with their Latvian counterparts—not because of some ideology of nationalism but simply because they could not understand the Latvians without using interpreters. The spread of Christianity was impeded for similar reasons.

The following brief review of the broad language relationships in northern Europe helps provide the linguistic context. Most European languages belong to the Indo-European language family, with branches such as the Romance, the Germanic, the Baltic, and the Slavic. Another language family is the Finno-Ugric, with branches such as Ugric (Hungarian), Volga Finnic (Mordvinian and Mari), and Balto-Finnic (Estonian and Finnish). In its grammar and basic vocabulary, the Slavic Russian is closer to the Germanic English than it is to Estonian. Estonian is about as distant from Hungarian as English is from Russian. In contrast, Finnish and Estonian are partly mutually intelligible in the way Spanish and French are; so too are Latvian and Lithuanian (which are both Baltic, in the linguistic sense).

A thousand years ago, the Slavic peoples already ranged from the Bulgarians in the south to the Russians in the north, and their languages were closer to each other than they are today. The same applied to the Germanic peoples, who ranged from the Alps to Scandinavia. A result was the availability of southern Germanic Catholic missionaries who could be understood in Scandinavia. Similarly, the conversion of Bulgarians to Greek Orthodoxy produced a missionary pool for the Ukrainians and Russians. (The Church Slavonic used by the Russian Orthodox Church is old Bulgarian, and the Russian Cyrillic alphabet has a similar origin.) Squeezed between the Germanic Catholicism in the West and the Slavic Orthodoxy in the East, the Baltic Lithuanians and Latvians as well as the Finnic Estonians and Finns had no such southern relatives. Consequently, it took Christianity an appreciably longer time to trickle down to them.

The advent of Christianity also meant a literate clergy, more advanced construction skills and weaponry, and notions of statecraft. The Baltic and Finnic people lagged on all these accounts, and their military strength could not last. The Swedes subjugated and Christianized the sparsely populated western Finland rather peacefully, from 1150 on. The Lithuanians were unified by a local prince (by the usual brutal means of state construction) and went on the offensive. In a magnificent anachronism, these worshipers of the ancient Indo-European gods built the largest state in Europe, in 1400, ruling Christian populations many times more numerous than the Lithuanians themselves. The Latvians and Estonians fell between the Finns and the Lithuanians in population density and in the degree of unification. They held their own against Swedes and Russians, but succumbed in the face of a new and more powerful adversary: the Germans.

German Conquest

After being defeated by Saladin in the Holy Land, the German knights were looking for an easier prey. The eastern shore of the Baltic fit the bill. The pope obligingly declared it the "Land of Mary"—somehow akin to the Land of Jesus in the Orient—as justification for a Christian crusade. Traditional history, as related by German chroniclers, describes the Baltic natives of the time as inveterate pagans who ignored the first bishop appointed by the pope to convert them and killed the second one when he tried strong-arm tactics. But more recent evidence of a number of churches existing in Estonia before the German conquest suggests that peaceful conversion had begun. This was the last thing the German invaders wanted, because conquest had to be justified as Christianization. They ignored the local Christians, often rebaptizing them as a sign of their political submission. Facing foreign invasion, the local Christians had to make common cause with their pagan brethren, thus reinforcing the pagan image of the country.[5]

The German onslaught across the Baltic Sea began with the arrival of an ambitious and militarily minded bishop who founded Riga, the present capital of Latvia, near a village of Finnic-speaking Livonians (1201). He founded the Order of the Knights of Christ, or the "Sword Brethren" (1202–1204), that attracted appreciable numbers of booty-seeking Germans. The Livonians (in present-day central Latvia) and the Latgalians (eastern Latvia) were soon subdued. Estonians resisted from 1208 to 1227. Under the leadership of Lembitu, the elder of a south Estonian *maakond*, they achieved concerted action but fell short of unification. Lembitu fell in battle (1217), and the Danes invaded northern Estonia (1219). The present Danish national flag is supposed to have fallen from the sky as they were on the point of losing the crucial battle to the Estonians; the heavenly gift encouraged the Danes to win. A Danish citadel was founded at the location of an Estonian trade center and became the present Tallinn, capital of Estonia. (The name probably comes from *Taan-linn*, the "Danish fortress.")

One of the ironies of history was that the Estonians were able to defeat handily a Swedish invasion of western Estonia (1220). Because of the lack of serfdom in Sweden and the relatively enlightened rule in Finland, submission to Sweden would have been the best course left to the Estonians. Their resistance collapsed under the weight of the two-pronged German and Danish attack. The two groups of invaders at times competed at baptizing entire villages with one scoop of water, occasionally executing elders who had dared to accept baptism from the other conqueror. German conquest of the island of Saaremaa in 1227 ended the struggle in Estonia. The submission of Curonians and Semgalians (southwestern Latvia) by 1285 completed the Livonian "crusade."

The Russians played a marginal and vacillating role while the competing brand of Christianity was imposed on their pagan neighbors. Responding to a Russian raid into Estonia, Lembitu took time off from the main struggle to invade Pskov, the major Russian city facing southeast Estonia (1212). As the German pressure increased, Estonians tried to find allies to the east, but the major common action involved only 200 Russians and ended in defeat (1224).

Raun (1991a:17) offers this explanation of the defeat of Estonians:

The failure of Estonian resistance can be attributed to three major factors: the numerical superiority of the invading forces; the military-technological superiority of the Germans and Danes; and the absence of a centralized Estonian political power, resulting in insufficient native mobilization and failure to secure significant foreign allies.

By 1200, the Estonians and Latvians acquired an unenviable geopolitical and geodemographic position that has bedeviled them ever since. The climate left them too marginal to sustain the demographic mass that enabled the Lithuanians to assert themselves in favorable times and to assure survival in bad times. But geopolitically, the Estonians were not sufficiently marginal to be left in relative peace, as the Finns have been. For the next 800 years, many parties all too often thought the land of the Latvians and Estonians worth fighting over—and without giving them any say in the matter. Repeatedly, sheer demographic survival became precarious. It still is. The interesting question is how the Estonians and Latvians managed to handle all these cliff-hangers.

GERMAN RULE, 1227–1561

The conquerors divided Estonia into three types of lands: northern Estonia under the suzerainty of the king of Denmark (but with 80 percent Germans among the local vassals); lands for the Order of the Sword Brethren in Latvia and southern Estonia; and interspersed with the latter, the domains of several bishoprics. After a severe defeat by the Lithuanians and Semgalians (southern Latvians), the Order of Sword Brethren became an autonomous branch of the Teutonic Order, centered in East Prussia (1237). A major uprising of Estonians (1343–1345) destroyed Danish control outside the city of Tallinn but was crushed by the Order. With the latter in military control of his domains, the king of Denmark had little choice but to sell them (1346). The bishops and the cities, all under German control, often quarreled with the Order, but it remained the effective ruler of Estonia and Latvia until the Reformation and even beyond. After the 1220s, the area technically belonged to the Holy Roman Empire, but the arm of the emperors never reached that far in any practical sense.[6]

The names of territories that came to be used are somewhat confusing. The entire realm, largely corresponding to the ethnically Latvian and Estonian area, was broadly called Livonia, or in hindsight, "Old Livonia," although the ethnic Livonians, on whose shores the first Germans had landed, were a vanishing breed being assimilated by Latvians. Only the northern, ex-Danish part of Estonia came to be called Estland. Western Latvia was called Courland, after the Baltic population of the area. That left southern Estonia and northern Latvia as "Livland," or Livonia in a narrower sense. The German names for cities in Estonia often have an Estonian origin. Reval (Tallinn) is derived from the Estonian name of the surrounding district, Revala. Tartu and its German name, Dorpat, both derive from the city's older Estonian name, Tarbatu.

Introduction of Serfdom

Imposed on the region was a feudal system on the German pattern, with villages subdued to estates of the vassals of the Order or the bishops. The estate owners were a motley crew of Sword Brethren and other Germans, adventurers of all origins, and a few Estonian elders who soon became Germanized. In the beginning, a large group of Estonian freemen remained, but they gradually were squeezed out through restrictions on peasant movements and growing indebtedness. The legal and economic standing of peasants continuously eroded, until they were reduced to utter serfdom. "Serfdom began in the second half of the fourteenth century, grew markedly in the fifteenth, reached near completion in the sixteenth, and received juridical confirmation in the seventeenth century" (Raun 1991a:20). By 1550, taxes in kind rose gradually to 25 percent of the crop. The first known case of a peasant being sold without an accompanying land sale occurred in 1495.

This loss of property and personal rights was only minimally counteracted by minor improvement in agricultural techniques, growth of cities with their new products, and the relative internal peace offered by a larger political unit. The extent of peace should not be overestimated, however; individual nobles feuded with each other and their suzerains, and war with Russians and Swedes was frequent. Peasants were drafted into auxiliary forces that suffered the heaviest casualties, and their dwellings were burned when the fortresses of the nobles could not be stormed.

Cities also developed on the German feudal pattern, under the leadership of German merchants, and joined the Hanseatic League. They offered a sometimes insecure haven to runaway serfs who formed an Estonian-speaking urban underclass and controlled some of the guilds (occupational associations) in Tallinn. Estonia's population in 1550 was about 250,000, and at least 6 percent were living in urban surroundings. Tallinn may have had 8,000 inhabitants, Tartu about 6,000.

Christianity remained superficial as far as the peasants were concerned. If it was not conveyed in Latin, it was in German. Pagan customs gradually intertwined with the Catholic cult of saints and continued after the Reformation. The clergy remained an elite German domain, in striking contrast with Swedish-ruled Finland, where many priests hailed from Finnish peasant homes and one became the bishop of Finland. Almost no Estonian entered the clergy before the Reformation. During three centu-

Ruins of Tartu cathedral, built 1250–1500 and destroyed by fire in 1624. ERKA-Foto, around 1935, *Meie Maa* III (1957), Eesti Kirjanike Kooperatiiv. Reprinted with permission.

ries, the written record in Estonian amounted to names in tax books and a few words and sentences. Nor did the Germans of Old Livonia contribute greatly to German culture. One is at a loss to name a Livonian-born cultural figure of the pre-Reformation period.

The tangible remains of this period include a number of churches and the medieval old city of Tallinn, probably the best preserved one north of Carcassonne in France. The ruins of the cathedral in Tartu impress me most. As a youth, I took them for granted when passing them on my sleighing trips, and although buildings seen during childhood later usually appear smaller, the arches of the Tartu Dome Cathedral seem to grow larger at every visit.

In many ways, the social structure of Old Livonia featured the typical medieval inequities. However, the ethnolinguistic differences worsened the oppression and cut off avenues of escape for peasants. They could not pass for someone else because their language would give them away. The peasant son could not join the clergy because he lacked language skills. As the special capitulation rights accorded to the island of Saaremaa were whittled away and the few Estonian vassals were eliminated or Germanized, the social gap became extreme. The gradual replacement of Latin by German as the literary language only increased this gap by boosting the prestige of German.

Ironically, this linguistic context also insulated the Estonians against Germanization. To the Livonian nobles, a German-speaking peasant had come unthinkable, and few were the intermediary jobs for which a limited knowledge of German would have been of use. There was no incentive for peasants to master German. Conditions were different in the cities, but these were few, and the rigid structure of guilds reduced opportunities.

Decline of German Rule

The conquest of Estonia represented the last stage of a German thrust that began three centuries earlier. The German knights and land-hungry peasants pushed the demographic border between Germans and Slavs back from the Elbe in 900 to the Oder in 1000. Split into two branches by Polish resistance, their northern thrust by 1300 reached the ancient Prussians, who spoke a Baltic language akin to Latvian and Lithuanian. Up to that time, the peasant could follow the knight because the conquest proceeded overland—the ancient Prussians were exterminated or assimilated in this process—but when leapfrogging to Livonia over the sea, the German knight left the peasant behind. The Teutonic Order was well aware of the need for a land bridge from Prussia to Livonia, but succeeded in holding Zhemaitia (Samogitia, western Lithuania) for less than a century. Lithuanian resistance blocked the Germanization of Livonia. The Germans in Estonia and Latvia remained a thin upper class of maybe 5 percent of the population.

Further German military advances came to a halt in a battle with the Russians on the ice of Lake Peipsi, at the Estonian-Russian border (1242). But irrespective of the outcome of a particular battle, the Teutonic Order lacked the demographic basis for consolidating any further gains. After 1400, the German hold on Old Livonia gradually weakened in the face of the increased power of Sweden and Russia and the union of Lithuania and

Poland; the Germans had failed to integrate Livonia internally. In addition, the Reformation rocked a regime based on a pseudo-religious order, which understandably opposed this movement, but Lutheranism spread quickly from Germany to the German cities in Livonia, where it became predominant in the 1520s. The landed nobility resisted until the collapse of Old Livonia.

One aspect of the Reformation did have an impact on the Estonian and Latvian masses: Martin Luther's insistence on preaching in a language the congregation could understand. Knowing some Estonian became important for clergymen, both for sermons and for hymns. The first services in Estonian were conducted in the 1530s. The first Estonian-language book (a few pages have been preserved) was printed in 1535—only eighty years after Johannes Gutenberg perfected the printing art. This Lutheran cathechism by Simon Wanradt (about 1500–1567) and Johann Koell (died 1540) was ordered removed from sale by the Tallinn city council because of obscure theological slippages, and the next Estonian book did not appear until many decades later. Nonetheless, this first book marked a change in attitude toward the language of the peasants. This period also produced the first cultural figure of some wider renown born in Estonia: the one-time Spanish court painter Michel Sittow.

By the mid-1500s, Old Livonia was visibly a sinking ship surrounded by sharks. Countrywide and local powerholders sought to sell themselves to outside powers at the best possible price. The debacle began with a Russian invasion in 1558; it was complete by 1561, when the Tallinn city council and the nobility of northern Estonia subjected themselves to the king of Sweden, while the southern parts of Old Livonia capitulated to Poland.

Old Livonia was dead, but the Livonian Wars (1558–1583) continued. Parts of Estonia were seized by Swedes, Poles, Danes, a Danish duke manipulated by Russians, Russians directly, and Estonian peasant insurgents. By 1583, Russia was out of the game. Poland-Lithuania held southern Estonia, Sweden the northern portion, and Denmark the island of Saaremaa. Wars continued until 1629, until Sweden gained control of the Baltic mainland up to the Daugava River in central Latvia. In 1645, Denmark yielded Saaremaa to Sweden, and Estonia was once more under a single foreign ruler. Of the prewar population of some 250,000, only 100,000 had survived war, famine, and plague. Although the Germans had lost sovereign political power, they remained the socioeconomic ruling class, and their power over the Estonian peasants even continued to increase.

In retrospect, the period of German rule is an overwhelmingly negative one in Estonia's history. After the desperate uprising of 1343–1345, the Estonians vanished from the chronicles as if they no longer existed, except as

vague *Undeutsche* (non-Germans), a term the Germans applied to all subjected people, from the Slavic Sorbs to the Latvians and Estonians.

Estonian historians have not purposely underplayed their people's role
as a way to stress the harshness of the German rule—one does not enjoy
being a nobody. In contrast, Finnish chroniclers stress the role of the peas-
ant-born decisionmakers and try to pass for a Swedish-Finnish commonwealth a political entity that appears a Swedish kingdom to the Swedes. If
any similar approach could be taken with Estonian history, it would appeal to the sense of national identity. But there is nothing to work on.
Writer Jaan Kross (1983) has concentrated on "recovering history" for the
Estonians by discovering famous people with an Estonian connection. The
earliest portrait in his gallery is Michel Sittow, the painter previously
mentioned. Despite the fond ideas of later German historians on the role
of the Germans as *Kulturträger* (carriers of culture) in the east, they rather
acted as culture spoilers in Estonia. Theirs was a sterile colonial rule overseas that foreshadowed the transoceanic conquests.

Of course, Estonia in 1561 had cathedrals and even a printed book in
Estonian, which it did not have in 1200. But this would be the wrong baseline for comparison in a changing world—no one had a printed book in
1200! Without foreign conquest, the ongoing voluntary Christianization
would have been completed rather soon. The colonial imposition of the
Church actually delayed Christianization, except in the most superficial
sense. As a means of spiritual resistance to conquest, paganism in Estonia
maintained a respectability it could not have in Scandinavia. Instead, the
proper baseline for evaluating the Sword Brethren as Christianizers is
supplied by the outcomes of various voluntary conversions in Europe,
ranging from Hungary and Scandinavia to Lithuania.

Even as foreign conquerors go, the Germans as *Kulturträger* in Estonia
appear as fakes or failures, compared with the Swedes in Finland. During
the span of nearly four centuries, the main innovation the Germans indis-
putably brought was serfdom.

SWEDISH RULE, 1561–1710

The period of Swedish rule was preceded and followed by such war,
famine, and plague that in comparison it seemed a happy period. The Estonian oral tradition calls it the "good old Swedish times," but a look at
the facts shows that the burden of the peasants actually increased. What
was new and encouraging was unprecedented talk about peasants' rights,
although in reality the privileges of the nobles were strengthened. In contemporary terminology, the situation might have been described as "lots
of glasnost but little perestroika."

Uninterrupted Swedish control began in Tallinn in 1561, throughout northern Estonia in 1583, southern Estonia in 1629, and Saaremaa only in 1645. It ended around 1710, during the Great Northern War. Thus, the Swedish presence in the different regions ranged from only 65 to 150 years (with an average close to 100), compared with over 300 years of German rule. It was a period of marked change throughout Europe, and ripples of it reached Estonia.

For a time, it looked as if the dividing line between Catholicism and Lutheranism might cut permanently across Estonia because Poland-Lithuania remained in control of southern Estonia. The competition made the Polish Counter-Reformation adopt some of the Lutheran attitudes toward local languages, as both groups tried to convert or confirm the peasants. The development of written Estonian and schooling for peasants profited from this rivalry. In the late 1500s, the Estonian peasants had become instant Lutherans as their German masters followed the north German trend. By the early 1600s, Estonian opinion began to matter.

In the long run, religious unification brought by the Swedish advance in 1629 solidified the Estonian identity. In contrast, the Latvian language area remained divided between Sweden (northern Latvia), Poland (Latgale), and a duchy of Courland that the last Grand Master of the Livonian branch of the Teutonic Order carved out for himself. The Catholic religion helped turn Latgalian into a virtually distinct language, but the equally marked differences between southern and northern Estonian were muted by the common religion. The Catholic interest in peasant education subsided with the end of religious wars. Efforts to increase literacy continued in Lutheran Courland and Swedish provinces but ceased in Latgale and Lithuania. By that time, the status of the Lithuanian language had fallen as low as that of the conquered Latvians and Estonians because the Lithuanian nobility had gradually become Polish-oriented culturally once they adopted Christianity.

The Swedes had a tradition of free peasantry, both at home and in Finland, and serfdom in their newly acquired overseas provinces was philosophically objectionable to them. Nevertheless, the loyalty of the Baltic German nobles was essential in view of the ever-present threat from Russia, and the need for Baltic grain was best served through large estates. Having lost political power, the Baltic German nobles concentrated on obtaining legal codification of their socioeconomic privileges; this became a fixation in the centuries to come. The unwritten traditional peasant rights, eroded during war, were conveniently forgotten. Periodic Swedish attempts to reduce the nobility's privileges only increased the estate owners' anxiety and counteractivities, and they got reprieves when the Swedish kings were occupied with emergencies elsewhere, which was the case most of the time.

The Diet of the Swedish duchy of Estland (northern Estonia) consisted only of nobles, and the responsibilities of the Swedish governor in Tallinn were limited to military security and tax collection from state lands. Kept in check under the Polish administration, the nobles of Livland (southern Estonia and northern Latvia) also gained appreciable autonomy when subjected to Sweden, though to a lesser degree than in Estland. "If there was any victor in the Livonian Wars, it was the Baltic German nobility. The field was cleared of two major rivals (the bishops and the Teutonic Knights), and a third threat, the cities, suffered relatively more than the nobility itself" (Raun 1991a:28).

War and plague had left many farms and even estates ownerless. Farms were usurped by estate owners for their direct use, which reduced the share of peasant lands. Ownerless estates were made Crown property but were usually turned over to local or Swedish nobles. Wartime population losses initially made peasants a scarce commodity. Hence their payments in kind and their corvée (labor duties on the manor land) were low initially. As the population bounced back and farms recovered their productive capabilities, the peasant burden increased rapidly. By 1700, the obligatory deliveries seemed to be 2.5 times higher than in 1600. Corvée demands doubled and became the predominant form of exploitation.[7] The Livland rural security regulations of 1671 formally bound peasants to their place of birth. They could not move, yet they could be sold without land. Thanks to the absence of major war, the well-being of peasants most likely was not reduced, but neither did it advance. When hard times returned, the peasants lacked any reserves, and the consequences were disastrous.

A potentially major positive step occurred when abolition of serfdom was ordered for the Swedish Crown estates in Estonia and Livonia, but the extent of implementation remains debatable. After 1681, the Crown retrieved the estates it formerly had given to the nobles, but it rented them back to the previous holders. This "reduction" and talk about abolition of serfdom made many Baltic Germans look toward the east. Compared with their fellow Lutheran and Germanic Swedes, the Russians were alien to the Germans. But at least serfdom was safe in Russia.

Education was the field in which the Swedish rule had the greatest impact. A university was founded in Tartu in 1632, four years before Harvard, and was preceded in the Swedish realm only by Uppsala and in eastern Europe by Vilnius. Tartu had been the site of a Jesuit college (1583–1601) during Polish rule, a precedent that probably influenced site selection. Instruction at the university was in Latin, and students were Swedes, Baltic Germans, Finns, and one Latvian, but no Estonians. As the threat from Russia increased, the university was transferred to Pärnu on the western coast in 1699 and closed in 1710, not to be reopened until a century later.

In primary education, some attention was paid to schools for peasant children. Finland supplied a pattern and also some personnel. Good intentions exceeded the deeds, but a conceptual breakthrough was made, not to be undone under subsequent Russian rule. Book printing in Estonian, hardly begun before the Livonian Wars, expanded to some forty titles, limited to religious literature. Two literary languages began to develop, based on the northern and southern dialects.

The Great Northern War (1700–1721) ended Swedish rule in Estonia, northern Latvia, and Finnish-inhabited Ingria (Ingermanland), which ranged from Estonia to St. Petersburg, founded during this war. The population of Estonia, which meanwhile had reached about 350,000, was reduced to 150,000 by war and a preceding period of crop failures and famine (1695–1697). The Estonian oral tradition often dated events from the onset of the famine rather than the war, indicative of its severity.

The war began at Narva, at the Estonian-Ingrian border, with a Russian onslaught the Swedes turned into a major Russian debacle (1700). However, as the main Swedish forces moved recklessly to then-Polish Ukraine and eventual defeat, the Russians gradually conquered Estonia (1704–1710). The usual plunder and murder were aggravated by a systematic scorched-earth policy ordered by the Russian tsar. The entire burgher population of Tartu was deported to Vologda and Kostroma in northern Russia in a foreshadowing of Soviet mass deportations. The event inspired the first known written poem by a native Estonian—a 32-strophe jeremiad (1708, first printed in 1902) by sexton Käsu Hans (Hans Kes, died around 1715):

> Then to Russia he did take
> all the city folks, by force.
> All the masters, mistresses
> sorrowfully shed their tears:
> Into Russia I will be.
> Tartu city, woe to me!

EARLY RUSSIAN RULE: THE PEAKING OF SERFDOM, 1710–1860

In the peace treaty of 1721, Sweden acknowledged the loss of its Baltic possessions as well as Ingria, where a new Russian capital city was built in Finnic-inhabited territory—St. Petersburg (later Petrograd, then Leningrad). Tsarist Russian rule in Estonia lasted 200 years, much longer than Swedish control but much shorter than German rule.

The economy and population gradually recovered. For the first time ever, a period of 150 years passed with no war or raids, though the peasants became subject to military service, which lasted twenty-five years. The half-million mark in population was reached in the 1780s—a threefold increase over seventy years. (Typical in their fertility were my patrilinear ancestors Jaan and Pibbi, of the Vaoküla village near the Latvian language border; they had six children, born from 1741 to 1750.)

Overshadowed by the port of St. Petersburg, Tallinn leveled off at no more than 10,000 inhabitants, and the urban share of the population (5 percent) remained lower than at the end of the Swedish rule or even the late Middle Ages. Industry was minimal. Tartu University remained closed, but progress in peasant education resumed. Teaching children to read at home became a tradition, and by 1800, about two-thirds of the adult peasants in southern Estonia could read—a vastly larger share than in Orthodox Russia or Catholic Lithuania.

The Baltic German attitudes during the Great Northern War were mixed, with some of the nobility going over to the Russians even while the battles continued. To win them over, the Russian tsars agreed to generous terms of internal autonomy and essentially kept their promises for more than a century. In peasant matters, Russia happily conceded everything Sweden had disputed. One and a half centuries after the collapse of Old Livonia, the Baltic German nobles reached the apogee of their socioeconomic power.

They also gained in political influence. The educational level of the Baltic Germans was ordinary in the Swedish realm but exceptional within the Russian empire. For two centuries, the Baltic Germans became a major pool for Russian officials, generals, and ministers. The closeness of the new imperial capital to the Estonian border (150 kilometers, compared with Moscow's 1,000) helped. At the same time, the Baltic Germans maintained their ties to Germany, where most of the clergy and tutors came from. But now the Baltic Germans themselves also became serious contributors to German and world culture and science.

The apex for the Baltic Germans conversely meant the nadir for their Estonian and Latvian serfs, at least in the beginning. At a time when only remnants of serfdom remained in France, it finally became complete and undisputed in Estonia. Hard liquor replaced the medieval mead and became a major solace and scourge for the serfs. The features of all-out slavery deepened, with individual peasants sold in the marketplace or exchanged for hunting dogs. When a demoiselle from the estate of Taagepera near the Latvian border married and moved near Tartu, around 1805, the dowry included Märt, a grandson of the aforementioned Jaan and Pibbi. I do not know whether he was consulted about the move; he was my grandfather's grandfather.

For the peasant, upward mobility was limited to a few lucky individuals. One of them was General Johann von Michelson, who briefly became the Russian commander-in-chief during the Napoleonic Wars. This former Estonian serf on at least one occasion so flaunted his origins as to infuriate the Baltic German nobles, but he did not try to affect the lot of his brethren otherwise.

The low point was reached around 1750. During the preceding five centuries, the deep undercurrent of history pulled the Estonians ever deeper to the bottom, Swedish efforts to the contrary notwithstanding. After 1750, the current seemed to reverse itself and pull the Estonians up again, various efforts to the contrary again notwithstanding.

By 1730, the pietist Moravian Brethren movement in Germany reached Estonia, and it could be said that Estonia finally was Christianized. Interacting with peasants in their homes and modest prayer houses, the pietists combated the spreading alcoholism and promoted literacy. The Lutheran clergy members were forced to compete with them and became more sensitive to the needs of their flocks. A negative aspect was pietist destruction of much of the Estonian folklore and material culture as being deemed overly worldly. In 1739, the full Bible was published in Estonian, after a full century of efforts and squabbles among the Lutheran clergy. The consequences were momentous: It lent prestige to the language and standardized the spelling. It also gave the northern dialect an edge over the southern and halted the development of multiple literary languages, a problem that has plagued many emerging nationalities, from the Basques on the Atlantic to the Finnic Maris on the Volga.

Other influences seeped in from Germany during the Enlightenment and affected Baltic German attitudes. Garlieb Merkel (1769–1850), a Livonian pastor's son, published an indictment of the Baltic socioeconomic conditions (1797). The book's message was overwhelmingly rejected by the nobles, but a formerly self-evident superiority had become one that needed justification.[8] The American Revolution probably was little noticed in the Baltic, since the independence for slave-owning American colonists was very much in line with the strivings for autonomy by the serf-owning Baltic Germans. The ideas of the French Revolution were something else: They attacked the foundations of serfdom. But a major agent of sociopolitical change came from a quite different quarter: romanticism.

Romanticism made the previously despised folklore respectable, including that of marginalized people like the Celts. In Germany, Johann Gottfried Herder's influential *Stimmen der Völker in Liedern* (1787) included eight Estonian folk songs,[9] and a new odd breed arose among the local Germans: Estophiles, that is, non-Estonians who appreciated the previously despised Estonian folk culture and songs. For the moment, they were drawn from the upper class, with little participation by the peasants themselves.

After Alexander I became tsar, Tartu University was finally reopened in 1802, giving instruction in German. Kristjan Jaak Peterson (1801–1822) became the first university student proudly to acknowledge his Estonian origin. But he died young and his poetry, amazingly modern despite the limitations of the peasant language, was not published until a century later. Briefly (1821–1825), an Estonian-language newspaper was published by clergyman Otto Wilhelm Masing (1763–1832), who never admitted to his Estonian origin. The economic basis for such a newspaper was still missing.

Meanwhile, the international constellation around Estonia was changing. The partition of Poland brought the last parts of the Latvian language area (Latgale and the autonomous duchy of Courland) and almost all of Lithuania (except Prussian-ruled Klaipeda/Memel) under Russian rule. The three Lutheran- and German-dominated provinces began to be designated collectively as the Baltic provinces: Estland (northern Estonia), Livland (southern Estonia and northern Latvia), and Courland (southwestern Latvia). Under similar conditions, the development of Latvians and Estonians was fairly parallel. Catholic Lithuania and Latgale followed a different and slower course in acquiring literacy and economic development. Sweden lost Finland, which received fairly extensive autonomy within the tsarist realm (1809). This shift reinforced a Finnish identity (even among the speakers of Swedish) and facilitated Estonian contacts with Finland.

A new phase began with the emancipation of serfs in Estland (1816) and Livland (1819), though actual implementation lasted more than a decade. Sales of humans and meddling with peasant family life ended. Family names were introduced. In some cases these names were assigned by the estate owners, which explains the frequency of German-sounding names among Estonians. In other cases the former serfs could choose their own. My grandfather's grandfather picked as his name the place of his birth.

Since serfdom continued in the Russian provinces up to 1861, the emancipation of serfs in the Baltic provinces visibly recognized their special status within the Russian empire. Some impetus for emancipation came from the Baltic Germans themselves. Resistance to emancipation was reduced because the deal offered advantages to the estate owners: The serfs were freed, but the masters kept their lands. In one sense, this was the final German conquest of Estonian soil. Serfdom often maintains a tie between the peasant and his land—one is usually not sold without the other—but this tie was now broken.

Indeed, abolition of serfdom at first made it worse for the peasants who called the new phase *teoorjus*, or corvée slavery. Working his oxen or serfs to death meant a loss of wealth to the estate owner, but the death of a "free" peasant didn't. For the use of a piece of land, heavy payment in labor could be exacted on a day's notice. In fair weather, the peasants had to work in the manor fields, leaving their own fields at the mercy of rain and cold. Shifting from corvée to money rents became a prime demand. The mid-1800s brought numerous peasant revolts in the form of strikes against excessive labor duty; these turned bloody when the estate owners attempted to break them by calling in the troops. The Russian government obliged but reluctantly. Well aware of the risks of larger uprisings, it pressured the Baltic landowners toward reforms.

In the 1850s, the estate owners' attitude toward money rent changed anyway. They now needed more cash, because they had discovered luxuries beyond the rustic pleasures of their forebears. Farms began to be rented for money or, by 1860, even sold to the peasants. Government credit for mortgages (typically thirty years) was made available, and favorable market conditions for Baltic flax and potatoes enabled peasants to make downpayments. Some forty-five years after his emancipation, my grandfather's grandfather bought a farm, and my father remembered the relief his parents felt at making the last mortgage payment.

Cultural development kept pace with the economic change and often was the driving force. The Estophiles founded the Learned Estonian Society (1838), and their ranks now included some university-educated Estonians, typically sons of manor officials sponsored by their masters. In Finland, the national epic *Kalevala* (The Home of the Kalevides) was compiled and published (1835), and the Estophiles dreamed of a similar feat. The task was outlined by Friedrich Robert Faehlmann (1798–1850) and completed by country physician Friedrich Reinhold Kreutzwald (1803–1882), both self-acknowledged Estonians. *Kalevipoeg* (Son of Kalev) was first published in a scholarly Estonian-German bilingual edition (1857–1861).

By 1840, the relations between the Baltic barons and the Russian government began to sour. The former still saw themselves as loyal feudal vassals of a suzerain who happened to belong to a different creed, but the Russian ruling circles were embracing the idea of a unitary bureaucratic state, with one creed and language. Baltic autonomy came under attack, and the Russian language was introduced into parts of courts and administration.

To weaken the Germans, the Russian government wanted to reduce their cultural influence on the peasants. Some officials encouraged the latter to convert to Greek Orthodoxy, sparking rumors that conversion to the emperor's faith would bring not only remission of corvée, head tax, and military service but also even the prospect of free land. Official disclaimers were of no avail. About 17 percent of the rural Estonians in Livland converted, but no worldly benefits resulted. Peasant sons were trained as Orthodox priests to serve the new flock, and their fluent Estonian contrasted with the poor language skills of most Lutheran clergy, who were largely imported from Germany. Once again, as in the times of the Polish-Swedish rivalry, the Estonian peasants profited from having their masters compete for their souls. Neither the Russians nor the Germans could imagine that the peasant culture could become an independent factor. Seventy years later, during the crucial phase of the Estonian war of independence, both the top political leader and the commander in chief hailed from families with some Greek Orthodox background.

ESTONIAN NATIONAL AWAKENING VERSUS RUSSIFICATION, 1860-1917

Although the cultural and economic ground had been slowly prepared for a long time, the Estonian national awakening visibly took place between 1860 and 1885. In 1850, a loosely defined mass of corvée peasants had some bits of mainly religious literature printed in a language with clumsy spelling and limited vocabulary. Within thirty-five years, they evolved into a nation with newspapers, theater, poetry, and mass cultural events, expressing themselves in a rapidly modernizing language and sustained by a vigorous farm economy. To the south, Latvian culture developed simultaneously, with different details but largely similar outcomes. To the north, Finnish-language culture had accelerated some twenty years earlier, and it offered encouragement and inspiration to the Estonians.[10]

How Cultural Nationalism Advanced Modernization

The previous German hegemony in the internal matters of the Baltic provinces changed into a triangular relationship as the Russian government's centralizing tendencies increased and the Estonian and Latvian peasant modernizers became active players. I use the term *modernizers* rather than *nationalists* because their activities consisted largely of developing agriculture, advancing education, and starting all-purpose newspapers. Political goals came later and were limited to control of city government and reducing the existing three provinces to two, to fit the Latvian and Estonian language areas. Political independence was not an issue before 1917. But yes, it was nationalism, from the very beginnings, because these newspapers and other cultural institutions used the peasant languages rather than German or Russian, thus setting themselves apart and creating new nations. Call it *cultural nationalism* if you will.[11]

The situation of the Baltic ex-serfs was in some ways similar to that of the South African blacks a century later, but their approaches differed. It would be hard to imagine the Estonian/Latvian peasants merely demanding education and jobs in a society that used German or Russian, consigning their own languages to the informal realm. It is equally hard to imagine the Xhosas and Zulus turning their back on both English and Afrikaans as well as areawide political issues, concentrating on farm improvement, schooling, and the press in their own languages and collecting folklore. Neither picture makes sense—indeed, this is not what happened. But why not? Could the outcomes have been the reverse had Herder included Xhosa instead of Estonian songs in his collection?

The outcomes are paradoxical. By making a fuss about their languages, the Latvians and Estonians introduced an additional element of conflict into an arena where economic issues by themselves were explosive. Areawide language wars could have distracted attention from local economic modernization, but this was not the strategy. The main effort took place on the microlevel: buying and upgrading one's farm and obtaining education for one's children (in any language, but preferably Estonian/Latvian). The language issue did not exacerbate the economic conflict. It possibly even exerted a moderating influence, because it created new positions in teaching and journalism that gave peasant children a chance to advance socioeconomically without displacing the Germans.

The many differences in the South African and Baltic conditions are obvious. Moreover, the long-term outcomes are not yet known. But in the short run, something went right in the Baltic provinces. The peasantry modernized rapidly, despite the extra burden of developing separate modern languages on the basis of a limited number of speakers. Despite or because? Losing one's cultural roots while undergoing radical socioeconomic change can be traumatic. Language and folklore supplied a polestar in a world in flux. Faced with the apparent need for a trade-off between tradition and modernization, the Estonians and Latvians largely succeeded in having their cake and eating it too.

Some highlights of this success story were the following. The first durable Estonian weekly was founded in 1857 and was upgraded into a daily in 1891. Its founder, former sexton Johannes Voldemar Jannsen (1819–1890), also started the first Estonian agricultural periodical and instigated the first nationwide song festival (1869). Attended by more than 10,000 people, this event was the beginning of a tradition that, much later, played a role in the popular mobilization of the late 1980s. Publication of a popular version of the national epic *Kalevipoeg* (printed in Finland, 1862) had a far-reaching psychological impact. Folklore collection campaigns (starting in the 1880s) gave even the most remote and humble people a sense of participation. Theater societies were founded in 1865, and soon the first original Estonian play was performed, written by Jannsen's daughter, Lydia Koidula (1843–1886), who emerged in 1867 as the first major Estonian poet. Romanticized historical novels came in the 1880s, socially critical ones from the 1890s on. A new orthography patterned on the Finnish was widely accepted in the 1870s, and the victory of the northern dialect as national language became complete. By 1881, the number of weekly newspapers rose to eight. Amateur orchestras (224 of them by the turn of the century) and choirs took musical culture into the countryside. Adult literacy, which was already around 90 percent in 1850, went to 96 percent in 1897.

All this was accompanied by changes in farm economy. The primacy of economics is widely accepted, but when we carefully compare the dates of major events, we may wonder to what extent economic modernization in Estonia was driven by the cultural awakening rather than vice versa (see Raun and Plakans 1990; Kahk 1990). The landless condition of the Baltic peasants became untenable once the Russian peasantry was emancipated and granted land (1861) and the Lithuanian-Polish peasants received a favorable agrarian law (1864). And although the Russian government pressured the Baltic nobles to abolish corvée and replace it with money rent on peasant lands (1868), corvée lasted until 1917 on the estates, which occupied about one-half of all agricultural land. The peasant-owned share of all agricultural land rose from about 4 percent in 1868 to one-third in 1898, but land hunger and anger against the estate owners nevertheless remained. Although 90 percent of the peasant-owned farms still carried a debt at the turn of the century, they offered a substantial economic basis for Estonian cultural life. At the same time, the mortgage debts of the German estates were also heavy, and by 1880 about one-fifth of the estates were run by Estonians, mainly as renters.

There were modest political changes also. Reforms imposed by Alexander II in 1866 made rural township elders and council members subject to elections, with limited voting rights even for landless males. This was the beginning of the practice of Estonian grassroots democracy.

By the mid-1880s, however, a mood of disillusionment began to surface. The establishment of an Estonian-language secondary school foundered on internal dissension. A joint-stock shipping company went bankrupt for lack of business skills (1893). Even earlier, a major rift had developed between the reformist and the radical currents. Whereas Jannsen had tried to appease the German nobles and clergy as much as possible, Carl Robert Jakobson (1841–1882), the son of a rural schoolteacher, introduced a new strategy of confronting them, seeking support from the Russian government. This approach looked radically new at the time, but its basic calculus was already outdated. The Baltic Germans were a fading factor, although they still were vastly superior to the Estonians in economic and political power. The strong ascendant Russian central government was bound to dominate the Baltic scene the moment it so decided. In the 1880s it did.

Russian Linguistic Imperialism

Russification measures started around 1885, after a new Slavophile tsar had ascended the throne. German unification in 1871 increased Russian fears that the Baltic peasants might become Germanized, inviting expansion by Germany. Estonian and Latvian nationalism proponents were not taken seriously by St. Petersburg, but it was decided to Russify those people as a preventive measure. Thus, the Germans supplied the motivation, but Latvians and Estonians bore much of the consequences.[12]

All administrative power in the Baltic provinces was put in the hands of Russians. In particular, the Baltic Germans lost control of police administration and courts (1888–1889). Instruction was shifted to Russian with a few years' notice, even though the overwhelming majority of pupils and teachers did not know the language. The only exception was teaching of Lutheran religion, because the Slavophiles did not want to make Lutheran texts available in Russian. Older teachers quit, and the younger teachers hastily acquired some Russian, but their poor command of this language impaired instructional content. Children speaking Estonian, even during recreation, had to be punished. It was an attempt at cultural genocide, with some gaps. In particular, Latin-script press and book publishing were allowed in Estonian and Latvian but prohibited in Lithuanian.

The Germans, Latvians, and Estonians were all affected, but in retrospect, the Baltic Germans lost the most, because they had more to lose. The German-language Tartu University became a Russian university, in language, faculty, and student body. For the Estonians, the loss involved only the basic schooling, the temporary hardship of shifting from German to Russian in middle and higher education, and the dashing of hopes of establishing Estonian-language high schools in the future. The number of Estonian (and Latvian) students at Tartu University was growing, economic development continued, and the sense of national identity was only reinforced by this new onslaught.

By 1894, there was again a new tsar, and the Russian government began to lose enthusiasm for Russification of the Baltic provinces. Once more, competition among their conquerors may have helped the Estonians. Exposure to Russian culture balanced out the earlier German cultural hegemony and helped Estonians discover Western Europe via the cosmopolitan St. Petersburg. "The seemingly contradictory effect of Russification was not to denationalize Estonian intellectuals, but rather to liberate them from the Baltic German cultural world" (Raun 1991a:77). Many Russification measures continued, but the Estonians and Latvians had successfully adjusted themselves. *Postimees,* the weekly newspaper founded by Jannsen, became the first Estonian daily (in 1891) and, after 1896, spearheaded the so-called Tartu renaissance, under the editorship of Jaan Tōnisson (1868–194?—death date in Soviet prison unknown even to the KGB).

It is time to discuss the Baltic Germans and their options. From coarse medieval conquerors, they had become a polished subsociety of nobles and burghers with some intellectual accomplishments. Tartu University had achieved a solid reputation,[13] and Estonian-born scientists had made significant contributions in many fields. But the Baltic German organs of local autonomy, completely dominated by the nobles, were by now so much out of step with modern realities that any attempt to modernize them looked dangerous to their survival. (Analogies with Soviet Communist rule around 1980 come to mind.)

Most important, the Baltic Germans by 1900 were demographically an extremely thin upper crust, less than 4 percent of the population in Estonia. Losses of educated people to attractive positions in Russia could be compensated only through a continuous inflow of professionals from Germany and Germanization of some of the Estonians and Latvians. When the national awakening reduced Germanization and the nationalist Russian government throttled new German immigration, the Baltic German manors became aging "houses of twilight" (the title of a 1914 novel by Count Eduard von Keyserling, 1855–1918) from which younger members tried to escape to Germany or Russia.

In Finland, a symbiosis of the Finnish-speaking masses and the Swedish-speaking upper class was worked out. Could the Baltic Germans, the Latvians, and the Estonians have conceivably achieved a comparable symbiosis? Mutually beneficial as it might have been, the proposal came much too late when one of Jannsen's sons first proposed it. After separation from Sweden, the upper class in Finland considered themselves Finlanders who happened to speak Swedish. In contrast, the Baltic Germans always considered themselves Germans who happened to live in the Baltic provinces. Having two different peasant languages impeded the development of a Baltic identity because branches of the same German family in Estland and Courland could not possibly communicate in either Estonian or Latvian. Above all, ever since the Middle Ages, the social and ethnic relations in Finland never were as antagonistic as they were in the Baltic provinces, thanks to serfdom. The Baltic Germans had reached a dead end.

Industrialization and urbanization took off in Estonia after 1860, when telegraph, railroads (1870), and telephone (1880s) reached it. The Kreenholm textile mills in Narva were among the world's largest. In the

1880s, Tallinn was the second-largest import center (after St. Petersburg) for the Russian empire, until displaced by Riga and Odessa in the 1890s. Labor came mainly from the nearby countryside, and Estonians became the numerically predominant nationality in the cities. By 1900, they began to replace the well-entrenched Germans in city governments. A young farm-born Estonian lawyer and newspaper editor, Konstantin Päts (1870–1956), engineered the victory of an Estonian-Russian bloc in Tallinn city elections in 1904. To the dismay of the Germans, who had counted on mis-representing the Estonians as separatists in St. Petersburg, a rather passive Russian was made mayor, with Päts as vice-mayor actually running the show.

The 1905 Revolution

The Russian revolution of 1905 altered the atmosphere (see Raun 1984b). Facing strikes and unrest (also in Estonia), the Russian govern-ment acceded to extensive reforms, then reneged. An All-Estonian Con-gress (November 1905) split into reformist and radical halves, but both groups demanded autonomy. The imposition of martial law ten days later provoked burning of manor houses and brought bloody indiscriminate repression. Päts became a fugitive abroad, with a death sentence hanging over his head. When it later was reduced to a one-year prison sentence, he returned and served it.

But the change was irreversible. Political parties were organized, le-gally or illegally. Estonians participated in the new Russian parliament un-til the tsar gradually choked it off, missing the last opportunity for gradual transition from autocracy to constitutional monarchy. Jaan Tõnisson was among the parliament members who signed a call for a tax boycott after the dissolution of the First Duma in 1906. Shaken by the revolution, the Baltic Germans increasingly began looking toward Germany.[14]

Rapid economic and cultural development continued. Agricultural societies formed federations, cooperative movement expanded, and Esto-nian credit unions multiplied from none in 1900 to 129 in 1914. By then, 22 percent of the population lived in cities, and Tallinn reached a population of 116,000. The lifting of censorship in 1906 led to a publishing explosion. In 1913 alone, 702 Estonian books and brochures were published, and the total for 1900–1917 exceeded the entire pre-1900 output. After 1906, in-struction in Estonian was allowed in private schools and in the two first grades of state-run rural schools. Estonians formed one-sixth of the stu-dents at Tartu University, and their total in all universities reached 1,000 in 1914.

World War I interrupted everything. About 100,000 (20 percent of Esto-nian males) were mobilized into the tsarist armed forces, and over 10,000 died. The German army conquered the southwestern half of Latvia in 1915 but did not advance any farther until 1918. Labor and consumer-goods shortages plus inflation brought increasing dissatisfaction.

HOW ESTONIA WAS PREPARED FOR INDEPENDENCE

As the Estonia opera theater in Tallinn was being completed (1913), a Baltic German leader warned the Russians that the Estonians were building their future parliament building. It never was used for that purpose, and Estonian political goals did not go beyond autonomy before the Russian debacle of 1917. Only the talented but schizophrenic poet Juhan Liiv (1864–1913) wrote that "once, what a sane thought, there will be an Estonian state" (1910). Russia's collapse and descent into chaos made independence not only possible but almost mandatory. When that moment came, Estonia was reasonably well prepared.

Estonia's literacy surpassed that of France. Basic education had been around sufficiently long to generate an appreciable pool of candidates for higher education in various fields. The days when a sexton with primary education edited the only Estonian-language newspaper were long gone. The first generation of educated Estonians had used mainly German at home and for serious intellectual conversation, for lack of suitable vocabulary in Estonian, but by 1900 they could and did use Estonian. Shops and restaurants that formerly agreed to serve customers only when they spoke German, Russian, or even French (French was a pompous inclusion because most restaurants had no personnel able to speak it) were faced with people like Tõnisson, visibly a gentleman, politely insisting on using Estonian. Estonian professional theater flourished in several cities. Beyond Germany, Estonian writers and artists had discovered Western Europe and its modern trends. The writers' circle Noor-Eesti (Young Estonia) had raised the slogan "Let's remain Estonians but also become Europeans!" and this goal was being implemented. The educational and cultural basis for independence existed.[15]

Political and administrative skills were more limited. Cooperatives and associations developed basic organizational abilities. Rural township government gave people experience with local elections (and practices like vote buying) and trained a large pool of clerks in the basic methods of administration. By 1900, more than half of the Russian government officials in Estonia also were Estonians. Practice in city government was acquired after 1900, and participation in the Russian parliament widened outside contacts. After 1905, Tõnisson could legally form an Estonian political party (Estonian Progressive People's Party), and many others participated in all-Russian parties. These skills could be rapidly upgraded for governing the country. For international interaction, the easy polished manners expected from diplomats were largely lacking. Military skills, formerly reserved to Baltic nobles, were acquired by Estonian peasant sons who entered the Russian military academies, and World War I gave them extensive practice as field and staff officers.

Economically, Estonia was catching up with Finland, which itself was catching up with Sweden. Out of a total population of 1.1 million, 22 percent were living in cities. Major business and banking in Estonia remained in Baltic German hands, with increasing foreign investment, but Estonian-owned stores, shipping companies, small factories, and credit unions multiplied, establishing a solid intermediary layer. Farming cooperatives were formed to sell produce and buy machinery and consumer goods. Estonia certainly was too small to practice autarky, but in a reasonably open world market it had salable products.

Population size was the major weak point. It had reached one million, but emigration and a rapid drop in birthrate reduced further growth to almost zero. At the time, independent countries with a lesser population existed in Central America and in Europe (Montenegro, Luxembourg), but none of them had an official national language distinct from their neighbors' languages. Awareness of the limited size of the language area was a major reason the Estonians set their goal at no more than extensive cultural and territorial autonomy.

Nevertheless, this territory was well defined: The sea on two sides and a large lake on the third delineated a quasi-peninsula with good maritime connections. Within this area (traditional Estland and northern Livland), Estonians formed 90 percent of the population (and close to 70 percent even in the cities)—quite a contrast to the mix of people and languages in the band ranging from Poland to Greece. There were no Estonian irredentas outside this area, apart from Narva (detached from Estland in 1803) and a small strip in Pskov province. The appreciable Estonian diaspora in the Russian empire (close to 200,000, mainly in St. Petersburg and the farmland south of it, Caucasia, and Siberia) were clearly seen as living outside Estonia (Raun 1986b).

Given the rapid formation of the modern Estonian nation, Western Europe was unaware of its existence until an independent Estonia emerged as if through spontaneous generation. The preceding considerations indicate, however, that a fairly solid foundation preexisted.

NOTES

1. For the entire period up to 1917, more details and references can be found in Toivo Raun, *Estonia and the Estonians* (1991a). See also Evald Uustalu, *The History of Estonian People* (1952); and Hans Kruus, *Grundriss der Geschichte des estnischen Volkes* (1932) and *Histoire de l'Estonie* (1935).

2. For prehistory, the major work is Lembit Jaanits et al., *Eesti esiajalugu* [Prehistory of Estonia] (1982). See also Toivo Vuorela, *The Finno-Ugric Peoples* (1964); Péter Hajdú, *Ancient Cultures of the Uralian People* (1976); and Karin Mark, *Zur Herkunft der finnisch-ugrischen Völker vom Standpunkt der Anthropologie* (1970).

3. For Estonia around 1200, see Gustav Ränk, *Old Estonia: The People and the Culture* (1976); Ivar Paulson, *The Old Estonian Folk Religion* (1971); and Harri Moora and Herbert Ligi, *Wirtschaft und Gesellschaftsordnung der Völker des Baltikums zu Anfang des 13. Jahrhunderts* (1970).

4. The location of this fortress is unclear. Tradition places it in present-day Tartu, but archaeological excavations show no Russian weapons inside the Tartu stronghold except arrowheads, which suggests siege rather than occupancy; see Ain Mäesalu, "Uut Tartu linnusest" [New information about the Tartu stronghold], *Eesti Loodus*, vol. 23, 690–695 (1980).

5. The major contemporary source on the German conquest is *The Chronicle of Henry of Livonia*, translated into English by James Brundage (1961).

6. For the period of German rule, see Eric Christiansen, *The Northern Crusades: The Baltic and Catholic Frontier, 1100–1525* (1980); and from a pro-German viewpoint, see William Urban, *The Baltic Crusade* (1975), and *The Livonian Crusade* (1981).

7. The estimates for increases in the peasant burden during the Swedish rule are based on lists of deliveries and labor duties in Jüri Parijõgi et al., *Eesti ajalugu noorsoole* [Estonian history for the youth] (Stockholm: Vaba Eesti, 1954), 98 and 121. For general agricultural conditions, see Arnold Soom, *Der Herrenhof in Estland im 17. Jahrhundert* (1954); and Aleksander Loit, *Kampen om feodalräntan: Reduktionen och domänpolitiken i Estland, 1655–1710* [Struggle over feudal rent: The reduction and demesne policy in Estland, 1655–1710] (1975).

8. Garlieb Merkel, *Die Letten vorzüglich in Liefland am Ende des philosophischen Jahrhunderts* (1797). The book was followed by Johan C. Petri, *Ehstland und die Ehsten oder historisch-geographisch-statistisches Gemälde von Ehsteland* (1802).

9. English translations of seventy Estonian folksongs are given in Juhan Kurrik, *Ilomaile: Anthology of Estonian Folksongs with Translations and Commentary* (1985).

10. For the period of national awakening, see Aleksander Loit, ed., *National Movements in the Baltic Countries During the 19th Century* (1985); Georg Kurman, *The Development of Written Estonian* (1968); and Juhan Kahk, *Peasant and Lord in Process of Transition from Feudalism to Capitalism in the Baltics* (1982).

11. See articles by Thaden (1984, 1985) and Raun (1986a) for comparisons with neighboring countries; and see Raun (1985b) on the role of journalism.

12. In Edward C. Thaden et al., *Russification in the Baltic Provinces and Finland, 1855–1914* (1981), the chapters by Toivo Raun, "The Estonians," and Michael H. Haltzel, "The Baltic Germans," are directly relevant for Estonia. Baltic German views are presented by Gert von Pistohlkors, *Ritterschaftliche Reformpolitik zwischen Russifizierung und Revolution* (1978).

13. For the impact of Tartu University, see Karl Siilivask, ed., *History of Tartu University, 1632–1982* (1985); and Gert von Pistohlkors, Toivo U. Raun, and Paul Kaegbein, eds., *Die Universitäten Dorpat/Tartu, Riga und Wilna/Vilnius 1579–1979. Beiträge zur ihrer Geschichte und ihrer Wirkung im Grenzbereich zwischen Westen und Ost* (1987).

14. For the post-1905 period, see Andrew Ezergailis and Gert von Pistohlkors, eds., *Die baltischen Provinzen Russlands zwischen den Revolutionen von 1905 und 1917* (1982).

15. For development of Estonian literature, see Arvo Mägi, *Estonian Literature* (1968); and Endel Nirk, *Estonian Literature* (1987).

THREE

Independence and World War II

For the peoples on the eastern shores of the Baltic Sea, World War I began as a Russian-German war and ended as a war of independence. From their viewpoint, the constellations and events at the western front were as secondary as the eastern front was for the Americans and West Europeans. The same can be said about World War II that quashed Baltic independence and imperiled the Finnish. Meanwhile, between the wars, the newly independent nation-states were an end by themselves to the nations concerned, whereas the Western world viewed them mainly as a *cordon sanitaire* against Soviet communism and, later, a weak link in the anti-Nazi defenses. The Baltic nations all too easily assumed that their survival was somehow in the interest of the West, but the Western powers equally easily assumed that the prime role of the Baltic nations was support of Western policies rather than their own survival.[1]

ACHIEVEMENT OF INDEPENDENCE, 1917–1920

The outbreak of the German-Russian war in 1914 was met by a different response by each of the east Baltic people. Autonomy of Finland and tsarist suspicion of its loyalty enabled it to steer clear of the hostilities. Finland contributed financially to the Russian war effort but escaped mobilization. Tsarist encroachments on their autonomy made the Finns sympathize with Germany, which was at a safe distance. The Lithuanians felt equally uneasy about a Russia that had, until 1905, prohibited Latin-script Lithuanian books and a Germany that was also uncomfortably nearby. The Baltic Germans either sympathized with Germany or were suspected of doing so. The Latvians and Estonians largely favored Russia because they viewed Germany as an ally of their Baltic German oppressors. The Baltic draftees formed a disproportionately large part of the Russian forces that invaded East Prussia in August 1914 and suffered heavy casualties in the ensuing debacle.[2]

41

By the fall of 1915, all of Lithuania was under German control, and Lithuania's quest for self-rule took place outside the context of events in Russia. Germany supported independence for the previously Russian parts of Poland but, as a counterweight to Polish ambitions, also came to support autonomy for Lithuania, preferably under the rule of a Prussian prince. As the German forces entered western Latvia, the Latvians pressed for their own regiments within the Russian army. These Latvian Rifles stopped the German advance on the Daugava River, in central Latvia, but at the cost of being used as cannon fodder by tsarist generals. Embittered, they became an easy target for radical agitation. Estonia hosted numerous evacuees from western Latvia but remained outside the battle zone.

Achievement of Autonomy

When the February 1917 Russian Revolution toppled the tsar, Estonian and Latvian demands for autonomy increased. In April 1917, some 40,000 Estonians carried out a major demonstration in the Russian capital, Petrograd (former and present St. Petersburg). This show of force scared the Russian Provisional Government, and it agreed to combine Estland and the Estonian-speaking northern part of the province of Livland into a single autonomous unit. The Estonian mayor of Tallinn, Jaan Poska (1866–1920), became province commissioner, and a national regiment was formed by May 1917. The Russian Provisional Government's stubborn resistance to autonomy demands by other nations contributed to the increasing appeal of Lenin's Bolsheviks among the non-Russians. Elections to various local bodies were held, and preparations were made for general elections throughout the empire. In Estonia, a representative assembly, Maapäev, was elected.

The Bolshevik seizure of power in November 1917 represented a political counterrevolution, because it destroyed the nascent Russian democracy and effectively reestablished tsarism under a new management. The Bolshevik rule later also turned into a feudal counterrevolution against capitalism when the empire became a quilt of territorially interwoven fiefdoms of the various ministries and the freedom of movement for most peasants was strictly limited. In the beginning, however, the Bolshevik promises of peace and national autonomy had considerable appeal throughout the empire and especially in areas close to the front. The Bolsheviks allowed the elections to the Russian Constituent Assembly to proceed as planned by the previous government. Despite their military control, the Bolsheviks won only 27 percent of the vote throughout the empire; they netted 39 percent in Estonia and as much as 72 percent in war-weary Latvian-speaking southern Livland.[3]

In Estonia, an uneasy coexistence initially prevailed between Maapäev and the new Bolshevik authorities led by an Estonian, Viktor Kingissepp (1888–1922). On 28 November 1917, Kingissepp led Russian troops to disband Maapäev, but the assembly had time to adopt a major resolution: Maapäev declared itself the supreme authority in Estonia. It was not yet a declaration of independence, but it was one of sovereignty. Maapäev said it alone had the authority to decide whether Estonia would join or rejoin another entity or pursue its own course.

By then the Germans had occupied the Estonian island of Saaremaa, and their advance into continental Estonia looked imminent in view of the Bolshevik failure to reach an accommodation with the Germans. The non-Bolshevik Estonian parties and press (which partly continued to operate openly) began to argue for an Estonian declaration of independence as a way to pull the country out of the German-Russian conflict and thus possibly prevent German occupation. As the price for their cooperation, the Bolsheviks were to retain power in this independent Estonia. The proposal was backed by all non-Bolshevik political groupings, from the center-right to Social Democrats to Socialists-Revolutionaries. Realizing he could not defend Estonia, Lenin responded favorably, although there was little hope that the German army would be deterred by a declaration of independence. However, in a surfeit of internationalism, the Estonian Bolsheviks refused the proposal—and that was a major mistake.

The Bolsheviks had alienated many Estonians with their virulence against the church, but the real disappointment came when the citizenry learned they refused to divide up the Baltic German estates: The highly principled Estonian Bolsheviks wanted to turn the estates directly into collective farms. Soon the Bolshevik slogan "Bread! Peace! Land!" began to sound hollow. Bread was as scarce as ever, peace was not in sight, and individual land for peasants was not forthcoming. Trying to improve their position, the Bolsheviks proceeded with the elections for an Estonian Constituent Assembly in January 1918, as planned by Maapäev. The Bolshevik vote dropped from 39 percent to about 37, and authorities stopped the ballot count. At the same time, the all-Russian Constituent Assembly briefly met but was disbanded by Lenin when it proved unwieldy. The Bolsheviks had betrayed democracy in Russia as well as national self-determination in Estonia.

Declaration of Independence

When the German-Bolshevik talks collapsed, the Germans quickly overran Estonia in late February 1918. The Red Army offered only token resistance. The first Estonian national regiment remained neutral, as it had during the Bolshevik takeover. A three-person National Salvation Committee empowered by the underground organs of Maapäev proclaimed Estonia independent on 24 February 1918. Estonians celebrate this date as their Independence Day.

At the moment, however, the declaration had little immediate impact; the Germans entered Tallinn the next day and ignored the Estonian authorities. The Estonian military units were disbanded. One member of the Salvation Committee, Jüri Vilms (1889–1918), fled to Finland and was executed by German and Finnish troops in Helsinki (April 1918). The most prominent of the committee members, former vice-mayor of Tallinn Konstantin Päts, was later sent to a German concentration camp in present-day Belarus.

Germany occupied all of Lithuania, Latvia, and Estonia until the German collapse in November 1918. It also sent an expeditionary corps to Finland in April 1918 during its civil war and maintained political influence there even after military withdrawal. Both in Finland and Lithuania, formation of kingdoms was proposed by national assemblies, with German princes as kings. In Lithuania, this was a move aimed to block the king of Prussia (i.e., the German emperor) from declaring himself king of Lithuania. Estonians and Latvians were not even left that option, as the Baltic Germans worked for a direct annexation by the Reich. To demonstrate popular demand for German protection, they summoned township elders to Tallinn and Riga to participate in instant assemblies in which the Baltic Germans took most of the seats for themselves. In Riga, the township elders of southern Estonia balked, declaring they had no mandate to decide on political matters, but the Baltic German majority voted for a separation from Russia anyway. Full Germanization of Estonia and Latvia was openly proposed. The university at Tartu opened as a German-language university and was boycotted by most Estonian students.

The surrender of Germany to the Western Allies (11 November 1918) altered the picture almost overnight. Provisional governments were set up in Lithuania, Estonia, and Latvia, but they were initially extremely weak in the face of the retreating German occupation troops. Lenin's Bolsheviks were surprised by the suddenness of the German collapse and only slowly began to marshal forces for a reconquest of the western territories. According to the capitulation agreement with the Western powers, the German troops were to withdraw from the Baltic lands but also were to resist advances by the Bolsheviks. This double obligation left some room for maneuvering by the Baltic Germans and those German officers who tried to maintain German influence in Latvia and Estonia. It was in their interest to keep the Baltic governments weak so that the Germans would appear as the only realistic defense against the Bolsheviks.

The first Bolshevik attack at the Estonian-Russian border (Narva, 22 November 1918) was repelled by German troops, but after they withdrew, the Bolsheviks took Narva and proclaimed an Estonian Workers Commune (29 November 1918), headed by Jaan Anvelt (1884–1937). As a counterweight to the Republic of Estonia proclaimed in February 1918, this fuzzy entity was too little, too late—the Estonian democratic government had been operating in Tallinn, however precariously, for several weeks. In terms of national emotions, a "commune" was no match for a "republic," and the commune government obviously was utterly dependent on the Russian Red Army commanders. Although appreciable numbers of Estonians sided with the Bolsheviks, the war immediately took on the character of an Estonian-Russian war rather than a civil war such as the one in Finland in early 1918.

War of Independence

For the Estonian government, the main enemy was its own lack of organization, especially in military matters, and the public expectation that Estonia could not possibly resist Russia. After four years of world war, the population was exhausted. Estonian mobilization orders were ignored. In some of the engagements, the Estonians actually had numerical superiority, yet retreated or even disbanded. By the end of December 1918, two-thirds of the country was in Bolshevik hands, and the front was a mere thirty kilometers from Tallinn. Then, however, a reversal set in on 7 January 1919. Within a month, nearly all of the national territory was recovered. What caused this reversal?

The Estonian civilian and military structures in Tallinn finally became sufficiently organized. Financial help received from Finland laid the basis for an Estonian currency. Konstantin Päts returned from a German concentration camp and assumed the premiership, determined to win Estonian independence. An able former tsarist staff officer, Johan Laidoner (1884–1953), made his way back from Russia and became commander in chief. A British navy detachment blocked a Bolshevik attempt to land behind the Estonian lines. The closeness of the front, as long as it did not create panic, shortened the Estonian supply lines but extended those of the Bolsheviks. Hard pressed on other fronts, the Red Army leadership underestimated the Estonian capacity to rebound and did not bring up reserves until it was too late. The arrival of some Finnish volunteers boosted Estonian morale. In sum, Estonians had desire to defend independence, some foreign aid, and ability to make maximum use of that aid. Once the Estonian counteroffensive began, the psychological reversal became self-reinforcing.

War continued until the end of 1919, and there were further difficult moments. Initially the forces on both sides numbered a few thousand;

there were a hundred thousand later on. In May 1919, the commander of the major Red Estonian regiment surrendered with one-half his men, and when the Red Army leaders packed their remaining Estonian allies off to other Bolshevik fronts, the last elements of an Estonian civil war disappeared. The Estonian Workers Commune quietly folded in June 1919. Twice during 1919, White Russian armies were gathered in Estonia, at the insistence of Western Allies, and tried vainly to take Petrograd. Estonian support for these endeavors was lukewarm, however, because these Russian elements were openly hostile to Estonian independence (see Kukk 1981).

A brief but intense battle in June 1919 against German units pulled Estonian reserves away from the eastern front and deserves a more detailed account: In early 1919, Latvia found itself in a markedly more difficult position than Estonia. The Baltic Germans retrenched themselves in Kurzeme (western Latvia) and arranged for a number of Reich Germans to be recruited as mercenaries, especially from among the retreating German troops. The fledgling Latvian government largely depended on them for defense. The advancing Bolshevik troops included the well-disciplined Latvian Rifles, and they took Riga on 3 January 1919. At this point, an observer might have thought a war of national liberation was occurring in Latvia, but with roles reversed compared with the Estonian situation: The largely Latvian Reds were fighting the essentially German Whites. It did not last. Bolshevik rule soon succeeded in turning the Latvian population against it, and the Latvian democratic government gained new credibility when the Germans toppled it in April 1919, replacing it with a puppet government. The mainly Baltic German Landeswehr and the predominantly Reich German Iron Division retook Riga from the Bolsheviks, but then turned against the Estonian-Latvian forces in northern Latvia, who beat them decisively at Cesis (23 June 1919). This victory enabled the democratic government of Latvia to reassert itself. Although the war against Soviet Russia lasted a full year and that against the Germans only a few weeks, Estonia later celebrated its Victory Day on 23 June. It symbolized the end of 700 years of domination by the German estate owners.

The Tartu Peace Treaty

As soon as its army reached the country's ethnic and historical borders, Estonia tried to end the war. When Soviet Russia became more amenable to this idea, the pressure to keep the war going increased on the side of the Allies, on whom Estonia depended not only for military supplies but also essential civilian aid. Finally, Estonia put its interests first and concluded an armistice (31 December 1919) and then the Tartu Peace Treaty (2 February 1920). For Soviet Russia, it was the first peace treaty it signed, to be fol-

Fight, fight, vote, vote: Elections for the Estonian Constituent Assembly at the front (5–7 April 1919) during the war of independence against Soviet Russian invasion. *Eesti Vabariik* (1968), Eesti Kirjanike Kooperatiiv. Reprinted with permission.

lowed by those with Latvia, Lithuania, and Finland many months later. For Estonia, it meant its first de jure recognition. Russia obtained transit facilities in Estonia, and the two sides agreed to trade relations.[4]

The border delineation in the Tartu Peace Treaty especially should be noted because this became a hot issue in Estonia's internal and external debate in the early 1990s. The Estonian declaration of independence spoke of its "ethnic and historical" borders, but these were not quite the same. The historical borders implied those of the predominantly Lutheran provinces of Estland and Livland; Livland was shared with Latvia, but areas of mixed Latvian-Estonian population were limited, and a mutually acceptable border was rapidly demarcated. The ethnic definition of borders added to Estonia a small adjacent area (about 1,000 square kilometers) in the Russian Pskov province, inhabited by Orthodox Estonian-speaking Setu, and raised the issue of the large numbers of Estonian farmers living in the Pskov and Petrograd provinces.[5] The Tartu Peace Treaty gave Estonia not only the Setu area but also about 1,500 square kilometers of predominantly Russian-inhabited land beyond the Narva River in the northeast and between the Setu area and the city of Pskov in the southeast (Raun 1991c). The expanded territory reflected the demands of the Estonian military for a defensible border. Incidentally, it also roughly balanced out the number of Russians in Estonia (about 100,000 within the Tartu treaty borders) and the number of Estonians in the Pskov and Petrograd provinces.

Already during the war, elections to an Estonian Constituent Assembly had been carried out (April 1919); soldiers at the front also participated. The assembly adopted a "Declaration of Independence and Sovereignty of Estonia" (19 May 1919), thus reconfirming the hurried statement of 24 February 1918. Outlined immediately was an extensive land reform to divide the large estates into family farms. Without such a reform, it would have been difficult to maintain morale among the draftees. By mid-1920, an ultrademocratic constitution was adopted, the consequences of which are discussed later. De jure recognition by major European powers followed in January 1921, but the United States held out until July 1922. Estonia became a member of the League of Nations in September 1921 (see Peters 1983).

Through at times quite different processes, by 1920 Finland, Estonia, Latvia, and Lithuania had reached the same political status: independent and essentially parliamentary republics based on a sense of community of language. The latter three countries increasingly came to be designated as the "Baltic states"; the earlier term "Baltic provinces" referred only to Latvia and Estonia.

In the case of Finland, a long period of autonomy had preceded independence, and the main conflict during the disturbed times of 1917–1920 was a civil war (with some involvement by German and Russian troops). In the case of Latvia and Estonia, the limited pre-1917 autonomy applied only to the Baltic German landed nobility. The main conflict in Estonia was an external defensive war with Soviet Russia, called the "war of freedom" in Estonian historiography. The initially many-sided conflict in Latvia also ended up as a Latvian-Russian war.

Lithuania lacked any autonomy before 1917, and military activities on its soil were relatively limited. It was partly sheltered from Russia by Polish forces (whose front in southern Latvia at one time made contact with the Estonian front in northern Latvia). But Lithuania lost its traditional capital, Vilnius, to Poland, and this seizure marred the countries' relations throughout the interwar period. Lithuania gained control of the Lithuanian-speaking but previously German-held Klaipeda (Memel) area on the Baltic coast, but its rule there remained disputed. The issues of Vilnius and Klaipeda cast a dark shadow over Baltic cooperation because Latvia and Estonia shunned involvement in these disputes. Once Lithuania was out of the picture, Latvian-Estonian cooperation seemed of little importance and remained minimal.

The independence of the Baltic states came about when both major powers in the region, Russia and Germany, were unusually weak, but that does not automatically mean the Baltic states were artificial creations. Their languages and the resulting cultures were very real and sooner or later were bound to have some political impact, but it also does not follow that independence was inevitable. The Balts were resourceful in making use of opportunities when these arose. Estonia was not created by the Peace Treaty of Versailles; it was created by its war of independence and by whatever it took to bring that war to a successful end, including the Tartu treaty. Foreign assistance was at times important, especially British naval intervention, but this aid pales compared with the crucial impact of French military involvement in the American Revolution. Rather than being either "artificial" or "inevitable," the formation of the Republic of Estonia between 1918 and 1920 falls into the broad zone in between these semantic extremes.

YEARS OF PEACE, 1920–1939

During the nearly twenty years of interwar peace, the new nation-states on the eastern shore of the Baltic went through a period of democracy and relative well-being and then faced the consequences of the world depression, which included the fascist and communist challenge to democracy. By 1939, the economy had recovered, but the degree of reassertion of democracy varied from country to country. In Lithuania, the last elections were held in 1926; they were soon followed by authoritarian rule that was partly relaxed only in 1938. In Estonia and Latvia, authoritarianism began in 1934. Estonia had new elections in 1938, but no similar relaxation yet occurred in Latvia. In Finland, democracy weathered a serious challenge from the extreme right without interruption.[6]

A common feature in all four countries was rightist exploitation of the threat from the extreme left, which was real enough, given the proximity to the Soviet Union. Authoritarianism in the Baltic states was more of the traditional conservative variety rather than the fascist. It involved individual powerholders with no mass party organization or heavy repressive machinery. There was no official anti-Semitism. The rulers' attitudes toward Nazi Germany were rather cool because nationalism in Latvia and Estonia was tied to resentment against the age-old Baltic German exploitation and because Lithuania was at odds with Germany over Klaipeda. By 1938, modest democratic recovery had begun in Estonia and arguably also in Lithuania. It is likely that Latvia would have followed the same pattern had peace in Europe continued.

The three Baltic states attempted to preserve neutrality regarding the great powers. In particular, all three countries signed nonaggression or neutrality agreements first with the Soviet Union (Lithuania in 1926, Latvia and Estonia in 1932) and then also with Germany (in early 1939). Neutrality laws patterned on the Swedish law of 1938 were adopted by Latvia and Estonia in December 1938 and by Lithuania a month later.

The Baltic states also remained rather isolated from each other. Finland kept aloof from its southern neighbors, much for the same reason its Scandinavian neighbors kept aloof from Finland: to avoid involvement with more recent national structures subject to possible Russian claims (see Raun 1987a). Latvia and Estonia did not want to be drawn into Lithuania's border disputes with Poland and Germany, and Latvian-Estonian cooperation looked too narrow to be worthwhile. An Estonian-Latvian defensive alliance in 1923 and a Baltic entente in 1934, which included Lithuania, remained largely on paper. On the positive side, all border disputes of any significance among the Baltic states and with Soviet Russia were settled in 1920. Relations were friendly or indifferent but not hostile.

Land Reform and Cultural Autonomy for Minorities

The nation's immediate concerns in 1920, once peace was achieved, were socioeconomic: repairing war damage, adjusting to the new borders, and solving longstanding social problems inherited from tsarist times. Cultural issues also were important in building a nation-state based on a formerly suppressed language.

The most urgent issues were achieving land reform, developing a new industrial production profile, finding new markets, and accommodating the ethnic minorities. It should be noted that Estonia did not face many of the usual problems of newly independent countries of the post–World War II era: There was no need to forge a new and somewhat artificial nation out of disparate parts of a colonial territory, because the Estonian-speaking population (88 percent of the total) already had a common national consciousness. An educated elite already existed, and literacy was universal. The country was economically fairly well developed, compared with the leading industrial states, and the disparity between the capital city and the countryside was unusually small (although it certainly existed). The elites felt no urge to spend heavily on armament or prestige projects; if anything, the reverse was the case—perhaps the result of the Protestant peasant's proverbial tendency toward economic caution. Estonia may have been the only country in the world to save on perforation of postal stamps: Until 1922, the stamps had to be separated with scissors.

Land reform was implemented within a remarkably short time, and it transformed large estates into small family farms. Very limited compensation was paid to the mainly German estate owners. In 1929, the average farm had about 18 hectares (including pastures and woodland), and half the farmland belonged to farms of fewer than 35 hectares (85 acres). A decade later, Estonia must have had the most equal farmland distribution in the world: Its Gini index of inequality (43 percent) was lower than any country's in the 1950s, including Communist-ruled Yugoslavia (44 percent) and Poland (45 percent).[7] The flip side was a lack of economy of scale. This was partly compensated by extensive development of cooperatives for various aspects of production, marketing, and land melioration. Dairy farming was the major trend, in imitation of Denmark, and Britain became the major customer (Hinkkanen-Lievonen 1983; 1984; 1986).

Industrial adjustment was less successful. The large factories in Tallinn and Narva were geared to tsarist military and naval uses or to the Russian market, which no longer could be easily reached. Trade with the USSR flourished for a while but then tapered off because of Soviet attempts at autarky. Industry had to be diversified and reduced in scale to suit the smaller domestic market. The number of industrial workers decreased. Management skills were limited, and blunders occurred. Influence peddling was naive rather than purposefully corrupt. Estonia was lucky to begin its recovery in a postwar worldwide boom era that helped to recover from war losses and start building a nation-state economy, but the ripples from the Great Depression arrived before the changeover could be completed. A suitable balance was found only in the late 1930s. The foreign debt incurred during the war of independence remained a burden.

In imitation of Finland, Estonia at first created a currency consisting of marks and pennies (1 mark = 100 pennies). Inflation was considerable in the early years of independence; the cost of a letter stamp went from 15 pennies in 1918 to 1 mark by 1921 to 10 marks by 1924. In 1928 the kroon was introduced (1 kroon = 100 sent = 100 previous marks), and for the next ten years its value remained stable at about 0.25 U.S. dollars.

Ethnic minorities in Estonia consisted mainly of Russians (8 percent of the population), Germans (1.5 percent), Jews (0.5 percent), and Swedes (0.5 percent). For geographically compact groups (Russians in the eastern borderlands and Swedes in the western islands), schooling in their own language was established through local township self-government. The more dispersed groups (Germans and Jews) made use of nonterritorial cultural autonomy, an approach for which Estonia still remains a model.[8] The authoritarian interlude in the 1930s had little effect on this cultural autonomy. German, Swedish, and Russian representation in the parliament was facilitated in the 1920s by nationwide proportional-representation rules (the negative effects of which are discussed later).

Participation of ethnic minorities in the elites was appreciable in the economy (Germans and Jews) but low in politics and the military (although the navy was headed by a German in the 1930s). The Estonians were busy with the first stages of building their nation, and the minorities on their part remained rather indifferent toward the new state. This applies, in particular, to the poorly educated Russian peasants in the eastern borderlands as well as the educated Russian Whites in their temporary status as international refugees. By today's Western criteria, one would note an insufficient integration of ethnic minorities. However, in the context of interwar Europe, the ethnic relations in Estonia are noteworthy for their peacefulness.

The Farm Mystique

Development of Estonian national culture continued throughout the democratic and the authoritarian periods. Education at all levels became available in Estonian. Tartu University switched to the Estonian language, and a technical university was founded in Tallinn. An Estonian Academy of Sciences also was founded. The Estonian language was purposefully modernized, an eight-volume universal encyclopedia was published, and world classics were translated into Estonian. Writers such as novelist A. H. Tammsaare (1878–1940) and poet Marie Under (1883–1980) made use of this more developed language. In particular, Tammsaare's five-volume *Tõde ja õigus* (Truth and Justice, 1926–1933) brings out a streak of recrimination and search for justice at any cost in the Estonian character that was to sound eerily familiar in the political debate of the early 1990s. A campaign to Estonianize family names (1936) motivated (and in the case of some state employees, pressured) perhaps a third of the Estonian population to change their names, but numerous Germanic names remained. My parents, for example, added a second "a" to the previous "Tagepera" so as to conform it to the actual pronunciation.

Most of this activity was oriented inward, and Estonia offered little to the outside world: Its best writers remained largely untranslated, scholarship at Tartu University was respectable but produced no major breakthroughs, and Estonia's foremost artists such as Eduard Wiiralt (1898–1954) were minor ones in Paris. Estonian society remained farm-oriented not only in economic terms but also in its mental outlook.

Acquisition of land had been the main goal for most Estonians during the preceding century, and this land hunger was largely settled only with the land reform of the 1920s. Meanwhile, city jobs continued to be seen as something alien. Farming was felt to be the only honorable activity, in principle, even by those numerous Estonians who had settled in the cities. As an urban child of a Tallinn-born mother, I read early on that "A tradesman's wealth is temporary, a farmer's permanent." The reasoning: "When the tradesman sleeps his trade stands at the wall; when a farmer sleeps his crops continue to grow."

It should be kept in mind that we are talking here about a very limited time span of twenty years and a very young culture in a modern sense. With few exceptions, these citizens were people who grew up on farms; they included a first-generation educated elite who received this education under quite adverse conditions. All too many of them were in their twenties before completing high school. Once free from Russian and German pressures, they still had to create the social, cultural, and material surroundings that normally form the atmosphere and springboard for unusual talent. That they were able to approach the world level in most aspects might be sufficient achievement for the first twenty years. A not atypical case was my father's situation:

Karl was born on a middle-sized farm. His mother had some four years of schooling and his father had less. They put him through high school in the city, somehow still expecting that he would return to tend the farm. The school was in Russian, in which he remained weak even by the time of graduation exams. Putting all his effort into it, he passed the Russian exam but was flunked anyway because the errors of Russian in his Latin exam were arbitrarily transferred to his Russian exam. Deeply hurt by this gap between Truth and Justice (as Tammsaare put it), he gave up on a high school diploma and entered a field of study for which no diploma was needed (veterinary). Despite this handicap, he eventually became an associate professor at Tartu University. Sharing in the farm mystique, he also bought a farm, ploughing and harvesting during summers instead of doing research. He had been a volunteer in the war of independence, and when I once asked him why, he said, "Because I was hungry," avoiding all heroic rhetoric. He had fled his home when the Red Army advanced and was alone in Tallinn when he volunteered. My father's blunt honesty instilled in me a self-confidence that he himself no longer could have.

From Ultrademocracy to Authoritarianism

In politics, Estonia initially created an ultrademocratic structure that stressed proportional representation and popular initiative at the expense of efficiency. All power was invested in a 100-member single-chamber parliament that made and unmade prime ministers and their cabinets every eight months on the average (for the period 1919–1933). The prime minister could not retaliate by calling for new parliamentary elections (as is usual in most stable parliamentary democracies). In an effort to avoid even the least possibility of executive dominance, the constitution provided for no head of state. The prime minister doubled as head of state, and during a cabinet crisis, the country lacked even a symbolic figurehead to bridge the gap.

In parliamentary elections, the entire country was effectively a single 100-seat district, and a 1 percent vote nationwide enabled a party to win a seat. Fourteen parties gained access to the parliament in 1923, and even the largest one (the Farmers' Union, of course) had only twenty-three seats. In terms of fractionalization, this apparently remained a world record until the Polish elections of 1991.[9] Cabinet coalitions were difficult to assemble and unraveled easily. By 1932, after the threshold on minor party representation was effectively raised to 2 percent, the number of parliamentary parties dropped to six, and the largest party won forty-two seats. The distribution of the 100 seats (closely reflecting the shares of votes) that resulted from the 1932 election was the following:

Communists	5
Socialist Workers Party	22
National Center Party	23
United Agrarian Party	42
Russian Party	5
German-Swedish Party	3

The reduction in the number of parliamentary parties shows that the system had some capacity for self-correction. However, it did not last. By 1934, several parliamentary groups had split up:[10]

Marxist Group	3
Leftist Workers Party	3
Socialist Workers Party	19
National Center Party	17
United Agrarian Party	19
Farmers' Union	20
Russian Party	5
German-Swedish Party	3
Independents	11

By this time, ultrademocracy had discredited itself in the public view. The hardships caused by the world depression also tended to be blamed on the political regime.

The first major challenge came from the far left, or rather from the east. In 1923, the communist front organization received a record 9.5 percent of the popular vote (and ten parliamentary seats), which may have encouraged its leaders to seize power. On 1 December 1924, a bloody communist putsch in Tallinn came dangerously close to seizing the radio building, and Soviet troops at the Estonian border were on high alert, waiting for a call for help. Three years earlier, Soviet troops had entered Georgia under somewhat similar circumstances, thus ending Georgia's independence. In Estonia, the outcome was suppression of communist organizations and a temporary rallying of all other parties in a government of national unity.

It is ironic that in the face of Soviet communist subversion, the otherwise superdemocratic regime felt obliged to resort to considerable repression, including life imprisonments and executions. Kingissepp, one of the former top leaders of the Estonian Workers Commune and later an underground Soviet agent, was court-martialed, shot, and buried in an unmarked grave in 1922. The USSR responded by renaming Iamburg, a Russian town close to the Estonian border, Kingissepp. Imprisonment of some Estonian communist parliament members, whose immunity had been revoked by parliamentary vote, raised strong protest among the Scandinavian Social Democrats.

The second major challenge came from the right, in the form of the League of Veterans of the War of Freedom, popularly abbreviated as the Vabs. This veterans' organization gradually became a populist political movement of the far right that demanded a strong presidency. A moderate modification of the constitution, supported by all nonleftist parties and also by ethnic minorities, was rejected narrowly (49 to 51 percent) in a 1932 referendum. A second attempt, pushed mainly by the Farmers' Union, fared even worse. Subsequently, a strongly presidential constitution proposed by the Vabs won by 73 percent of the votes (October 1933). Presidential elections were scheduled, and the Vabs expected to win. When signatures were collected for nominations, their candidate surpassed by far the combined total of the three other candidates. Increasingly, the Vabs applied strong-arm tactics, threatening their opponents with dire retaliation once they gained power.

Meanwhile, however, Prime Minister Päts became acting president. He decided that the broad powers that accrued to the president in the new constitution applied to the acting president too. He declared a state of martial law (March 1934), arrested some 400 Vabs, prohibited all political parties, deactivated the parliament, and postponed any further elections. "Since the postponement of elections by decree was expressly forbidden by the Constitution of 1933, Päts had, in effect, carried out a coup d'état" (Raun 1991a:119).

From Authoritarianism Toward Democracy

The Vabs had been beaten at their own game, but in so doing Päts also ended democracy. Given the alternatives, the democratic parties yielded. A putsch attempt by the Vabs (November 1934) was nipped in the bud, and Päts ruled by decree until 1938. A referendum on a new Constituent Assembly formally legalized his caretaker regime in 1936. However, no public opposition activity was permitted before the referendum or during the elections for the Constituent Assembly, members of which were largely handpicked by Päts and followed the guidelines he set. His tactic was to claim, correctly so, that the 1933 constitution gave the president dangerously strong powers—and then he slipped in even stronger ones. The new constitution provided for an utterly toothless first chamber of the parliament to be elected in eighty single-seat districts, and a second chamber largely appointed by the president. In subtle ways, presidential powers were increased, compared with the Vabs constitution, and became in many ways much stronger than those in the United States.[11]

One of the most cunning sleights of hand was the procedure of presidential election. Candidates could be nominated only by majority in each of three bodies: the second chamber, which consisted largely of Päts's appointees; the assembly of local governments, which also consisted largely of Päts's supporters; and the first chamber, the only body by which someone other than Päts could conceivably be nominated. The only party label allowed during the parliamentary election was Päts's own Popular Front for Implementation of the Constitution. In many districts, several opposition candidates were nominated and split the anti-Päts vote. With 47 percent of the popular vote, Päts's supporters carried 55 percent of the seats—a fairly typical bonus when one-seat districts are used. Ten more deputies later jumped on the winners' bandwagon. All three bodies nominated Päts for president, and in the face of such orchestrated unanimity, he was anointed without any popular election in early 1938.

Like Mikhail Gorbachev fifty years later, Päts did not submit himself to direct election. Both men proceeded through assemblies that themselves were elected under conditions of imperfect competition. Both men probably would have been elected, though we will never know for sure. Was the process democratic? Far from it—but in both cases, it was an improvement on the previous state of affairs and left the door open to further developments.

Compared with the Vabs' leaders and their fascist-sounding rhetoric, Päts was by that time a traditional conservative and used his new powers with some caution. His talk about a shift toward more democracy seemed sincere. It should be remembered that in 1938 democracy seemed on the decline and did not receive the universal lip service it does today. Ever since 1919, Päts had played the democratic game, repeatedly assuming the premiership, then stepping down when voted out in the parliament. But by 1935 he had become skeptical about the maturity of an electorate who had supported the Vabs constitution, and he wanted the return to democracy to be slow.

Päts became accustomed to power, and the prime ministers he chose were yes-men. In 1936, the face of Päts replaced Estonia's coat of arms on the main series of stamps, which loudly proclaimed that Estonia had become Pätsonia. His pettiest act was the sequestration of *Postimees*, the newspaper of Jaan Tõnisson, his archrival since 1900. Tõnisson had frequently been prime minister in the 1920s. Initially more conservative than Päts, he was now leading the centrist opposition. The worst factor for Päts was that at the same time he retrenched himself in the presidency, his

Jaan Tõnisson, the most prominent democratic leader of the 1930s, was prime minister and head of state 1919–1920, 1927–1928, and 1933. Place and date of death in Soviet prison unknown. *Eesti Vabariik* (1968), Eesti Kirjanike Kooperatiiv. Reprinted with permission.

mental capacities may have become affected by health and age, just when international clouds were darkening.

In another irony, the authoritarian interlude was a period of no executions or political murders in Estonia, in notable contrast to the embattled democracy of the 1920s.[12] The communist underground collapsed in the early 1930s as a result of steady official pressure and lack of popular support. Most of those Estonian communists who sought refuge in the USSR were executed as nationalists by Stalin; they included Jaan Anvelt, once the head of the Estonian Workers Commune. By 1938, Päts felt so secure that he granted amnesty to all political prisoners (except a few dozen espionage cases), both communists and Vabs.

The economy improved in the late 1930s, as Estonia recovered from the depression, to the degree that some emigrants returned from the United States. The political system had slipped from ultrademocracy to authoritarianism, but was shifting back toward a balance of presidential efficiency and some democratic features like parliamentary elections. Cultural development and cultural autonomy for minorities had not been affected by the political roller coaster. Foreign relations were peaceful, and there were no unsolved border disagreements. The country was still heavily rural demographically (29 percent urban in 1935) and even more so in its outlook. The birthrate was low and natural population increase practically zero. Per capita income remained low compared with Scandinavia, but the gap was closing.

In sum, the critical early period of state building was over. Left to its own devices, Estonia could look to a reasonably bright future. It was not left alone.

THE MOLOTOV-RIBBENTROP PACT AND THE FIRST SOVIET OCCUPATION, 1939–1941

A Soviet-German nonaggression agreement concluded 23 August 1939 between Soviet Foreign Minister Viacheslav M. Molotov and his German counterpart, Joachim von Ribbentrop, enabled Hitler to attack Poland and Stalin to end Baltic independence, among other consequences. The Molotov-Ribbentrop Pact (MRP) grew out of a triangle of negotiations: Western-German, in which the West tried to persuade Germany to desist from expansion, an effort that largely ended after the fiasco in Munich; Western-Soviet, which attempted to build a barrier to German expansion and failed when the West reluctantly disagreed with the Soviet demand to control the countries between Germany and the USSR; and Soviet-German, which succeeded when Germany agreed to split this zone with the USSR.[13]

The Pact and Soviet Bases

Publicly, the resulting MRP was merely a German-Soviet nonaggression agreement. The delineation of Soviet and German spheres of interest in East-Central Europe was hidden in a secret additional protocol. Its basic contents leaked out almost immediately. Documentary evidence was found by Western Allies in 1945 in German archives, and in December 1989 the Supreme Soviet of the USSR confirmed its existence. For Estonia, the crucial sentence was the following:

> In the event of a territorial and political rearrangement in the areas belonging to the Baltic states (Finland, Estonia, Latvia, Lithuania), the northern boundary of Lithuania shall represent the boundary of the spheres of influence of Germany and the USSR.[14]

Most of Lithuania was transferred to the Soviet sphere in late September 1939, after Hitler had broken the Polish military resistance and Stalin had stabbed Poland in the back and occupied its eastern territories.

The MRP left the meaning of "spheres of influence" vague. At its softest, it could merely mean exclusion of any other outside influence. At its harshest, it could mean outright annexation. Recent developments offered examples in both directions. The Czech lands had been annexed by Germany, but Slovakia remained a formally sovereign German satellite; Mongolia had a similar relationship to the USSR. Not even knowing the exact text of the secret protocol of the MPR and unable to undermine a Soviet-German alliance, the Baltic governments hoped for the softest interpretation.

As mentioned earlier, the Baltic states early on had concluded neutrality or nonaggression treaties with their large Soviet neighbor. As the German presence made itself increasingly felt, similar treaties were signed with Germany in early 1939 (see Ahmann 1989). Neutrality laws patterned on Sweden's were adopted by the Baltic states in winter 1938–1939. Depending on prior expectations, one can view neutrality as a glass half empty or half full. Accustomed to Swedish neutrality but hoping to include the Baltic states in the anti-German alliance, the Western Allies felt Baltic neutrality was pro-German but that of Sweden was acceptable. Germany, precisely because it did not expect to win the Baltic states to its side, was satisfied with their neutrality. Paradoxically, precisely because they tried to be neutral, the Baltic states suddenly appeared nonneutral to both sides.

Participation of the Baltic states in a *cordon sanitaire* against Germany was prevented not only by their desire to keep out of great-power competition but also by Soviet insistence on terms that made "alliance" akin to Soviet occupation of the Baltic states (and Poland). To the Western powers, blocking Germany was primary—preserving Baltic independence was tertiary. They were annoyed by the Baltic and Polish objections, but did not feel quite comfortable overriding them completely to strike a deal with the USSR. Thus, the USSR got a better deal from Nazi Germany, which was not as squeamish about Baltic independence as Western democracies felt obliged to be.

When he had occupied his half of Poland, Stalin suddenly shifted 160,000 Soviet troops from Poland to the Estonian border and demanded military bases in Estonia. The proposed Soviet garrisons (25,000) surpassed in size Estonia's army (16,000). Having a common border with Poland, Latvia and Lithuania had partially mobilized so as to handle border crossings by the defeated Poles; Estonia had not. It now faced a ten-to-one superiority at the border, Soviet warplanes flying low over Estonian cities, and no time to mobilize. Germany not only refused any diplomatic support, but also made clear it would not tolerate any sea transport of arms to Estonia from the West. Latvia and Lithuania distanced themselves. On 28 September 1939, Estonia accepted a pact of defense and mutual assistance with the USSR. Latvia's and Lithuania's turn came in early October. Stalin probably picked Estonia first because it was the smallest, had not mobilized, and was far away from Germany, whose reaction Stalin could not be certain of in view of the vagueness in the MRP secret protocol.

Once the Soviet bases had been established, military defense of Estonia against further encroachments became as impossible as it was for Czechoslovakia after it ceded the Sudeten to Germany. The only course left was to avoid the least provocation and wait for the world situation to change. Until May 1940, the Soviet government and garrisons also adopted a fairly cautious attitude. When Finland refused Soviet demands and was subjected to an attack it possibly could not withstand for long, the Estonian government leaders congratulated themselves for their coolheadedness. One year later, the Finns had more reason to congratulate themselves.

Soviet Military Occupation

The USSR chose to occupy the Baltic states when Germany was preoccupied with the conquest of France and the world's attention was riveted there. Germany seemed resigned to such an eventuality in late 1939, when Hitler ordered all Baltic Germans to "repatriate" to Germany (a country many of them had never seen before). However, given the vagueness of the MRP, Stalin could not be sure of Hitler's reaction to an actual occupation. On 28 May 1940, as the German army closed in on the British beachhead of Dunkerque in northern France, *Pravda*, the Soviet main daily, suddenly lashed out in an article captioned "Political Feelings in Estonia," chiding the Estonians for liking Britain and disliking Germany. Unfounded accusations against Lithuania followed. This time Stalin tackled Lithuania first, possibly to seal off the entire Baltic area from any conceivable German counteraction. In the face of an ultimatum, Lithuania capitulated, and unlimited Soviet troops streamed in on the very day (15 June 1940) German troops paraded into Paris.

Latvia and Estonia received similar ultimatums on 16 June 1940, with six to eight hours to respond. Without even trying to produce any serious evidence, the USSR falsely accused them of violating their pacts and plotting against the USSR. It demanded unlimited entry of Soviet troops and formation of pro-Soviet government cabinets. Lacking any support from abroad and caught between the Soviet forces at the border and those in the bases within the country, Estonia and Latvia capitulated. By 18 June 1940, the occupation was complete.

The immediate goals of the occupier had parallels to the sexual rationale of an abductor and were twofold: reduce the victim's resistance by denying any intention of rape, and establish a fake record that the victim was eager and willing. In other words, the purpose was to prevent spontaneous popular uprisings by denying any intention of annexation and to present an external military occupation as an internal uprising. (I neither subscribe to nor take credit for the sexual metaphor; it was first introduced by Mikhail Gorbachev, who in 1989 and 1990 kept calling annexation "marriage," thus adding insult to injury.)

To reduce resistance, the USSR denied any intention to annex Estonia, and Soviet plenipotentiary Andrei Zhdanov dictated the composition of a cabinet of leftists that initially included no persons known to be communists. This signaled that Estonia might remain even more autonomous than Mongolia. To establish willingness, the occupation authorities staged a crude but elaborate charade of "popular uprising" four days after military occupation. The props included the puny 133-member Communist Party of Estonia, Soviet civilian workers from the Soviet military bases masquerading as local demonstrators, and coerced local citizens. Out of sight in official photos, Soviet armored cars accompanied and supervised the "popular demonstrations" that preceded the promulgation of the puppet government on 21 June 1940.

Real power lay not with the "People's Government" but with the Soviet emissary Zhdanov operating from the Soviet legation. All non-Soviet-controlled public activity was proscribed, including the Boy Scouts. The Communist Party emerged as the only political organization allowed. Police were replaced by a militia recruited from large factories, and arrests began. Senior administrators and army officers were fired, but massive layoffs were delayed because of Soviet inability to find any replacements more trustworthy.

Choiceless elections to a fake "People's Assembly" were carried out on 14–15 July 1940. The Soviets pretended to follow the existing electoral laws but grossly violated them in practice. The period for presentation of candidates was reduced from thirty-five days to three days. Only legally functioning organizations could nominate candidates, and only Communist-dominated organizations remained legal. The Soviet-organized slate of the Estonian Working People's League (EWPL) was meant to be the only one. In comparision, the semifree elections of 1938 looked like model democracy.

However, the procedures and tactics used in 1938 were still fresh in the people's minds, and noncommunist groups managed to present candidates in sixty-six of the eighty single-seat districts. Zhdanov ordered the puppet government to require that all candidates submit a written platform within a few hours—and the instructions sent out to local election commissions suggested there was no need to inform the candidates of the new demand. Most non-EWPL candidates still managed to comply. Threats made some of them withdraw thereafter; in other cases, their platforms were declared either contrary to people's interests or parallel to the EWPL platform and hence redundant or insincere. A few candidates were certified by local communist electoral commissions, which recognized that formal requirements had been met; these officials were told to nullify such decisions. By election day, only one token non-EWPL candidate remained on the ballot. Elsewhere the elections had been "de-choiced" completely.[15]

In seventy-nine of the eighty districts, the ballot carried only the Soviet-assigned candidate's name; hence interest and electoral participation could be expected to be low. But the press, by now fully Soviet-controlled, openly threatened potential nonvoters. As the new main daily *Rahva Hääl* (People's Voice) put it: "It would be extremely unwise to shirk elections. . . . Only people's enemies stay home on election day" (14 July 1940). The extent of actual participation remains unclear. The officially reported 81.6 percent includes large-scale falsifications. In one known case, local election officials computed the votes needed to show 99.6 percent participation and counted out the necessary number of used and unused ballots (Taagepera 1983).

The only way to register opposition to the single candidate was to strike out the name, but use of a private voting booth was strongly discouraged. Soviet Army personnel were used in transportation and guarding of ballot boxes; in Tartu, they were even present in the polling room. The elections in one sovereign state were physically conducted by the armed forces of another.

The vote count was often cynically falsified to satisfy the requirements from higher-level officials. The one non-EWPL candidate allowed to remain on the ballot, Henn-Rajur Liivak (b. 1912), was arrested during elections on a trumped-up forgery charge. Despite this slander, his precinct representatives reported him leading two to one in vote counts, but he was declared loser, with no figures given. He was arrested in early 1941 and sentenced to fifteen years, but survived to publish his memoirs in 1988.[16] The overall pro-EWPL vote of 92.9 percent reported by the occupation authorities is meaningless in view of intimidation, elimination of choice, and shameless falsification.

Soviet Annexation

Prior to the fake elections, the occupation authorities vehemently denied any plans to incorporate Estonia into the USSR. Hence, abolishing Estonia's independence was not among the campaign issues, and the new assembly had no mandate whatsoever to tamper with it, even if the assembly had been properly elected. However, after 15 July the propaganda tune changed sharply in the direction of annexation. The puppet People's Assembly convened on 21 July 1940, with Soviet troops initially present in the assembly hall. Within an hour, a Soviet socialist republic was proclaimed by acclamation, and the next day an application for membership in the USSR was formulated. Expropriation of most industrial, financial, and commercial property was decided unanimously, without debate. The timing of the events was exactly the same in Latvia and Lithuania, betraying the hand of a common orchestrator.

The by now ailing President Päts meekly signed all the illegal documents the occupation authorities presented to him, including his own resignation, on 22 July 1940. This was the man who in his youth had contributed perhaps more than anyone else to Estonia's independence, who later had played the democratic game fairly, accepting his defeats, and who much later had become a nonelected president. He now lent a veneer of legality to Soviet occupation. He had been tough in internal politics and had concentrated all power in his hand, but now he was not up to the supreme responsibilities it entailed. Was it high treason? The jury of history still is debating his acts. Päts was deported to Ufa in the Urals on 30 July 1940. At that time, Estonia was still formally an independent state, and the deportation of its leading statesman by the neighboring state was a low point in the history of modern international relations.

The Supreme Soviet of the USSR received the Soviet-dictated Estonian request on 1 August and pretended to ponder it for five days before annexing Estonia formally on 6 August 1940—less than two months after the initial Soviet ultimatum and military occupation. Estonian diplomats abroad refused to return home and continued their functions wherever possible. Only Nazi Germany and the compliantly neutral Sweden recognized the annexation of the Baltic states officially, though some governments recognized it de facto. Others, including the United States, refused and continued to deal with the Estonian diplomatic representatives for the next fifty years.

Until August 1940, Stalin had acted in the Baltic states ruthlessly but with a cautious eye regarding possible repercussions. In an emotional urge to recoup some of the borders of the tsarist empire, he probably miscalculated and acted with excessive haste in formally annexing the Baltic states. Annexation offered the USSR no tangible advantages and several disadvantages, as compared with a satellite status the USSR had successfully experimented with in Mongolia. Soviet military position in the Baltics did not depend on the formality of annexation, and July 1940 had proved that Stalin could control the Baltic states through the puppet governments as fully as he cared to.

The disadvantages of hasty annexation were both external and internal. By not maintaining a "decent interval" between occupation and annexation, Stalin blocked paths of gradual recognition of the changes by some major powers. Once the puppet regimes were accepted internationally and the Baltic legations and consulates abroad were turned over to them, it would have been hard for any country not to recognize a later decision by puppet governments to "join" the USSR. By telescoping the issues of occupation and annexation, Stalin kept the Baltic legations abroad out of his reach and the Baltic question alive indefinitely (see Kochavi 1991).

The internal consequences may have been even more serious. The Westernized Soviet Baltic republics could not be quarantined from the USSR, which meant an injection of Western ideas into a previously sealed-off empire. To minimize this undesired effect, Sovietization of the Baltic states was carried out at top speed, only to maximize dislocation and resistance; the approach played into German hands in 1941. Those Baltic communists who thought in terms of a "Mongolian status" were rational, except for failing to take into account Stalin's irrationality. When given the opportunity to annex Poland after the war, Stalin declined, although Poland, like the Baltic states, had been largely within the borders of the tsarist empire. By then, Stalin probably had realized the costs of annexing the Baltic states.

Once undertaken, annexations are difficult to undo. One can imagine how much more complex Soviet politics would have been had the USSR annexed Poland. One can also picture how much less entangled Soviet politics would have been, especially around 1990, had Stalin kept the Baltic states as satellites outside the USSR.

The First Year of Sovietization

The year after the annexation of Estonia is covered here only briefly. Native communists of long standing were appointed to the two top positions in the province (called "republic"): Karl Säre (1903–1943?—death date in German hands uncertain) as first secretary of the Communist Party of Estonia (CPE), and Johannes Lauristin (1899–1941) as chairman of the Council of People's Commissars (local prime minister). The figurehead role of the formal head of state (chairman of the Presidium of the Supreme Soviet) went to Johannes Vares (1890–1946), the prime minister of the interim puppet government and one of the thousand-odd "July Communists," so named for joining the CPE only in July 1940. All these people and bodies served merely as channels to implement the decisions made by the extremely centralized party government in Moscow. Soviet legal codes were copied with minor modifications.

Existing native administrators were retained until they could be replaced. Colonial officials were imported from the USSR in large numbers; by June 1941 they formed 37 percent of the CPE membership. The CPE now consisted of 124 preoccupation members (nine having been purged as early as September 1940), 2,600 July Communists and other local joiners, and 1,000 imports.

Chronic shortages arrived with the Soviet army, who emptied the stores because their rubles were pegged at an artificially low exchange rate. Instead of the former market value of ten to fifteen rubles, Estonians received only 1.25 rubles for one Estonian kroon. Shortages were aggravated by dislocations caused by expropriation of all banks, most commercial enterprises, factories with more than ten to twenty workers, and houses exceeding about 200 square meters (2,000 square feet). The portions of bank accounts that exceeded 1,000 rubles (equivalent to about U.S.$400 in 1992) were confiscated, as were the contents of all safes. (This is how my mother lost her table silver.) Individual craftsworkers were coerced to join cooperative artels, whereas existing consumer and producer cooperatives and credit unions were disbanded: Only nonvoluntary cooperatives seemed to be acceptable.

Salary increases for low earners soon were matched by price increases. My calculations on detailed price lists indicate that between early 1940 and early 1941, the purchasing power of median wages dropped 15 percent for food and 65 percent for textiles. Housing became scarcer as apartment dwellers were evicted on short notice to make room for colonial military and civilian personnel. The working class—in whose interest the occupation regime pretended to act—lost its autonomous institutions as trade unions were converted into management tools to strengthen labor discipline. Leaving employment without the manager's permission was punishable by two to four months in prison; so was refusal to transfer to another plant. The last strike on record, at Red Krull in December 1940, was broken through attrition tactics.

Changes were slower in agriculture. Only nine collective farms were established, all of them in the partly Russian-inhabited eastern borderlands. Elsewhere, farms not worked by the owner (about 3 percent of the total) were confiscated; so was any land in excess of 30 hectares (75 acres), a measure affecting some 20 percent of the farms. In a country that already had excessively small subsistence farms, parceling out up to 12 hectares to smallholders and landless people only increased farm unviability—which was an intentional move in view of later collectivization plans. Obligatory deliveries to the state were established at about one-sixth of the fair market price and involved 30–50 percent of a farm's production.

In education, private schools were taken over, and bookstores were ordered to cut out unsuitable pages from textbooks until new ones could be printed. (My first-grade reader was missing a page; I quickly discovered it had a picture of the now-prohibited Estonian flag.) Publishing houses and printing shops were consolidated into a single State Publishing House so as to facilitate censorship. The number of periodicals was reduced, as was their total circulation, and they became bland providers of one-sided propaganda. Lists of banned books were published and included thousands of titles in history, politics, philosophy, and fiction. These books were to be removed from all bookstores and libraries and often were burned. At Tartu University, 70,000 volumes of theological literature were destroyed. Church holidays were abolished, but church organization remained, subject to heavy taxation and excluded from education and social work.

The existing cultural organizations were disbanded (including the Estonian Academy of Sciences), and branches of the Soviet "all-Union" societies of writers, composers, and other artists were established. Some cultural figures welcomed the new order, at times forswearing their own previous writings, but the majority chose silence or translation from Russian and world classics. The major cultural monthly *Looming* presented an odd mix of works ranging in orientation from strong non-Marxism to strident Sovietism.

Red Terror

The population tried to cope with the dislocations and hardships as best they could. Active collaborators with the occupation regime numbered only in the thousands, not in tens of thousands; also minimal initially was active resistance, however, in line with the pacifist attitude of the last Estonian government. But resistance was created by the Soviet need to find enemies. One by one, government leaders and other elite members were arrested, although they had not resisted Soviet aggression and had not worked against the occupation regime. People of any social standing who made critical comments as they were accustomed to doing would vanish. The NKVD (People's Commissariat of Internal Affairs), the Soviet insecurity organ, had arrived in Estonia with the first garrison troops in the military bases and soon after full occupation began to make arrests, which reached 300 per month. Insecurity of the individual became a cardinal element in the maintenance of order.

The pace of arrests accelerated but remained on the level of "spot terror." On 14 June 1941, indiscriminate mass terror began; 6,640 people were deported in a single night.[17] Families were awakened, given a few hours to pack, taken to railroad stations, and separated without forewarning. The men, technically "arrested," were sent to northern slave labor camps, while women and children, technically "exiled," were to fend for themselves on Siberian collective farms. Deportation lists were haphazard, and patriotic mentality mattered more than social class. Hence, 28 percent of the deportees were workers and 26 percent salaried personnel (or their family members); 30 percent were children under 16. Affected disproportionately were city people, including urban minorities such as the Jews. Some deportees died of thirst even before the 490 boxcars crossed the Russian border. As the process continued, the total number of deportees surpassed 10,000 (1 percent of the population).

Arrests and executions accelerated after Germany attacked the USSR, and forced evacuation looked little different from deportation. The same applied to the 33,000 young men conscripted into the Soviet army and then sent to perish in labor camps (Taagepera 1986b). Combined losses have been estimated at 60,000 (6 percent of the population) in a single year, excluding about 30,000 voluntary evacuees. Latvia and Lithuania suffered similar losses. Later, Soviet sources tried to justify the Baltic deportations of 1941 as a precaution against German attack, but Stalin practiced deportations from 1929 to 1949. Moreover, the USSR was singularly poorly prepared for an attack by Stalin's German ally.

The deportations were not caused by an active Estonian patriotic resistance—but they created one. Until then, passive resistance was limited mainly to boycott of Soviet political activities, verbal ridicule, and observation of old now-prohibited holidays. A few unarmed underground groups had been formed in various cities, and by March 1941 some of them began to interact. But widespread armed resistance in the woods was triggered by the June 1941 deportations. It inevitably took a pro-German turn after the German attack, but the original cause was Soviet terror. As an eight-year-old boy, I overheard my parents saying sometime in spring 1940: "At the rate things are going, even a German rule would have been better." I remember my surprise, because the Baltic Germans were the historical enemy. Within a year, Stalin had succeeded in turning the Estonians around.

Every cloud is supposed to have a silver lining, and scholarly tradition demands a balanced handling. The silver linings of Marxist-Leninist regimes have acquired a distinct tarnish even when not Stalinist. To say anything positive to "balance" the account of the first year of Soviet occupation of Estonia, I would have to lie. It was an unmitigated disaster.

GERMAN OCCUPATION AND SOVIET
REOCCUPATION, 1941–1945

Germany attacked the USSR on 22 June 1941. By early July the German columns reached southern Estonia, and by 21 July a thrust east of Lake Peipsi nearly cut Estonia off from Russia. Guerrilla units became active in the Estonian woods. Some numbered several hundred men, led by former Estonian army officers. In much of southern Estonia, Soviet administration was replaced by an Estonian one, days and even weeks before the arrival of German main forces. In particular, Tartu was under full or partial Estonian control from 10 to 28 July, and Jüri Uluots (1890–1945), the last pre-occupation premier, convened a council there but did not dare to proclaim a government. The Germans had already responded with arrests to such attempts in Ukraine. In northern Estonia, where about 5,000 guerrilla fighters were active, the Soviet resistance stiffened. The Germans took Tallinn on 28 August and the last major Estonian islands by October 1941. Among the Soviet Estonian top administrators, "Prime Minister" Johannes Lauristin perished in evacuation; CPE First Secretary Karl Säre was captured by the Germans, became an informant, and was treated as a traitor in Soviet historiography.

If the goal of Soviet occupation and annexation of Estonia was to ensure the Soviet northern flank against Germany, the results were counterproductive. The Germans penetrated 500 kilometers into the Baltic area in seventeen days—one of the fastest advances during World War II. Their thrust probably would have been less rapid if they had faced the Baltic armies defending their homelands against the age-old German enemy and the Soviet forces trapped in Estonia would have been spared for the defense of Leningrad. The speed of the German thrust is at least partly explained by Stalin's feat of turning the Baltic populations friendly toward the Germans, an accomplishment that had no previous counterpart.

Massive deportations had occurred one week before the German attack. Hence, most of the population welcomed the arrival of the Germans, at least passively, but the German actions, right from the beginning, did nothing to preserve this goodwill. The Estonian guerrilla units were disbanded as soon as firm German control was established. The new masters also brushed aside a cautious memorandum by Uluots arguing for reestablishment of Estonian independence. Apart from being allowed to fly the national flag, Estonia was treated as another conquered part of the USSR.

Between Two Wolves

Documents in German archives, such as the *Generalplan Ost*, indicate that the Nazi leadership intended to annex Estonia to the Reich, expel one half of the Estonians toward the east, and fuse the more "Nordic" half with German colonists. However, the Germans' immediate goal was to win the war, and until then they kept their later plans secret so as not to upset the population. Compared with the Soviets, who had practiced genocidal deportations, the Germans were temporarily the lesser evil for most Estonians.[18]

Administratively, Estonia was made a general district within the German occupation area of Ostland, along with Latvia, Lithuania, and Belarus. Apart from the German administrative apparatus, the Germans also appointed an Estonian "Self-Administration" (Selbstverwaltung) with narrow administrative and advisory functions. Its members came mainly from among those who had gone to Germany during a second repatriation in January 1941; no nationally known prewar politician agreed to serve. The Self-Administration had about as little say as the Soviet Estonian government that preceded it, but occasionally its members could speak up a bit more. Recommending a declaration of independence to facilitate mobilization in 1943, Director for Internal Affairs Oskar Angelus (1892–1979) wrote in a memo to the Germans: "The average Estonian is saying: If I am treated badly in my own homeland now, during an exhausting war, then what will they start doing with me when peace comes?"[19] No member of the Soviet Estonian government could have survived after revealing such sincerity.

The Germans saw the Estonians mainly as providers of farm products, labor, and also later as cannon fodder. Private property expropriated by the Soviets was not restored but taken over by special German firms. (In 1943 some token reprivatization took place as part of a morale-boosting campaign.) Another confiscatory currency exchange (10 rubles to 1 ostmark) reduced any prewar savings, already decimated by conversion to rubles, to about one-tenth of their original value. Censorship was almost as heavy as under the Soviets. Nazi tenets were introduced into biology and history textbooks. Tartu University was opened late and reluctantly. Cultural and religious life was left relatively alone.

About 5,000 Estonian citizens were murdered or sent to death camps elsewhere by the Nazis and their local henchmen. The most killings occurred just as the Germans arrived. Of the 5,000 Estonian Jews, most escaped to Russia (including maybe 200 deportees). About 1,000 remained and perished.

Compulsory labor service in Germany involved maybe 15,000 Estonians, including university freshmen who had first to serve one year in the Reichsarbeitdienst (State Work Service), probably as a planned prelude to Germanization. Military service was in principle a prerogative of the Germans, but war losses made the use of Estonians increasingly attractive. It began with a few security units, later called police battalions, largely staffed by volunteers and eventually totaling about 10,000 troops. Many joined to avenge deportation or murder of close ones.

In early 1943, an Estonian legion of some 11,000 troops was formed of "volunteers" who chose military service over the labor battalions with their widely known poor conditions. The regular German army (Wehrmacht) required German citizenship. However, the bylaws of the Waffen-SS (the Nazi Party armed units) specified nothing about citizenship; therefore, ironically, all non-German legions were attached to this elite army. Despite the partial failure of various conscription attempts in Estonia, the German top leadership obstinately refused to sugarcoat the pill by giving Estonia even a Slovakia-like limited statehood.

As the Soviet army again reached the Estonian border in early 1944, the prewar Premier Uluots switched his stand on German conscription, reasoning that large numbers of Estonians armed under any pretext could become useful against both Germans and Soviets. He even succeeded in hinting at it on the German-controlled radio, suggesting that Estonian troops on Estonian soil have "a significance much wider than what I could and would be able to disclose here" (Misiunas and Taagepera 1983:58). The nation understood. Some 38,000 registered—more than the Germans expected and could (or dared to) arm. The cumulative Estonian enrollment in the German army was at least 70,000 troops. More than 10,000 died in action, and another 10,000 reached the West after the war ended.

To escape German conscription, some 5,000 people fled to Finland. About 3,000 of them were persuaded to join the Finnish army, which included a special Estonian regiment. About 1,800 returned to Estonia in August 1944, under a German amnesty, to join the local units and to be in readiness during the critical times of German retreat.[20]

Estonian Provisional Government and Soviet Reconquest

Patriotic resistance to German occupation was made difficult because it could play into the hands of the Soviets. In early 1944, a blanket underground organization was formed that joined all the major prewar political tendencies. This Republic National Committee had good channels to Finland and Sweden but suffered heavily from 200 arrests by the German Gestapo in April 1944. The aim of the committee was to install a provisional government in the interval between the expected German retreat and the Soviet arrival. This was the desperate ploy of a weasel caught between two wolves, but on 18 September 1944 it succeeded, supported by Estonian units of the German and Finnish armies. These units clashed with the retreating Germans and set up defense positions east of Tallinn, but it was too late to organize efficient resistance.

The Soviet troops broke through the makeshift Estonian defenses and occupied Tallinn on 22 September 1944. The provisional government had been in partial control for four days and fell into the hands of the Soviets; only acting president Uluots reached Sweden. However, the symbolic point was made: The Soviet occupation forces did not "liberate" Tallinn from the Germans, but seized it from the Estonians.

The Soviet reconquest of Estonia began in January 1944, proceeded rapidly in September, and was almost complete in October. The Estonian Red Army conscripts of 1941 were mostly sent to perish in slave labor camps. In 1942 the survivors were formed into an Estonian corps in which the peak number of native Estonians may have been 18,000 (Taagepera 1987a). Of these, 800 surrendered at the first engagement (December 1942); the remainder were kept later in reserve and saw symbolic use in reoccupation of Estonia. Thereafter, a new Soviet conscription netted up to 10,000 soldiers, including many who had served in the German army. Indeed, cases exist of Estonians having served in five different armies during and immediately after World War II (Estonian, Soviet, Finnish, German, and the U.S. "guard companies" in occupied Germany).

The Soviet reoccupation brought new deportations. In late 1944, some 30,000 people were sent to "labor service" outside the labor-short Estonia. Over 60,000 had fled to Sweden and Germany, mainly in September 1944, to escape prospective deportations. (My family was among them.) Consumer goods were in shorter supply than ever, and fuel shortage became extreme in winter. Because the Soviets collected but did not exchange the German ostmarks, there was a short moneyless period. Soviet control, initially patchy and superficial, was gradually tightened. The general mood of the population was one of "wait and see." There was some relief that the worst expectations did not materialize immediately, and some joy at refinding relatives evacuated to Russia in 1941 and given up for dead.

In January 1945, Estonia lost 5 percent of its territory and population, as the right bank of the Narva River and most of the southeastern Petseri district were attached to the Russian Soviet Federated Socialist Republic (Russian SFSR) (see Anderson 1988; Raun 1991c). By the end of World War II, Estonia had lost about 30 percent of its pre-1939 population, the result of Soviet deportations, flight to the West (to avoid deportations), territorial cuts, German and Soviet executions, and warfare. Estonia's losses were among the heaviest in Europe, surpassed only by those in Latvia and Lithuania and matched in Poland.

Compared with most occupied nations of World War II, Estonia and the other Baltic nations faced not one but two occupying powers—an unenviable situation. The Germans, coming second, had an unfair advantage: They did not have to destroy the national elite—the Soviets had already done this dirty work. Therefore, the Germans evoked less local resentment. Estonians could suspect Hitler of wanting to deport them, but Stalin had already begun doing so. Consequently, the Estonians saw no advantage in weakening Hitler against Stalin. As the war ended, they still found themselves under Stalin's genocidal rule.

WHY INDEPENDENCE DID NOT LAST

The question of why independence was only temporary may sound naive and the answer self-evident, yet different people would offer different answers. Most Estonians would say that Estonian independence did not last because it was crushed by overwhelming Soviet power in disregard of international law. Many outsiders, especially those from large nations, might say that Estonia was too small to exist as an independent nation and hence did not resist occupation. Neither explanation suffices.

On the one hand, if overwhelming force were the answer, why did Finland survive? Indeed, if a USSR-Finland population ratio of 200 to 4 proved resistible, how can one say with certainty that the USSR-Estonia ratio of 200 to 1 was not? Did the Estonians yield too easily?

On the other hand, if Estonia was too small to exist, why was the nation still around fifty years later, despite severe denationalization pressures, to assert its independence? And how could it have reached independence in the first place, when Estonia was as exhausted from World War I as were Russia and Germany? Both short answers are simplistic, and hence the question remains: Why didn't independence last? (I'll ignore the counterfactual claim that Estonians voluntarily joined the Soviet Union.)

The critical threat to independence arose with the Molotov-Ribbentrop Pact and the resulting demands by the USSR. The different reactions to these demands by the Estonian and Finnish governments cannot be explained by rational calculations of force ratios alone. Archival evidence suggests that the Finnish government did not expect the Soviets actually to attack, once their bluff was called; the Finns were flabbergasted when the attack materialized. Finland partly blundered into its heroic Winter War. It mistakenly expected Swedish support, yet its defense preparations were also superior to Estonia's.

Then why did not Estonia fortify its border somewhat more? (Note that Finland's "Mannerheim Line" was pathetic compared with the Maginot and Siegfried lines on the Rhine.) Estonia's land border with Russia was less than 100 kilometers; even including the 150 kilometers of the Lake Peipsi shoreline, it was more Thermopylae-like than the thousand-kilometer Finnish-Soviet border. Finland could not resist for much more than three months, but this delay in submission proved crucial. With moderate peacetime preparations, Estonia might have resisted for as long. If such preparations were not made, despite the European climate after the mid-1930s, one is pushed to the rationale of lack of will and foresight rather than inherent defenselessness.

The timing of Soviet demands for bases disfavored the Estonians. They were caught by surprise in late September 1939; the Finns had another month thereafter to brace themselves. But it is hard to imagine Finland yielding even when tackled first. Indeed, Stalin probably counted on the Finns to be softened up by seeing their southern neighbors yield.

Did it make any difference that Finland had remained solidly democratic but that Estonia still had an authoritarian president, combined with an elected parliament? Could it be that the Finnish governing circles felt solid popular support behind them, whereas Päts in Estonia lacked it? The answer is a qualified no. From the time of its 1918 civil war, Finland was more deeply divided than Estonia. Opposition to Päts's authoritarian strands was an internal matter, and foreign threats tend to rally support around any government. Of course, absence of public debate because of press restrictions made it easier for Päts and his yes-men to yield, once they decided on that course, than it would have been for the Finnish government to make that choice. But why did the Estonian leaders decide to yield?

One may get closer to the answer when one compares the commanders in chief of Finland and Estonia, who in both countries were the same in 1918 and 1939: Carl Gustaf Emil Mannerheim (1867–1951) and Johan Laidoner (1884–1953). Both were bright staff officers in the tsarist army. But Carl Gustav Emil came from a long line of Swedish-speaking aristocrats; Johan came from a peasant family. This was somewhat typical of the two elites. When the Soviet demands came in late 1939, the psychological gut reaction of the Finnish leadership was that of aristocrats used to getting their way more often than not. The gut reaction of the Estonian leadership, first-generation nonpeasants as they were, was rooted in serfdom four generations down the line—they had experience with being bossed around. This is no indictment: To the contrary, this generation did a heroic job, lifting themselves by their bootstraps from farmhouses to cities and then creating a state to fit the nation. But 1939 was more than they could handle sociopsychologically.

Given ten more years, independent Estonia would have had a new generation in charge, raised by educated urban parents rather than peasants with grade school education—a generation that would have taken independence for granted and not as an incredible strike of luck, as it may have looked to the generation of Tõnisson, Päts, and Laidoner. I still remember an aged physician of that generation vehemently trying to persuade me that Estonians had mental capacities equal to those of members of any large nation—something my generation found self-evident on the basis of the achievements of our parents.

Ten years later, the Estonian reaction to a major crisis could have been different. Could. But it also was different in the fifty years to follow. Although bashed around externally, the Estonian elites nonetheless were to acquire something they never had before: some college-educated grandparents. And that contributed to making the loss of independence a temporary reversal.

NOTES

1. For more details and references for the entire period of 1917–1945, see Toivo U. Raun, *Estonia and the Estonians* (1991a); and Evald Uustalu, *The History of Estonian People* (1952). For Baltic comparisons, see Georg von Rauch, *The Baltic States: The Years of Independence, 1917–1940* (1974); Romuald J. Misiunas and Rein Taagepera, *The Baltic States: Years of Dependence, 1940–1990* (1983); August Rei, *The Drama of the Baltic Peoples* (1970); and V. Stanley Vardys and Romuald J. Misiunas, eds., *The Baltic States in Peace and War, 1917–1945* (1981).

2. Additional sources on achievement of independence are Stanley Page, *The Formation of the Baltic States* (1970); Hans Kruus, *Grundriss der Geschichte des estnischen Volkes* (1932) and his *Histoire de l'Estonie* (1935); Estonian National History Committee, *Estonian War of Independence, 1918–1920* (1968); and articles by Arens (1982) and Hiden (1987).

3. The 72 percent figure often has been attributed to Latvia as a whole, but it should be stressed that it applied only to northern Latvia, where evacuation from western Latvia had wrought dire hardship both on the evacuees and their hosts. Lenin's promises of national self-determination had brought an illusion of a convergence of Bolshevik and Latvian national goals. Because of that, the Latvian regiments were the only ones in the entire tsarist army whose officers largely sided with the Bolsheviks. Consequently, these were the only disciplined troops under Lenin's control in the beginning; they supplied his bodyguard and the first commander of the Red Army. Most of the Latvians soon became disillusioned with Bolshevik practices.

4. For a discussion of the Tartu Peace Treaty that focuses on its recent implications, see Walter C. Clemens, Jr., *Baltic Independence and Russian Empire* (1991), 40–44.

5. The area south of Petrograd originally had a Finnic-speaking Vote and Karelian population, complemented later by Finnish Ingrians. The founding of St. Pe-

tersburg brought a large influx of Russians and, even later, of Estonians. These Estonian settlements were annihilated under Stalin.

6. Additional sources on the period of independence 1920–1940 are J. Hampden Jackson, *Estonia* (1948); Henry de Chambon, *La République d'Estonie* (1936); Artur Mägi, *Das Staatsleben Estlands während seiner Selbständigkeit* (1967); John Hiden and Aleksander Loit, eds., *The Baltic in International Relations Between the Two World Wars* (1988); John Hiden, *The Baltic States and Weimar Ostpolitik* (1987); and Tõnu Parming, *The Collapse of Liberal Democracy and the Rise of Authoritarianism in Estonia* (1975).

7. Rein Taagepera, "Inequality Indices for Baltic Farm Size Distribution, 1929–1940," *Journal of Baltic Studies* 3:1 (Spring 1972), 26–34.

8. Karl Aun, "The Cultural Autonomy of National Minorities in Estonia" (1953). See quote by Lijphart (1984) in Chapter 1. See also Temira Pachmus, "Russian Culture in the Baltic States and Finland, 1920–1940" (1985).

9. Rein Taagepera and Matthew S. Shugart, *Seats and Votes: The Effects and Determinants of Electoral Systems* (1989), 83. Several countries (Latvia, Czechoslovakia, Chile, Ecuador) have had more parties represented in their parliament, but they also had some fairly large parties; Estonia had none. See McHale (1986) for comparison of Baltic party systems.

10. Artur Mägi, "Rahvahääletus ja rahvaalgatus Eestis" [Referendum and popular initiative in Estonia], in Kivimäe, Arnold, et al., *Omariikluse taustal* [Against the backdrop of statehood] (Uppsala: Raimla, 1955), 11–53.

11. The myth that Päts moderated the presidential powers, compared with the Vabs constitution of 1933, has been one of the most successful in Estonian history, and my previous writings have propagated it, too. I faced some surprises when I applied the recently developed Shugart-Carey checklist of presidential powers to the Estonian constitutions. On the Shugart-Carey scale (in its 1991 form) the figurehead Irish president rates 0 points, the United States reaches 13, and the record of 26 points goes to pre-1969 Chile. Estonia 1933 rated 13, but the Päts constitution of 1937 reached 24 points! Because Päts had majority support in the parliament, he did not have to show his full powers in practice; these would have become apparent once he lost parliamentary majority. For the scale, see Matthew S. Shugart and John M. Carey, *Presidents and Assemblies* (Cambridge: Cambridge University Press, 1992).

12. A major Vabs leader, Artur Sirk (1900–1937), fell to his death from a hotel window in Luxembourg in what may or may not have been a suicide.

13. The literature on the Soviet occupation and annexation of the Baltic states is extensive. For example, documentary evidence is presented in *Third Interim Report of the Select Committee on Communist Aggression* (1954) of the U.S. Congress; August Rei, ed., *Nazi-Soviet Conspiracy and the Baltic States: Diplomatic Documents and Other Evidence* (1948); Dietrich A. Loeber, *The Soviet-German Secret Agreements of 1939 and 1941 in Retrospect: A Selection of Materials* (1989); and Arno Köörna et al., comps., *1940 god v Estonii: Dokumenty i materialy* (1989). Legal commentary is given by Boris Meissner, *Die Sowjetunion, die Baltischen Staaten und das Völkerrecht* (1956); Alexander Shtromas, *The Soviet Method of Conquest of the Baltic States: Lessons for the West* (1986b); William J.H. Hough III, "The Annexation of the Baltic States and Its Effect on the Development of Law Prohibiting Forcible Seizure of Territory," *New York Law School Journal of International and Comparative Law* 6:2 (Winter 1985), 301–533; and

several articles by Shtromas (e.g., 1984, 1985). Broader panoramas of the first year of occupation are given by Ants Oras, *Baltic Eclipse* (1948); Henry de Chambon, *La tragédie des nations baltiques* (1946); August Rei, *The Drama of the Baltic Peoples* (1970); and Czeslaw Milosz, "The Lesson of the Baltics" (1984).

14. Raymond J. Sontag and James S. Beddie, eds., *Nazi-Soviet Relations, 1939–1941: Documents from the Archives of the German Foreign Office* (1948), 76–78.

15. Rein Taagepera, "De-Choicing of Elections: July 1940 in Estonia" (1983).

16. Henn-Rajur Liivak, "Mälestusi käidud eluteest, " [Reminiscences from a life course], *Looming*, no. 6 (June 1988), 813–825.

17. Vello Salo, *Population Losses in Estonia, June 1940–August 1941* (1989), 211. This book has a list of names, birthdates, and residences of 9,632 deportees. For many names, location after deportation is also given; sites were mainly Kirov (between Volga and the Urals) and Novosibirsk oblasts. Statistical data are given for 59,967 persons murdered or involuntarily removed from Estonia.

18. For the German occupation, see Seppo Myllyniemi, *Die Neuordnung der baltischen Länder, 1941–1944* (1973); and Alexander Dallin, *German Rule in Russia, 1941–1945: A Study in Occupation Policies* (1957).

19. Oskar Angelus, memorandum, 15 March 1943, in Bundesarchiv R6/76, as cited in Myllyniemi (1973).

20. Evald Uustalu, *For Freedom Only: The Story of Estonian Volunteers in the Finnish War of 1940–1944* (1977).

▪ FOUR ▪

Soviet Occupation

Soviet military occupation of Estonia was complete by 18 June 1940 and in many ways continued even after reachievement of independence in 1991, but it was at its severest from 1945 to 1980, the period I focus on in this chapter. For as long as World War II continued, some hope remained that further unforeseen reversals of fortune could take place, possibly for the better. From 1980 on, something new was in the air, and in retrospect it proved to be the starting point for the momentous changes of the late 1980s. But from 1945 to 1980, the Soviet empire was firmly in control of the lands it occupied during World War II, Estonia included. Three subperiods can be distinguished: the years of genocide (1945–1953), when Stalin carried out a war against the Estonians (among many other peoples) after the end of the international war; the years of hope (1954–1968), when conditions became better without ever getting good; and the years of suffocation (1968–1980), when active genocide did not return but hopes for improvement also were gone.[1]

YEARS OF GENOCIDE, 1945–1953

The initial Soviet approach to reoccupied Estonia was a mix of ruthlessness and caution. The occupation authorities restructured city life but only gradually extended effective control into the countryside, where proindependence guerrillas continued to hold on. The attitude of the population was one of submission to manifest force, combined with passive resistance and continual mental reservations about the more absurd aspects of Sovietization. The wartime coalition of Western democracies and Stalinist totalitarianism was so incongruous that many in Estonia expected a Western-Soviet armed conflict soon after the common Nazi enemy was defeated. Reinforced by virulent anti-Western propaganda in the Soviet press, this belief not only sustained passive and guerrilla resistance but also discouraged would-be collaborators from jumping too early on a bandwagon that already had been derailed once in 1941.

The occupation regime lacked qualified and politically reliable personnel. Moscow distrusted anyone, including native communists, who had not undergone twenty years of Sovietization in the USSR. Russian personnel were imported on a large scale, but they were of limited use because Estonian language skills were needed in many positions. This is where the "Russian Estonians" came in—people whose families had emigrated from Estonia to Russia between 1850 and 1920 (see Raun 1986b). Tens of thousands of them migrated to Estonia in the late 1940s because of superior living conditions but also because they saw major advancement opportunities as bilingual agents of Sovietization. They filled many middle-level posts and, as described later, seized the top administrative posts in 1950 and kept them until the late 1980s. The local population considered them uncouth and often arrogant, also ridiculing their accent (a questionable habit of Estonians that slowed the integration of immigrants).

Demobilization and disbanding of the Estonian corps of the Soviet army released many native Estonian Communist Party (CPE) members into civilian life, but even after that the CPE was heavily colonial in character. There were fewer native Estonians in the CPE in 1946 (about 1,900) than in 1941 (2,400). Of its 7,139 members in January 1946, Russians represented 52 percent, Russian Estonians were about 21 percent, and native Estonians only about 17 percent. Thus the CPE was not just taking orders from the outside but predominantly consisted of colonists. Its composition reflected both the reluctance of Estonians to join and the preference of the colonial regime for their own kind. As occupation lasted and seemed more permanent, more careerists joined, but even in 1949 homegrown communists still numbered only 6,000 and represented about one-third of the CPE membership.

The top Soviet administrators in the country had been lost during the Soviet retreat; they were at first replaced by other native communists: Nikolai Karotamm (1901–1969) as first secretary of the CPE and Arnold Veimer (1903–1977) as chairman of the Council of People's Commissars (renamed Council of Ministers in 1946). "July Communist" Johannes Vares continued as the ceremonial head (chairman of the Supreme Soviet Presidium) of the Estonian Soviet Socialist Republic (ESSR) until he committed NKVD-assisted suicide in 1946. In a foreshadowing of the practices to come, he was not replaced by a native but by a Russian Estonian, Eduard Päll (1903–1989). Overall control was exerted through a newly created Estonian bureau in Moscow, which was abolished around 1948. Fake elections to the ESSR Supreme Soviet were delayed until 1947, and local council (*soviet* in Russian, *nõukogu* in Estonian) elections until 1948, because of the tenuous Soviet control in the countryside. Preoccupation administrative subunits were initially maintained, then gradually replaced by standard Soviet units (districts and village council areas) and constantly revamped.

Guerrilla War

On the other side, the proindependence guerrillas may have at times reached a strength of 10,000—about 1 percent of the total population, which is high for any guerrilla force. The attrition rate was high—the estimated average active period of service was two years—so that over eight years of visible guerrilla war (1945–1953), some 30,000 may have been *metsavennad* (forest brothers), as they were called. Their motivation for participating was complex (Misiunas and Taagepera 1983:81–82):

> Why did people join the forest brotherhood now, although they had submitted peacefully to the Soviet invasion of 1940? Why did they decide to resist under the much less favorable postwar occupation conditions? Patriotic idealism was an important motive. In 1940 it had been tempered by the desire not to die, but by 1945 war and both occupations had engendered a feeling that one might die soon anyway. Fugitive life had become familiar to many, and scattered arms had become plentiful. However, the prime direct reason for resistance was the Soviet terror during the 1940–41 occupation, and its reintroduction after re-occupation. Terror affected many more than just the wealthy or the German collaborators. Anyone with democratic views was a likely target, including Social Democratic workers. Anyone who had voiced a preference for national independence instead of Russian or German domination was a target. Anyone complaining about some aspect of Soviet bureaucracy or unable to adjust to its demands (such as farm grain deliveries) was a target. The sloppy randomness of the MVD [Ministry of Internal Affairs] and MGB [Ministry of State Security] repression units, and lack of due process, in fact made practically everyone a potential target, the more so since the Soviets considered everyone who had survived the German occupation a Nazi collaborator of sorts. People went to the forests mainly when they could no longer take the insecurity of civilian life.

The first wave of guerrillas consisted largely of willing and unwilling German collaborators and draftees as well as ex-members of the Finnish army; they were soon followed by Soviet army deserters and avoiders of conscription. Social dislocations such as land redistribution and Soviet screening and arrest campaigns produced new waves. The last one came with forced collectivization, as described later.

Guerrilla groups ranged in size from several hundred people down to single individuals. Many were simply hiding, taking no action against the occupiers unless attacked. Even for larger groups, the main objectives were to discourage collaboration and maintain combat readiness while waiting for an expected Western-Soviet conflict. Because some guerrillas would return to cities with forged papers and some supporters in villages might fill in for casualties, it is impossible to draw a firm line between the guerrilla and the civilian population.

The forest brotherhood operated in nearly every county. In the early years, entire townships were for weeks outside Soviet control and church towers flew national flags. Elsewhere, Soviet occupants and collaborators retrenched themselves at night in stone buildings and moved in armed convoys. Offices and bridges were blasted, and collaborators were forced to turn in their Communist Party or Komsomol (Communist Youth) cards and ordered to go easy in carrying out Soviet orders under threat of death. Close to 1,000 collaborators may have been murdered over eight years, and guerrilla casualties must have been many times higher.

Afraid of Soviet infiltration, which was a very real danger, Estonian guerrilla groups avoided interaction, and hence not even countywide organization materialized. This dispersal contrasted sharply with the Lithuanian guerrillas, who desperately tried to maintain a unified nationwide command, attempted contacts with the West, maintained city intelligence, and published mimeographed information for the population at large. There is no evidence of any of this type of activity in Estonia. Comparisons with the Estonian and Lithuanian styles of resistance to Germans in the 1200s come to mind.

As time went on, groups became smaller. From aboveground huts in 1945, the guerrillas shifted to poorly ventilated and humid underground bunkers that rarely fitted more than three people. Soviet arms obtained by raids replaced the original German weapons, but ammunition rotted rapidly and remained a major concern. Food and clothing were supplied by the population, but this supply dwindled after forced collectivization. From then on, resistance continued largely because there was no way out: The Soviet authorities had broken all their previous promises of amnesty, arresting those who surrendered a few weeks later.

The Soviet repression forces had the advantage of superior numbers, armament, and mobility. They could concentrate on one forest at a time, but the forest brothers lacked two essential ingredients of successful guerrilla activity: internal mobility and external support. In the absence of the latter, even the better-organized Lithuanian resistance was doomed. Throughout the Baltic states, fighting ceased after Stalin's death in 1953. Guerrillas reentered civilian life using forged documents or turning to a 1955 amnesty the Soviets did honor. Some individuals continued to hide. As late as 1978 a lonely survivor drowned himself rather than surrender.[2] The Estonian proindependence guerrillas obviously enjoyed extensive popular support. In the face of the heavy odds, their persistence in fighting for eight years defies imagination.

Collectivization Through Deportation

Forced collectivization of agriculture was the step that not only broke the guerrilla resistance but also eliminated the last segment of private enterprise. It was preceded by four years during which land redistribution was aimed at eliminating the large farms, with the goal of forming unviably small new ones and creating social tensions between those who lost and those who gained land. Increasing taxes and obligatory deliveries at ridiculously low prices made individual farming well-nigh impossible by 1948. The tax reached 75 percent of the "estimated income" for those branded as large farmers (even if their holdings had been reduced meanwhile to 5 hectares) and close to 30 percent even for acknowledged smallholders. The first kolkhoz (state-controlled "collective" farm) in postwar Estonia was formed in November 1947, and 8 percent of the farms were "collectivized" by 20 March 1949. CPE leader Nikolai Karotamm estimated that further tax squeeze would force most farmers to follow suit within two years, but this was too peaceful an outcome for Stalin. He ordered massive deportations of farmers in March 1949 in all newly seized territories, from Estonia to Moldova.

In a few days and nights, starting on 23 March 1949, at least 20,000 people, mainly farmers, were deported from Estonia, with the help of special MVD troops fresh from Russia.[3] As the Soviet Estonian main daily put it: "When collectivization started in our country, the Russian working class gave tens of thousands of its best representatives, who helped to create a new happy life in our villages" (*Rahva Hääl*, 30 December 1952). The memory of this cruel "help" is bound to color the present ethnic relations in Estonia. The victims had between ten minutes and two hours to pack their things. After weeks in boxcars, they were dropped off in west Siberian and northern Kazakh kolkhozes to fend for themselves: build cavelike huts, tear up ground to grow food, and survive somehow meanwhile. Preferring kolkhozes in Estonia to those in Siberia, the remaining farmers hurriedly "collectivized." Within a month, the collectivization rate jumped from 8 to 64 percent. It reached 80 percent by the end of 1949 and 92 percent by late 1950, as the impossibly heavy taxes made the last smallholders give up.

One might think that the Soviet next step would have been to ease the conditions, so as to demonstrate the advantages of the kolkhozes, but this was not the case. Prevented from farming individually, Estonian farmers were not allowed to carry out rational collective farming either. They were kept in a halfway house gradually wrecked by order-spewing spooks from various levels of bureaucracy.

The classic description of the kolkhoz misery is *Tondiöömaja* (The Spook Hostel) by Heino Kiik (b. 1927), published with some delays in 1970. Total strangers were "elected" kolkhoz chairmen on an hour's notice. Harvesting at planned dates ignored the degree of ripeness of crops. State deliveries left no grain for the kolkhozes, and farmers competed with city people in buying scarce but cheap bread from city stores. The price received for a bull fell short of the price of a bottle of state-sold vodka. The daily pay for work on collective land fell to 3 kopeks, yet a pack of cigarettes cost 3 rubles (300 kopeks). Farmers avoided collective work, surviving on their one-acre private plots (which were heavily taxed). By spring 1953, cows had to be carried out of stables and were blown over by the wind, according to later reports in the official Soviet press. Production gradually dropped to about one-half the prewar figures, and villages looked as if they had undergone years of warfare. They had.

Colonization

In the cities, Sovietization made its mark sooner than in the countryside, in the form of high-speed industrialization that served as the pretext for wide-scale Russian colonization. Still, for those not affected by arrests, city life proceeded toward postwar normalization. Streets were cleared of bombing rubble, and food rationing ended in 1947, earlier, for instance, than in West Germany or Morocco. The flood of food-seeking *kotimehed* (bagmen) from Russia eased a year later, and clothing and shoes became available in stores, though firewood remained scarce at least until 1954. Reconstruction of war-destroyed cities was largely completed by 1950, but influx from the countryside and from Russia made for a permanent housing shortage. The last small servicing enterprises were expropriated in 1947.

For both economic and political reasons, expansion of industry was high on the Soviet priority list. Along with Latvia, Estonia represented a skilled-labor reserve unique in the USSR, and its substantial physical infrastructure was relatively undamaged by war. From the Soviet viewpoint, all those existing roads, factory buildings, housings, and schools could be used more intensively than free-enterprise Estonia had done. Night shifts could be added, and more workers could be crammed into existing apartments. Thus, the relatively balanced development of production and welfare during independence became the basis for lopsidedly production-oriented expansion during Soviet occupation.

But imperialist considerations often outweighed the economic. Industrialization offered a path to colonize the country with Russians and establish a civilian garrison among a reticent Estonian population, as a prelude to their total assimilation. It made no economic sense to deport tens of thousands of skilled people from a labor-short area to destinations where their skills went largely unused, and then import so many more Russians.

Indeed, colonization became a goal in itself rather than a means of industrialization.

By 1949 the size of the rapidly growing industrial labor force surpassed the prewar level, and so did production. Despite increasing mechanization, work efficiency did not increase. For example, in oil-shale mining, which was Estonia's main industrial base, the amount produced per worker was slightly lower in 1950 than in 1939. Oil shale is largely neglected in the world because its energy content is low compared with coal. Independent Estonia had become the world pioneer in oil-shale development to reduce its dependence on imported coal. The occupation authorities vastly expanded the mining, largely with labor imported from Russia. Oil shale was gasified onsite in an effort to deliver energy to nearby Leningrad. The Kohtla-Järve oil-shale center in northeastern Estonia is only 50 kilometers from the Russian border. Boosting the existing industry in the border city of Narva and mining low-grade uranium at Sillamäe, between Narva and Kohtla-Järve, created a near-continuous industrial zone that was purposely Russified: Estonians evacuated from the area during the war were discouraged from returning and were resettled in western parts of the country.

Although forced collectivization of farms opened up a major internal labor reserve, the largest influx into the cities came from Russia. Some were attracted by Estonia's relative well-being, but others were actively recruited or brought in against their will. Forced labor used in Estonia included many non-Russians; because they usually knew more Russian than Estonian, they too were made to play an involuntary Russifying role. An idyllic view of the process was presented in the official *History of the Estonian SSR* (*Eesti NSV ajalugu*, vol. 3, 1971:577):

> During the years of building socialism, the specific weight of other nationalities increased within the Estonian working class, but the identical interests and goals and common work linked the settlers from fraternal republics to the local workers. Both were formed into a single Soviet Estonian working class. . . . Political educational work was used in trying to help workers to free themselves from the influence of the bourgeois-nationalist propaganda.

The last sentence confirms that the Estonian workers did not perceive any "identical interests" in an industry based on Russian investment, largely Russian imported labor, management by Russians according to goals set by Russians, and export of most of Estonia's product to Russia. The entire show was called "Estonian" industrial growth only because the Soviet authorities decided to run it on Estonian soil.

The Russian influx was heaviest in the early postwar years, but it never stopped, and its denationalizing effects were aggravated by the guerrilla deaths, arrests, and deportations of Estonians. The share of Estonians in the country's population decreased from about 94 percent in early 1945 to about 72 percent by 1953, the latter figure including the Russian Estonians. At least 60,000 native Estonians were lost in the period 1945–1953. Approximately the same number of Russian Estonians immigrated, largely depleting their remaining available pool in Russia. About 230,000 Russians and other non-Estonians also came, and their pool remained unaffected. At this rate, the Estonians could become a minority in their ancestral land within another ten years.

Was it genocide? The answer depends on the definition of the word. The process was not a holocaust in which all people belonging to a given group were slaughtered. At one extreme, one can make the definition of *genocide* so unreasonably stringent that the Turkish genocide against the Armenians and even the German genocide against the Jews are made debatable. At the other, one can devalue the term to include any killings of members of another group. The crucial criterion is whether a group's very existence is jeopardized by killings and deportations. In the Estonian case, the answer is affirmative, as it is in the other cases mentioned and also those of Crimean Tatars under Stalin and Cherokees in the nineteenth-century United States. Within the criterion of jeopardy to group existence, genocide allows for degrees in both intention and execution. The pace of the Estonian genocide was slower than in the aforementioned cases, but had it continued, it would have led to minority status within another ten years and extinction of the Estonian language as a cultural medium within a generation, especially when combined with the cultural repression, described next. It was slow genocide—and it was intentional.

It remains to ask which groups stood to profit from the genocide. Blaming one person—Jackson (U.S. president during the Cherokee expulsion), Hitler, Stalin—is too easy a way out, and the same is true of political organizations. Some entire nations profited. True, many Germans also suffered under the Nazis and many Russians under Soviet communism. But the beneficiaries of the Cherokee, Armenian, Jewish, Crimean Tatar, and Estonian genocides were, respectively, the white Americans, Turks, Germans, Russians, and Russians. History cannot be undone, but it can be acknowledged. Symbolic amends can be made, the very least of which is desistance from further encroachments.

The Purge

Cultural life and higher education in postwar Estonia were strongly affected by the flight to the West of maybe one-half of those with a higher education. The immediate effect was negative; later, the resulting surge of upward mobility brought rejuvenation, but the reverse trend set in with the aging of the age cohort of individuals who occupied all cultural positions around 1950. In sum, the normal generational alternation was disturbed. Culture was one area in which injection of Russians and even Russian Estonians was difficult. Soviet-style textbooks were printed, but many native teachers had to remain in their positions for many years. Participation in the communist youth organizations (Pioneers and Komsomol) increased only slowly, despite strong-arm tactics and material incentives. By 1950, 44 percent of students had joined.

Religious organizations (excluding the Marxist-Leninist quasi-church) were quickly silenced and infiltrated. Two successive bishops of the Estonian Lutheran Church were deported in 1945; in 1949 a bishop satisfactory to the occupation authorities was appointed, with a Soviet agent as chief secretary. A non-Estonian-speaking bishop was appointed for the Estonian Orthodox Church. Nazi-destroyed Jewish synagogues were not reconstructed (see Segal 1988).

An initial relaxation in cultural Sovietization followed reoccupation. By 1946, it gave way to a "struggle against apolitical culture" that engulfed all of the USSR. Literary activity in Estonia remained low. Those writers who had not fled remained silent or tried to adjust to ideological demands; they sacrificed quality, yet still failed to satisfy the new masters. Poet Heiti Talvik (1904–1947) was arrested and died in prison. But the axe really fell in 1950.

The great Estonian purge of 1950–1951 began with culture, quickly shifted to the CPE leadership, and then swung back to culture. In early 1949, numerous passive cultural figures as well as those who tried to collaborate were forced to condemn themselves publicly for "formalism." Charges of nationalism followed in the July 1949 issue of the cultural monthly *Looming*, and people were required to condemn their colleagues or be themselves doomed.

In March 1950, the Soviet Politburo passed a resolution on "The Shortcomings and Errors in the Work of the Central Committee of the Communist (Bolshevik) Party of Estonia." Presented at a CPE plenum, this resolution gave the signal "to unmask a bourgeois nationalist anti-popular group who had forced their way into the party and caused great harm, especially on the ideological front," as *Rahva Hääl* later put it (4 April 1951). Nikolai Karotamm, first secretary of the CPE, was accused of "rightist opportunist errors" and "peaceful coexistence with class-hostile elements." Dismissed but not imprisoned, he finished his days as an economics researcher in Moscow. He was replaced by a Russian Estonian, Ivan Kebin (b. 1905), whose family had emigrated from Estonia to St. Petersburg in

1910 and who later re-Estonianized his name to Johannes Käbin. At the time, he was fully prepared to denationalize a culture he did not know, appoint Russians to key positions, extend the use of the Russian language, and be subservient to everything Russian.

In the course of the following eighteen months, the ESSR premier, several ministers, and numerous CPE Central Committee members were fired, expelled from the CP, and at times sentenced to twenty-five years of forced labor. The latter sentence was especially ironic in the case of Vice Premier Hendrik Allik (1901–1989), who also had been sentenced to twenty-five years in 1924 for subversive activities against the Republic of Estonia. Hundreds of other functionaries and intellectuals were deported. The purge extended from Tallinn to Tartu, with its university, and to minor cities.

What caused the great Estonian purge? In marked contrast to the deportations of 1949, it did not extend to other newly annexed territories of the USSR. Attempts to connect it to the purge of supporters of Zhdanov in Leningrad are based solely on geographic proximity and Zhdanov's fleeting role in Estonia 1940. They do not explain why an intra-Russian power struggle should lead to a purge of nonparty intellectuals in Estonia. What is documented is that Karotamm actively pleaded for a slower pace of collectivization and for sending the deported farmers to the labor-short Estonian oil-shale mines rather than Siberia. Once he had thus aroused Stalin's suspicions, Karotamm's obedient execution of the deportations might actually have worked against him. Estonia's collectivization pace exceeded that of the neighboring territories, and Stalin may have concluded that a breakthrough could have been obtained even earlier had Karotamm not been timorous. Once Karotamm was removed, every one of his underlings became suspect in turn.

One also has to consider the role of the Russian Estonian mafia who chafed under the command of the more cultured native communists to whom they felt superior because of their Soviet upbringing. They certainly tried to undermine Karotamm, and they were the main beneficiaries of the purge. By late 1952, not a single homegrown ethnic Estonian remained among the four CPE secretaries or even among the twenty-six ministers of the "republic." Some positions were held by Russians (a couple of them born in Estonia), but the Russian Estonians obtained most of the posts. In particular, the ESSR premiership went to Aleksei Müürisepp (1902–1970), who had been in Russia from 1908 to 1941. Two reservations are in order. The Russian Estonian Päll, who became the formal head of the ESSR in 1946, also was demoted in 1950 for glorifying "reactionary bourgeois nationalist ideas" and was replaced by a homegrown writer, August Jakobson (1904–1963). More important, the Russian Latvians, who were numerically even stronger than their Estonian counterparts, did not succeed in triggering a similar purge in Latvia or exporting the Estonian purge there.

The Historical Gap and the Role of Estonian Diaspora

The intracommunist political purge soon spilled over to what could be called cultural genocide. Popular playwright Hugo Raudsepp (1883–1952) was deported to his death. Estonia's major novelist Friedebert Tuglas (1886–1971) became a "nonperson" whose name was not to be mentioned in the press after first being drenched with invective: "He tried to cover up the stench of putrefication of the bourgeoisie's corpse," as *Rahva Hääl* put it on 7 July 1951. The previous day, Moscow's *Pravda* had severely admonished *Rahva Hääl* itself for not unmasking "the rotten bourgeois culture of the West." On a different level, a childhood friend of mine was warned in 1952 not to wear a wedding ring when teaching school; it could be considered bourgeois.

Collaboration proved no safer than passivity, because unwitting ideological mistakes could be interpreted as subversion. A writer who had joined the transitional puppet government in 1940 and later authored Soviet Estonia's pro-Russian anthem was suddenly found to be "the meanest enemy of the Soviet people and literature," and the anthem from then on could be played but not sung. History was blatantly falsified to present Russians as Estonia's saviors throughout the ages, and Russians were presented as superior to Estonians and other nations. The tone resembled that of Nazi propaganda, only with the term "German" replaced with "Russian."

Ten years later, this period came to be called the "historical gap," because of its dearth of cultural output. Quantitative analysis of Soviet Estonian anthologies and art books bears it out: The number of presentable works dropped to its twentieth-century low in the period 1949–1953. The cultural output of the 60,000 Estonian refugees in the West vastly surpassed that of Soviet-occupied Estonia.

The refugee activities also contributed to the Soviet Union's failure to gain international acceptance for its annexation of Estonia. The USSR tried hard, especially at the Paris conference of 1946, to obtain recognition and United Nations seats for the Soviet Baltic puppet governments but was rebuffed. Independent Estonia's diplomatic representatives continued to be accredited in countries such as Great Britain, the United States, and Canada (see Liivak 1987). In addition to promulgating some clumsy repatriation propaganda, the Soviets reacted to the refugee culture by isolating it from the homeland. In the Soviet Estonian media, the refugees were mentioned only in negative generalities. Listening to foreign radio was punishable; so too, in fact, was receiving any mail from abroad. Nonetheless, awareness of fellow Estonians abroad persisted in Estonia. The existence of the refugee communities also made it harder for Stalin to toy with the idea of even more drastic genocide measures, because nothing done in Estonia could completely obliterate the Estonian culture.[4]

Surprising as it may seem, the Estonian deportees also had some impact on the USSR through their interaction with other inmates of slave labor camps. One such inmate was Aleksandr Solzhenitsyn, who befriended Arnold Susi (1896–1968), a member of the ill-fated Estonian government of September 1944. In his *Gulag Archipelago,* much of which was written in the relative security of the south Estonian countryside,[5] Solzhenitsyn says:

> To understand the Revolution I had long since required nothing beyond Marxism. . . . And now fate brought me together with Susi. He breathed a completely different sort of air. . . . I listened to the principles of the Estonian Constitution, which had been borrowed from the best of European experience, and to how their hundred-member one-house Parliament had worked. And, though the *why* of it was not clear, I began to like it all and store it all away in my experience.[6]

The hundred-member one-house parliament Solzhenitsyn refers to is the one created by the 1920 constitution, not that of 1938.

From the vantage point of 1952, every year since 1939 had brought Estonia major changes; since 1944, there had been a succession of shattered hopes. The guerrilla resistance was broken, and hopes for relief by the West had to be abandoned. On the personal level, the hope to escape terror had to be given up. Terror had reached German collaborators and anti-German Estonian patriots, then private farmers, intellectuals, and native communists. Terror had become an expected norm, and in this sense things had normalized.

The spirit of irony and mental resistance that met the first Soviet measures in 1940 had dissipated. The Estonian population was numb, and terror had outlasted its purpose, if there ever was one. In 1952 the scene altered in a major way in that it no longer changed appreciably. Arrests and the decay of the kolkhozes continued, but no new major population groups were targeted. It was an eerily quiet year. In March 1953 Stalin died. On 1 December 1953 an Estonian prisoner in a slave labor camp wrote a poem titled "Portrait of Norilsk" (Norilsk was a major center of arctic camps):

> Cold. Wind from hills. Barbed wire.
> That blooming Soviet land.
> We walk an old men's walk—
> no room for carefree stride.

Stride carefree, hit the wire,
a guard's lead in your chest.
The snow would hide forever
life like beggar's bag.

Cold. Snow. Hills. Barbed wire.
Take these and paint Norilsk,
and drowning in your torment,
paint it a robe with blood.

Composer, turn to notes
the song of lips closed tight—
an ode to fit the graveyard
they call USSR.[7]

YEARS OF HOPE, 1954–1968

As 1953 ended, the future of Estonia looked grim. Terror had proceeded at a genocidal rate a mere few years earlier and could be reactivated any time. The only hope had been the imperial dictator's death, but this death had come and the empire and its political system had survived. None of the Stalinist decrees were rescinded, and some of the practices were even tightened. Life in the cities showed little improvement, and culture was at a standstill. The forcibly collectivized countryside was sliding even further toward despair as it was subjected to new senseless orders such as to sow corn, which does not ripen so far north. Society was atomized, because the threat to national survival was overshadowed by a concern for one's personal survival. All the gains of the period of independence had been undone, and in many ways it was worse than during the tsarist Russian rule.

Small signs of hope appeared. Social norms remained harsh, but at least they remained stable, so that adjustment became possible. Indeed, being sanctioned only when overstepping known bounds, however narrowly set, sounded like a happy dream, after nine years of shifting demands and erratic terror. One wanted to hope, yet did not dare to—hope had been quashed too many times before. Still, as terror subsided, so did resistance. When the choice seemed to be between *surm siin või Siberis* ("same death, either here or in Siberia"), one might as well fight. But now it became a choice between death and collaboration, and few chose death.

By 1954, the Soviet control of Estonia no longer was viewed as a temporary occupation. If the Soviet authorities were not considered morally entitled to proclaim laws, at least it was accepted that they were fully able to enforce their laws, and thus one better behave as if the Soviet rule were legitimate. The habit of mentally challenging every Soviet command slowly shifted into the less stressful habit of submission. In this most passive sense, the Soviet control of Estonia had become "legitimate." From struggle against a foreign *occupation*, the population largely shifted to working for one's interest within the framework of foreign *rule*. This shift was involuntary and survived only as long as the repression machinery, at levels below indiscriminate terror, was maintained. The awareness of being an occupied country reemerged quickly in the 1980s, but meanwhile, it was buried in the deeper levels of consciousness of most people.

The Thaw

The period of relative relaxation in Soviet life, called the "thaw," began in late 1953 and in many ways ended in 1956 with the Soviet aggression in Hungary (although chills and new thaws alternated throughout the Nikita Khrushchev era). In Estonia, however, some of the most visible results actually came later, after Khrushchev's denunciation of Stalin. Immigration of non-Estonians largely ceased in 1953, as people and officials took a wait-and-see attitude. Forced labor brought to Estonia began to leave, deported Estonians to return. Because many of the rural deportees returning to Estonia stayed in the cities, the scarcity of living space there reached a postwar high in 1955 and 1956. On the administrative level, the struggle for succession in the Kremlin enabled the top administrators of the various Soviet Socialist Republics (SSRs) to gain some minimal degree of autonomy, and denunciation of Stalinism (1956) furthered this trend. As early as summer 1953, a Russian was replaced by a Russian Estonian as second secretary of the CPE, whose role was to act as Moscow's chief watchdog in Estonia.

The size of Soviet repression forces was reduced, and the political uncertainty made some colonial functionaries leave. As a result, CPE membership dropped from 13,400 in 1952 to 12,100 in 1956, and the Russian share in it decreased. The number of new membership applications reached the 1952 level only by 1956. Hoping to advance the national cause within the communist framework, many young Estonians began to join the CPE around that time—an act they themselves might have considered treasonable just a few years earlier.

In 1957, regional economic councils (*sovnarkhozy*) were established throughout the USSR. They represented a definite increase in economic autonomy, at least in the case of the Baltic SSRs. During the public discussion that preceded the change, Müürisepp, the Russian Estonian premier of the ESSR, strongly criticized previous centralism in an article published in Moscow (*Izvestiia*, 22 September 1956), making these points: The policy of interdependence prevented Estonia's industry from using local raw materials, forced Estonia to export its output before its own needs had been met, and dispersed Estonian specialists throughout the USSR, causing a pointless influx of Russians.

The new system made each SSR a separate unit for economic planning, and control of local industry was largely shifted to the republic ministries. In the resulting reorganization, many incompetent Russian and Russian Estonian Party stalwarts were replaced by better qualified Estonians, and the Communist Party monthly admonished "those responsible workers who have lived for many years in the country and whose success in learning the Estonian language is insignificant" (*Kommunist Estonii*, May 1957:15). The Russian Estonians preserved their top positions, but former ESSR premier Veimer, demoted in 1951, became the head of the Estonian *sovnarkhoz*.

In agriculture, a real breakthrough came in 1958, when the machine-tractor stations (MTSs) were abolished in the USSR. Until then, incredible as it is, the kolkhozes and the sovkhozes (openly state-owned farms) were not allowed to own their own machinery and remained at the mercy of the MTS, the operators of which often acted negligently because they faced no product-delivery pressures. The Estonian kolkhozes eagerly purchased the equipment from the MTS, mostly with state-supported credit. Compulsory product deliveries were also abolished, and prices were set at nonconfiscatory levels. Production rose and the rural population escaped from the "spook-hostel" syndrome into relative well-being.

Although still dominated by Russian Estonians at the top, the ESSR administration was searching for some symbolic legitimization by the population. In 1957, Estonian athletes began to sport "EESTI" (Estonia) on their uniforms instead of the previous "EESTI NSV" (Estonian SSR), and university student caps similar to those of preoccupation fraternities appeared. Republic prizes for science and arts were instituted. The first postoccupation Baltic soccer games were held in 1958.

Modest ideological concessions also were made. Rudolf Sirge's (1904–1970) otherwise pro-Soviet novel *Maa ja rahvas* (The Land and the People, 1956) created a sensation with a realistic 1941 deportation scene. Unpretentious posthumously published poems by Ilmi Kolla (1933–1954) caught brief attention by what some of them lacked—political rhetoric—and maybe also by what was a foreshadowing of the consumerism of the 1970s:

> Minu sõbral on nüüd oma masin,
> Leningradist ise ostmas käis.[8]
> [My boyfriend now has a car of his own,
> he went to Leningrad to buy it.]

The tone was a far cry from the tenor of 1949:

> Aga harva näen ma oma päiksekiirt,
> tema on ju tähtis, karjabrigadiir.[9]
> [But I rarely get to see my sunshine maid,
> for she's busy leading our cattle brigade.]

These modest concessions whetted the appetite, especially among the young, for whom it was easier to forget the years of genocide. The students of the Tallinn Polytechnic Institute tried to form a new nonpolitical student organization apart from the Komsomol, but were rebuffed in 1956. The Hungarian Revolution obviously struck a responsive chord among the Estonians, and in response the regime adopted a reactionary stance, attacking nationalism and establishing clearly the narrow limits of what it considered acceptable.

The Soviet repression agency, by now renamed the KGB (State Security Committee), continued its activities. Its thoroughness and pettiness are illustrated by the one case the Soviets decided to advertise as a warning, in contrast to their usual quashing of information about repression. In 1958 a student at Tartu University, Mart Niklus (b. 1934), was sentenced to ten years merely for sending abroad uncomplimentary photos of shoddy construction and a radio-jamming station. The total number of imprisonments for similar offenses is hard to estimate because of lack of records.

In sum, by early 1959, the atmosphere in some respects had changed almost beyond recognition, compared with 1953; yet some matters remained very much the same (Misiunas and Taagepera 1983:150):

> Those who measured the gap still remaining between the Western and Baltic degrees of cultural freedom correctly saw very little change indeed. Those who compared the foul air of 1959 to the suffocation of 1953 saw the immense difference between cultural survival and death. There was new hope, and the coming decade was to see a veritable resurrection of Baltic cultures. The fact that it did not come about easily only added to its significance.

The demographic situation in 1959 also had improved. Most survivors among the deportees had returned, and the percentage of Estonians in the country's population increased slightly; it probably peaked around the first postwar census (January 1959) at 74.6 percent.

Although the struggle for cultural autonomy was successful, the struggle for political autonomy soon failed. It meant failure in ability to control excessive immigration and boded ill for the fledgling economic autonomy. In 1957, Khrushchev had defeated all his rivals and no longer needed to court the provincial chieftains.

The crunch came in Latvia. Up to then, changes in the three Baltic countries had proceeded at approximately the same pace, although Lithuania's top administrators were homegrown, Estonia's were imported from Russia, and Latvia's were mixed. Possibly because Latvia's demographic constellation was the most precarious (62 percent Latvian in 1959), "national communism" was the most intense in Latvia, where there was a 1958–1959 effort to block further Russification and to re-Latvianize the party and government apparatus. In summer 1959, the Soviet regime showed that it still was an occupation regime: It unleashed a two-year purge comparable in scope to that inflicted in Estonia in 1950–1951.[10] By 1961, Latvia's top administration was fully in the hands of Russian Latvians. Throughout the USSR, Khrushchev took a course toward rapid Russification as he consolidated his power, but Latvia was hit especially hard and served as warning to Estonia.

Reemergence of National Culture

These developments strengthened the position of Russian Estonians and reduced their urge to gain some popular approval by pressing for autonomy. The last homegrown Estonian was eliminated from the top circle when the ailing Jakobson was replaced in 1958 by Russian Estonian polar biologist Johan Eichfeld (1893–1989) as chairman of the ESSR Supreme Soviet Presidium, a figurehead position. He was succeeded in this post by Müürisepp, who retired in 1961 from the ESSR premiership and was followed by another Russian Estonian premier, Valter Klauson (1914–1988). The replacement of Khrushchev by Leonid Brezhnev in 1964 had little political impact in Estonia, but the resulting abolition of the *sovnarkhozy* in 1965 soon reintroduced utmost centralization.

The Estonian share of the CPE membership gradually rose from a low of 41.5 percent in 1952 to 52 percent in 1966 (including the Russian Estonians). It then leveled off, much below the Estonian share in the population. Despite their higher level of education (as shown by their preponderance among the college-educated specialists), Estonians were grossly underrepresented in the power structure. It is impossible to say to what extent the CPE discouraged Estonian membership and to what extent Estonians chose not to join, because the two factors were inseparable under colonial conditions: Given the policies of the Soviet Communist Party leadership, which often were anti-Estonian in their impact and yet were obligatory for all CPE members, many Estonians would "choose" not to join. Some other Estonians would join for the sake of personal career advantage, and still others would join in an effort to soften the implementation of anti-Estonian policies.

Estonians were generously overrepresented (with around 85 percent) in the powerless ESSR Supreme Soviet, a rubber-stamp assembly that met for a couple of days per year to approve anything submitted to it. In the more powerful Central Committee of the CPE, however, homegrown Estonians remained a grotesquely small minority; in 1966 the 111 members included 26 Russians, 45 Russian Estonians, and only 26 native Estonians. In cultural matters, however, the picture was different.

The sudden resurgence of Estonian culture around 1960, once part of the repression had been lifted, can be explained by the simultaneous appearance of three age cohorts: those whose time had come, those whose time had been overdue since 1945, and those whose promising beginnings in the late 1930s had been stopped short. Poet Betti Alver (1906–1989) best represents the latter group. In "Sõnarine," a nonsensical name very close to "Wordfront," she writes:

> Kuulasime kohisevaid ajakoski.
> Taga Tarbatut lõi paistma tume Tartaroski.[11]
> [We listened to the roaring rapids of time.
> Behind Tartu loomed suddenly the dark Tartaroski.]

This transparently "Tatar-Russian" appearance is followed by an invitation to become extinct, which the "Wordfront" protagonist defiantly declines to accept. Among the delayed cohort, Jaan Kross (b. 1920) eventually emerged as the foremost postwar novelist; the Soviet occupation authorities had held him in a slave labor camp between 1946 and 1954 solely because he had earlier been imprisoned by the Germans, a sign that he was an Estonian patriot. Among the youngest cohort, poets Jaan Kaplinski (b. 1941) and Paul-Eerik Rummo (b. 1942) have withstood the test of time (see Kitching 1988).

The cultural reemergence began first in poetry, expanded to short stories and novels, and continued with development of a theater of the absurd in the late 1960s. Estonian classics and refugee authors were published; so were Franz Kafka and Fyodor Dostoyevski, both still prohibited in Russia at the time. In abstract art, Tallinn became a third major center in the USSR (along with Moscow and Leningrad). Vive Tolli (b. 1928) gained recognition with her semiabstract graphic style. The first Soviet jazz festival was held in Tartu around 1964, and composer Arvo Pärt made his international debut with dodecaphonic music.

Cultural emancipation was achieved and maintained in an uphill struggle against the imperialist forces. The movement was successful in ridding culture of obligatory sloganeering; political neutrality became acceptable. Art for art's sake, like all allowed art in the USSR, was actually subsidized by the state. But that's where the new freedom stopped. Art's function as social criticism remained severely limited throughout the USSR—counterproductively so, because the lack of criticism contributed to Soviet collapse twenty years later. Some good exposés of Stalinism were published in Estonia, but most of modern history remained off-limits; so did serious critique of the present, apart from indirect hints like Alver's "Wordfront." In the short run, what mattered was that world-level cultural activities became possible, and this increased people's self-respect.

Contacts abroad underwent similar controlled expansion. Western tourists, including some Estonian refugees with Western passports, could visit Estonia, and a trickle of carefully selected Estonians could go abroad. Finnish television became available in northern Estonia and, over time, had appreciable impact.

Education remained strongly ideological. Its format underwent numerous changes. In 1965 an eleven-year curriculum prevailed in Estonia and the other Baltic states; ten years was the norm in the USSR. The extra year was a modest victory for the Estonian language, although much of the extra time was allocated to the study of Russian, which was made an optional subject in theory but mandatory in practice. Christian religious practices dwindled once the Soviet authorities began to devise dignified substitute ceremonies for church weddings and first communions.

Economic autonomy peaked in 1962 and remained limited even then. Formally, 80 percent of the country's industrial production was subordinated to the Estonian *sovnarkhoz*. In 1962 suprarepublic regional *sovnarkhozy* began to infringe on the republic prerogatives, and in 1965 all *sovnarkhozy* were abolished. Most industry was placed under joint "Union-republic" jurisdiction, in which the USSR ministries effectively dominated their republic-level counterparts. Less than 15 percent of industry remained under the control of Estonian ministries. Production and consumption grew steadily, and Estonia and Latvia established themselves as the wealthiest Soviet republics. At the same time, they kept falling ever further behind their Finnish and Scandinavian neighbors. Agriculture improved markedly, but the farming population still depended heavily on their tiny private plots. Housing became less cramped, but still remained far below Western standards.

The Limits of Hope

The list could be expanded, and the story would always be the same: There was considerable or even dramatic improvement, compared with the years of genocide, and Estonia had the best conditions in the entire USSR—and yet the conditions continued to be utterly miserable when compared with those of Western neighbors that Estonia had been catching up with during independence.

Two aspects did not improve. Pollution of the environment became worse, and little could be said much less done about it, given the centralized and compartmentalized nature of Soviet administration. And immigration began to increase again in the 1960s.

At times, jobs in Estonia were better advertised in Moscow or Leningrad than in Estonia, indicative of purposeful Russification. The immigrants often received the scarce housing for which Estonians had been waiting for years. Newcomers sometimes would simply invade newly finished apartments—no Estonian official would dare to evict them and risk being charged with nationalism. The Soviet slogan of "friendship of peoples" meant humble acceptance of Russian colonization. The colonists acted like a master class, superior by their language even when they were unskilled workers. They were unable and unwilling to integrate with the national language and culture, the existence of which they barely recognized. On the contrary, they expected the Estonians to assimilate with them. For Russian children, the Estonian language was an optional subject in school, and most did not bother with it.

For 1965, the Nazi "Generalplan Ost" (described in Myllyniemi 1973) had envisaged 520,000 German colonists in the Baltic states. Instead, by that date they had received over a million Russian colonists. Soviet reality surpassed Nazi plans. In 1970, Estonians were down to 68 percent of Estonia's population.

In the border city of Narva, the Soviet authorities made a special effort to extirpate the very memory of its non-Russian Western-oriented past. The ruins of the medieval city, burned in World War II, remained standing until the early 1960s and could have been restored. Instead, bulldozers were sent in, and people were forbidden to save any pieces of venerable medieval portals.[12] The Estonian Lutheran Church of Narva, also destroyed during the war but restored by congregation members by 1960, was confiscated and turned into a clubhouse.

Despite all this, some hope remained, although it was wearing thin, until the Soviet aggression against Czechoslovakia in 1968. The regime was still very oppressive, but progress made since the years of genocide encouraged optimism about further changes. The pace of reforms slackened during the 1960s, but a feeling of making some headway lasted. There seemed to be some small measure of reciprocal good feeling (Misiunas and Taagepera 1983:193):

> Readiness to cooperate within the Soviet framework increased, and confrontational tactics were avoided for various reasons. The Soviet debit in foisting Stalinism on the Baltic nations was gradually being cancelled out by credit for overcoming it. Russia evolved, and so did the Baltic image of Russia. The renascent Baltic culture was increasingly appreciated by Russian cultural circles. This recognition, combined with grudging Baltic respect for Soviet stability, for the first time added a fleeting element of goodwill to the complex mix of Baltic feelings toward the regime, a mix which previously had

mostly ranged from passive total negation to abject slavish eagerness in some cases. It seemed that problems could eventually be talked out with Moscow on a rational level based on respect for mutual interests.

All this changed when Soviet troops invaded Czechoslovakia. Estonia braced for a purge. It did not come, but Brezhnev's regime had squandered the fleeting goodwill. August 1968 was a psychological watershed, marking the end of a cooperative evolution. The years of hope were over.

YEARS OF SUFFOCATION, 1968–1980

Soviet aggression in Czechoslovakia ushered in a period of hopelessness and loss of vigor in Estonia and, indeed, throughout the Soviet empire. In contrast to the cruel and senseless dynamism of the Stalinist period a few decades earlier, a sense of winding down developed, especially after 1975. In politics, I have called it "softening without liberalization": Ever more rigidly conservative in its outlook, the regime ran out of energy not only for reforms but also for repression (Taagepera 1984a). Estonia (and various other parts of the empire) may have escaped purges after 1968 not because Leonid Brezhnev did not wish to have any but because he was too listless to carry them out.

Several subperiods can be distinguished. Between 1968 and 1975, consumer goods became more plentiful, and a tacit pact could be said to exist between the Soviet population and the regime: butter in exchange for freedom. But the regime supplied the consumer goods only by borrowing from the future, and by the last half of the 1970s, it no longer was able to honor its end of the tacit pact. The shift was accelerated by a series of harvest failures, but underinvestment during the previous times never allowed the regime to catch up again. Even worse, it left any future reformist government with nothing to work with, and this was Brezhnev's biggest crime: squandering precious time and reserves when it was high time for reforms. As for the would-be reformers, they also marked time, as did their colleagues in Franco Spain waiting for the aging ruler to die. Both Franco and Brezhnev held death at bay much longer than people expected.

In the Soviet perspective, a third phase of stagnation could be said to begin with Brezhnev's death (1982) and end with Konstantin Chernenko's (1985). However, dissent in Estonia became so active by 1980 that the benefit of hindsight permits one already to distinguish the confused beginnings of a new era. Also, although in the USSR the term *stagnation* has come to characterize the late Brezhnev era, I prefer to use *suffocation* for Estonia because of the almost painlessly slow but relentless squeeze on the national psyche through colonization and infringement of the Russian language on ever-new aspects of social life. At the same time, direct contacts with the West expanded, and in its shrinking range, Estonian culture and lifestyle continued to develop in a Western direction.

The Estonian population reacted in different ways to the obvious fall of the curtain on reforms in 1968. Resigned to the indefinite continuation of the system, many adopted a cynical stance of consumerism, pursuing material goods that were still scarce but could be obtained when one put his soul (and sole!) into it. Others became dissidents in spirit or, in very few cases, even acts. Dissent, barely noticeable during the period of hope for reforms from above, was born. It was peaceful but nonetheless confrontational.

The Peak of Consumerism

The period 1968–1975 was the high time of consumerism. After prolonged scarcity, the material good things of life now became available, if one focused on getting them and did not rub the system the wrong way. Status symbols shifted from power (especially power to affect other people's lives in a negative direction) to conspicuous consumption: a car, a summer cottage with a sauna bath, fancy food (by Soviet standards), elegant furniture and tableware, trips abroad, and even a new "Estonian Soviet Encyclopedia" and other cultural books made scarce through oversubscription by other similar consumerists. The concomitant collaboration with the regime was considered inevitable and also was rationalized away: One supposedly voiced one's complete opposition to the communist ideology by going through all the required motions with an ironic meticulousness.[13]

There were things to buy—or to obtain by other means. (It was officially estimated that 30 percent of all gasoline assigned to state enterprises and kolkhozes was pilfered for private use.) Car sales in Estonia quintupled from 1971 to 1972, obviously starting from a very low baseline. Waiting times could be several years, and on the island of Saaremaa the *right* to buy a car (not the car itself!) was made a major prize in a socialist competition. Although bank checks (in rounded-off hundreds of rubles only) were introduced, most customers still paid for their cars with wads of thousands of rubles. Services remained so limited that a new eight-pump gas station with no repair facilities in Tallinn rated a first-page photo in the Soviet Estonian main daily.

The market became saturated with washing machines, and vacuum cleaners, refrigerators, and tape cassettes became available fairly widely. Estonia-Stereo was the first stereophonic radio set in the USSR. The traditional Soviet sellers' market shifted partly to a buyers' market, with "socialist commercial advertising," buying on credit, and trade-ins. All this seemed to fade after 1975.

Popular culture also changed. Telemania expanded, although the TV programs were unbelievably dull (at least to my taste, as I dutifully tried to watch them from Finland). Because about 75 percent of Soviet programs available in Estonia were in Russian, the habit also had a Russifying ingredient, but in northern Estonia this was counterbalanced by Finnish television. Youth culture visibly imitated the West. Shocked teachers accused television of promoting long hair. Despite dress codes, leather jackets and Beatle outfits invaded the school dances, where weirdly dressed bands performed rock music. Two books on sex and family were published in massive quantities. The first comic book was published (Donald Duck, translated from Finnish rather than English, to judge by the nature of translation mistakes), but no others followed. By 1975, Estonia even got its first funeral home.[14]

The regime's attitude toward consumerism was hesitant. The emphasis on private consumption did not square with the official interpretation of Marxism and drew away idealistic supporters of the regime. However, the idealistic opposition lost even more because consumerism faced the nascent political dissent with something more powerful than harassment and arrests: a mix of ridicule and boredom. Dissent may have looked morally imperative to the dissenters themselves and criminal to the regime, but to the consumerist it appeared merely foolish. The emphasis on material things, therefore, weakened the ideological underpinnings both of the regime and of dissent.

Immobilism and Russification

The official politics was dominated by immobilism in the Soviet Estonian administration, as it was in Moscow. In line with Brezhnev's general policy of lifelong job security for cadres, the Kremlin's top lieutenants in Estonia remained the same for long periods. CPE First Secretary Käbin, who made his way up in 1950 as a Russifier, later made his peace with the Estonian cultural establishment, as long as its members did not make waves, and became some sort of a buffer between them and Moscow. He remained in office until 1978. ESSR premier Klauson remained in office from 1961 to 1984. Another Russian Estonian, Artur Vader (1920–1978) became the ESSR chairman of the Presidium of the Supreme Soviet upon Müürisepp's death in 1970 and remained there until his own (1978), which produced a convenient opportunity to have Käbin kicked upstairs to that figurehead position. Moscow felt so safe with the Russian Estonians that they even occupied the position of the second secretary, reserved for a

Russian in most SSRs. However, when Vader vacated this post in 1970, he was replaced with a Russian.

In sum, Russian Estonian gerontocracy continued in the Soviet Estonian top administration, and their tactic for staying there was not to show any initiative but merely to go through the motions upon receiving new impulses from Moscow (which were becoming rare). Thus, immobilism in Estonia surpassed even that in Moscow. As time passed, the available pool of Russian Estonians was reduced by mortality and some renativization, whereas the indigenous pool of available talent expanded in both numbers and party seniority. Käbin's retirement became the focal point of the native Estonians' expectations.

Moscow had always tolerated native top administrators in Lithuania, and a native Estonian, Vaino Väljas (b. 1931) seemed positioned to become the next CPE first secretary. He was one of the several nonranked third secretaries and seemed quite subservient to Moscow. In the mid-1970s, I systematically asked visitors from Estonia whom they expected to succeed Käbin, and the answer invariably was Väljas. Instead, Karl Vaino (b. 1923), a lackluster Russian Estonian CPE secretary, was anointed. Born in Siberia, he had come to Estonia around 1948, reputedly under the Russianized name of Kiril Voinov, and he never mastered his ancestral language. His appointment was a slap in the face to native CPE members, a way of telling them in effect that their career chances were nil however subservient they tried to be.

Under Vaino, stagnation and hopelessness deepened, and Russification intensified. The remaining topmost native Estonians were eliminated: An ESSR vice-premier was demoted, and Väljas soon (1980) accepted the post of Soviet ambassador in Venezuela, where he reputedly achieved the reputation of being the first Soviet ambassador who acted like a live human being.

A Russification campaign was launched throughout the USSR with a secret decree of the USSR Council of Ministers (13 October 1978) that most likely represented a delayed reaction to the 1970 census results: Among the Soviet children under ten, the Russian share had fallen to 47 percent. The cause of the Russian decline was birth explosion in Central Asia, but the reaction extended all the way to Estonia. Formerly introduced in third grade, Russian began to be taught in the first grade, starting in the middle of the school year. Nursery schools were ordered to use Russian for one-half of the day. High schools, universities, the media, and even amateur theatrical groups were ordered to use more Russian. The Pedagogical Institute expanded the training of Russian teachers for Estonian-language schools, but prepared absolutely no teachers of Estonian for Russian-language schools in Estonia.

Vaino proclaimed that Russian was the lingua franca in Estonia and the key to world culture. The most disingenuous "proof" for the latter claim came in *Rahva Hääl* (25 August 1982): "Of all world scientific literature 75 percent is published in English or Russian." (I venture the complementary claim that some 65 percent of world scientific literature is published in Estonian or English!) During the 1980 Estonian song festival, for the first time, all speeches at official receptions were in Russian only; in public speeches Estonian was partly maintained. Unbeknownst to the population at large, the documents of the CPE Central Committee began to be printed in Russian only.[15]

The Estonian reaction, after initial shock and despair, registered swiftly: In the 1979 census, the percentage of Estonians who declared fluency in Russian dropped (from 29 to 24 percent). In the other Baltic states and throughout the USSR, an increase was reported. There was no concerted campaign in Estonia to understate one's knowledge of Russian, though rumors circulated that an increase in such knowledge could be used as an excuse for reducing Estonian-language book publication. Instead of Russian, many Estonians apparently reported fluency in Finnish, which they had picked up from television, although the census question specified that only "languages of the USSR" should be reported.

The success of the Russification campaign was mixed. The Estonians were determined not to yield a single cultural or educational position without argument and delay. The most important consequence of the campaign may have been its effect on the consumerists. The shortages since 1975 had already shaken their belief that a material good life was possible within the Soviet framework. Now they were forced to give up the illusion that opportunistic collaboration for personal gain did not really threaten national survival. The empire had turned too blatantly Russian-chauvinist. Pleas for support in the West were smuggled out by some who had never before taken such risks. At this point, it is time to return to the birth of organized dissent around 1970.

Dissent

Unorganized dissent had always been latent. It manifested itself in refusal to speak Russian when addressed in that language. There were often flowers on the grave of Julius Kuperjanov (1894–1919), a hero of the Estonian war of independence, although he had no living relatives. When a Czech hockey team beat the Soviets in April 1972, students from the Tallinn Polytechnic Institute spilled into the streets shouting "We won!"—obviously making the connection to the Soviet aggression four years earlier. At Tartu University, a thousand students roamed the streets in December 1976, shouting anti-Soviet slogans, after a pop concert was prohibited. Once again, the authorities who were not sufficiently liberal to tolerate mildly political lyrics were too soft to take strong action in the face of the riot.

The first hints of organized dissent came in the midst of the Prague Spring, in the form of a July 1968 underground essay "To Hope or To Act?" Arguing against Andrei Sakharov's recent moderate thoughts, this samizdat essay called for a more specific program of action for the USSR: renunciation of aggressive foreign policy, a democratic form of government, and national self-determination—essentially Mikhail Gorbachev's platform twenty years later, except for self-determination. Although the essay was signed by "Numerous Members of Estonia's Technical Intelligentsia," its contents made it seem a part of the intra-Russian debate. The same was definitely the case for an underground Union for Struggle for Political Rights uncovered in 1969 among Soviet navy officers in Tallinn. Its membership extended from Leningrad to Kaliningrad; Estonian involvement was limited. Throughout the 1960s, numerous Estonians were arrested and sentenced on grounds of secret organizing, but names and details did not become available at the time, and publicity is an essential aspect of all successful dissent.

The birth of well-published and definitely Estonian dissent can be dated to an October 1972 joint memorandum by the Estonian National Front (ENF) and the Estonian Democratic Movement (EDM) addressed to the United Nations General Assembly; it was accompanied by a cover letter to Secretary-General Kurt Waldheim. These documents described Russification in Estonia and demanded restoration of an independent Estonia through UN-supervised elections. The membership of ENF and EDM must have been minimal, and they disagreed on one issue: EDM wished to include Russian democrats residing in Estonia; ENF did not (Taagepera 1984a:30). It took the memorandum almost two years to reach the West.[16]

The UN did not react, but the Soviet authorities did, thus rescuing the memo from oblivion. House searches in December 1974 resulted in arrests and the subsequent sentencing (October 1975) of four engineers: Artjom Juskevitš (1931–1982), Mati Kiirend (b. 1939), Kalju Mätik (b. 1932), and Sergei Soldatov (b. 1933). Sentences ranged from five to six years—a far cry from the ten years Mart Niklus received under Khrushchev's rule for a couple of snapshots, not to mention the almost standard twenty-five years under Stalin for almost anything. For determined people, six years was a nonfrightening price to pay for one's convictions. The regime had gone too soft to lash out in a stronger manner, yet had not become sufficiently liberal to overlook the memo that Waldheim had ignored. After 1974, this pattern was to repeat itself over and over: Half-hearted repression gave dissent the publicity it needed to survive. In a new appeal to Waldheim, dated a few days after the initial arrests, the EDM/ENF survivors declared:

> In spite of these gloomy events, we consider that our primary goal has been achieved. . . . The monopoly of the Soviet Estonian puppet regime to represent the Estonian people has ended. No one can state any more that the Estonian nation as a whole agrees with the thirty-five years of occupation and perspective of assimilation.[17]

They were right. The pendulum was beginning to swing back from surviving under Soviet rule to chafing under Soviet occupation.

Further statements of dissent on issues of human rights and independence followed. A May 1977 letter by "Eighteen Naturalists" protested against Soviet oil-shale and phosphate mining practices, which turned large stretches of land into a moonscape. This was exactly ten years before the "Phosphate Spring," the ecological mass protest that triggered fundamental political changes, but at the time the great majority of the Estonians did not even hear about the dissident activities—and those who heard often preferred not to hear.

Cooperation among dissidents in all three Baltic states began at least by 1975 and reached a peak with a common declaration on the fortieth anniversary of the Molotov-Ribbentrop Pact (August 1979). This so-called Baltic charter, signed by thirty-seven Lithuanians, four Latvians, and four Estonians, asked that the secret protocols of the MRP be nullified.[18] It appeared a brave but quixotic demand; yet ten years later the USSR Supreme Soviet obliged. The sudden expansion of the Estonian dissent in 1980 is described in the next chapter.

Stagnation

Meanwhile, Russian colonization continued, although the pace slowed, thanks largely to a decrease in the Russian birthrate twenty years earlier. The 1979 census showed Estonians at 64.7 percent of their country's population (compared with 68.2 percent in 1970). Only 13 percent of the Russians deemed themselves fluent in Estonian. Many of them were footloose migrants; for every 100 arrivals to Estonia, there were about 80 departures. This transiency reduced the colonists' social power and vested interest but also impeded their integration. They were guests who for the most part ignored Estonian language and culture and expected their hosts to adjust themselves—an attitude that obviously created resentment.[19]

Housing shortage remained a major social problem, although the urban living space per capita finally returned to the preoccupation level. Such lack of progress hardly could be blamed on a war that occurred thirty years earlier. Personal reasons such as divorce were no grounds for receiving new housing, and many ex-couples, sometimes remarried, were forced to live side by side in cramped quarters; one can imagine the tensions and frictions. In schools, a large portion of older children attended night shifts because of space shortage—and that in a country with a low birthrate! The number of abortions surpassed that of live births because abortion was effectively the only birth control device available. Inadequate housing was the primary reason women mentioned for avoiding having even a single child.

As mentioned earlier, food shortages became more frequent after 1975. Estonians spent some 62 percent of their income on food, but even at this cost it was hard to obtain. Meat, coffee, onions, and even the lowly potatoes would vanish for shorter or longer periods. Russian "tourists" from regions with even poorer supplies raided city stores, sending packages home and aggravating the situation. Alcohol consumption was 50 percent higher than in Russia or the United States. Group drinking at workplaces was widespread.

Control of the economy remained concentrated in Moscow, but it would not be quite accurate to call it centralized, because the different ministries were becoming independent from each other. It was rather a form of feudalism, with the estates of the various lords interspersed geographically.[20] Estonia's metallurgy and machine construction industries were subject to fifteen different agencies, most of them outside the country. The USSR ministries often had a single plant in Estonia and carried out its day-to-day management from a distance of 1,000 kilometers. Industry could be expanded into cities where communal facilities were already badly strained because the ministerial planners did not have to consult with city agencies; they often learned about the new plant only when the walls were going up. Estonian pleas to pay more attention to integrated "territorial management"—as opposed to "branch management" by specialized production ministries—fell on deaf ears in Moscow.

Ecology was a prime victim of this attitude, because pollution is eminently territorial.[21] Oil-shale and phosphate mines and paper and other industries were geared to production plans—the ecological side effects were of no concern to the producers, and even minimal preventive measures were usually neglected. Negligent handling of fertilizers in agriculture also contributed heavily to pollution. Estonian concern about ecology began with a debate about pesticides in 1965, and DDT and various highly toxic compounds were completely banned. An ESSR water code was promulgated in 1972, which among other measures prohibited construction of new plants without pollution-control devices. However, a republic-level code was not binding on a USSR ministry operating in the republic, and hence such legislation lacked teeth. During the 1970s, the freshwater fish catch decreased by a factor of eight, and several beaches had become seriously polluted.

Agriculture was a relatively bright spot. It remained largely under ESSR control, and its efficiency surpassed that of the USSR by large margins. Enterprise self-management, a catchword throughout the USSR in the 1970s, approached reality in the Estonian kolkhozes. Auxiliary industry, legalized in 1967, was a major factor: Kolkhozes could process their own products and built mills, canneries, and wine factories. They also branched into light industry based on outside raw materials. The Kirov fishing kolkhoz near Tallinn received much of its income from fur animals, furniture, garden products, and souvenirs. It had its own store in Tallinn and became a showcase of collective well-being shown to visiting VIPs. Collective farmers' average income actually surpassed that of urban workers, causing a moderate flow of labor back to the farm. Nonetheless, a large part of farmers' income still came from the tiny private plots. On the basis of about 6 percent of total arable land and a heavy input of labor, these plots supplied 17 percent of Estonia's marketed agricultural produce and probably about 30 percent of the total agricultural output.

The Estonian agricultural efficiency surpassed the Soviet average, but it fell short of the Scandinavian average by equally wide margins. Once again, the best in the Soviet realm was crude by West European standards.

If this litany of social, economic, and ecological woes had been presented in the early 1980s, many a Western reader would have judged it "anti-Soviet" unless some positive features had been artificially included to balance it. But given the subsequent Soviet socioeconomic debacle, my description of Soviet-occupied Estonia of the 1970s must be considered, if anything, overly positive. The crisis was in the making for a long time before it became manifest. Indeed, most areas in the USSR, including central Russia, were worse off than the Baltic states. Estonians were in the best position in a poorhouse they were not allowed to leave.

Cultural development continued, supported by an expansion of Western contacts. A regular boat connection with Finland began in 1965, but initially took mainly Finnish "vodka tourists" to Estonia. In 1970, about 1,700 Estonians could visit Finland, and the flow later must have expanded somewhat. Estonian artistic performances abroad multiplied, and scholars sometimes stayed in Western Europe or North America for an entire year, sometimes with spouses, but children were usually left behind as hostages to make certain their parents returned to the USSR. Many travel requests were denied, even when relatives abroad guaranteed all expenses. Obstruction of travel forced many a talent to seek permanent emigration. Two cases stand out. Conductor Neeme Järvi was well known in the West by the time he emigrated in 1979 and had even greater success later. Composer Arvo Pärt, also allowed to leave in 1979, had considerable difficulty in establishing his reputation in the West, but finally succeeded. In both cases, Soviet bureaucracy seemed to prefer a total loss of talent to sharing it with the West. After they left, Pärt and Järvi became unmentionable back home, except in a few scurrilous articles.

Modern Western culture became largely available in Estonia. *West Side Story* was staged as early as 1965, probably the first American musical to make it past the Soviet borders, and Samuel Beckett's *Krapp's Last Tape* was published and staged—the list is long. Estonia's own culture continued to make the most of the allowed limits. Lennart Meri (b. 1929) produced remarkable ethnographic films of Finno-Ugric peoples, and Veljo Tormis (b. 1930) used the motifs of folk songs (some of them dating to the pre-Christian era) in modernistic compositions. Hando Runnel (b. 1938) wrote simple poetry in a tragicomic vein that appealed to the youth but infuriated the Soviet authorities with its innuendos.

Socioeconomic suffocation in the 1970s proceeded so slowly that it was hard to notice, either by participants or outside observers, in the light of counterpoints such as cultural achievements and the prowess of the dissenters. (One can notice when a noose gradually closes but not when the air in an entire room gradually is depleted of oxygen.) In most respects, all peoples in the Soviet empire were suffocating in the closed room held airtight by the Marxist-Leninist regime. As a nation, Estonia furthermore was smothered through colonization.

WHY SOVIETIZATION FAILED

In the Estonian context, Sovietization meant pursuit of two goals: state socialism and Russification. Both goals were quite evident from policy statements and actual practices from 1940 on.

The first goal applied to Russia as well as to other Soviet-ruled countries, from Yakut to Ukraine to Czechoslovakia. At its root was the Marxist doctrine with its Leninist contortions. Marxism called for abolition of the existence and the spirit of free enterprise and establishment of the reality and spirit of social ownership. It called for the decay of the state machinery and for a versatile people who followed the work style of the ancient Athenian slaves and who governed the society the way Athenian citizens did theirs. Leninism grafted the Russian tradition of a centralized state on this Marxist stock: accepting the socialist part but replacing the decay of the state with its very opposite, the all-powerful state. Tsarist state power had been limited by private enterprise, but the Leninist state could have been reined in only by citizens who fitted the Marxist versatile ideal. However, such citizens did not yet exist, and the totalitarian state nipped citizen participation in the bud or, worse, turned it into a parody. Far from producing citizens who could do factory work in the morning and govern in the afternoon, the mature post-Stalinist Soviet regime molded people who were unable even to switch from one type of work to another as needs changed.

The Soviet regime was successful in establishing a norm of equality among the rank and file (but somehow not among the established elites) and a sense of dependence and expectation of lifelong state support with the concomitant loss of personal initiative (except for considerable skills in procuring scarce goods and services, legally or illegally). As demonstrated by the popular resistance to change around 1990, this socialist goal was achieved, at least in Russia, to a degree the rulers themselves had not dared to believe possible.

The second goal, Russification, flowed naturally from the premises of a centralized state and was reinforced by the Marxist notion that a worker has no homeland. This goal obviously did not impinge on the Russians and, indeed, established a bond between the Russian Marxists and those anti-Marxists intent on keeping the empire intact. Nor was it applied to any serious extent to Soviet-dominated areas in Central Europe. But Russification was very much a central goal in non-Russian areas within the borders of the USSR and at times even overruled the goal of socialism. The periodic elimination of native Marxist administrators in the various "republics" when they showed signs of leadership certainly made Marxism less palatable to the nations affected.

In Estonia, Sovietization could register considerable success in many aspects, yet turned out an overall failure. Russification was successful in the sense that as colonization proceeded almost uninterruptedly (except for a few years in the mid-1950s), it brought Estonians ever closer to a minority status in their own country. The impact on Estonian language and culture was imperceptible in the short run, but still added up to noticeable changes over several decades. If prolonged over several more decades at the same pace, Russification could have become irreversible. However, the pace was slowing. Extreme Stalinist methods (full-scale deportation as in the case of the Crimean Tatars) were never used, probably because of logistic difficulties a population of one million presented and the visibility of the Baltic states in the West. Slower methods may have seemed sufficient in the 1960s, and they produced much less internal resistance and external protest.

However, Estonian culture had considerable resilience and attractiveness. No Estonians were denationalized in Estonia, and most younger Russian Estonians became renationalized over time. The progeny of mixed marriages more often than not opted for Estonian nationality (if they resided in Estonia) when a choice had to be made at age sixteen when people received their internal passports. Expansion of Western contacts came in time to counteract the Russian cultural pressure. The Central

Sovietization as cultural genocide: Soviet soldiers' graffiti on the walls of the Estonian National Museum, used as storerooms and stables by Soviet armed forces from the 1940s to the late 1980s. Photo Mart Niklus, December 1990. Reprinted with permission.

Asians might be persuaded that Moscow was one of the centers of world culture, but Estonians were more impressed with Helsinki, not to mention the great Western capitals.

The 1970 colonization rate, however, could not be maintained. From the 1960s on, the continuously low Estonian birthrate was matched by an equally low Russian birthrate. Central Russia was becoming a demographic wasteland where deaths exceeded births—the seemingly inexhaustible reservoir of would-be colonists was drying up. By 1980 (or even 1990), the danger of Russification through colonization was by no means past, but the odds against its success were decreasing.

As for the socialist aspects of Soviet goals, success was complete in eliminating private enterprise (and voluntary cooperatives), introducing state-oriented socioeconomic institutions, and having the population get used to them and accept them almost unquestioningly. The very skills needed for private enterprise disappeared in generational change that, over forty years, was extensive. What did not disappear was a dim sense of having lost something valuable. This sense was anchored in a Protestant work ethic that was much more deeply rooted than Lutheranism itself and was felt to be part of the besieged national culture. Renewed Western contacts helped to maintain this sense of loss.

Sovietization had made considerable headway in Estonia by 1980, both on the level of institutions and in individual psychology and habits. But this success was not yet complete, forty years after the first Soviet occupation and after thirty-five years of uninterrupted Soviet control. That in itself was a failure—because for the advocates of Sovietization, time was running out.

NOTES

1. Most of this chapter is condensed from a much longer presentation, with detailed references and data tables, in Romuald Misiunas and Rein Taagepera, *The Baltic States: Years of Dependence, 1940–1980* (1983), 74–259. See also Toivo Raun, *Estonia and the Estonians* (1991a), 169–220, Aleksander Kaelas, *Das Sowjetisch besetzte Estland* (1958); Andres Küng, *A Dream of Freedom: Four Decades of National Survival Versus Russian Imperialism in Estonia, Latvia, and Lithuania, 1940–1980* (1980); and Dietrich A. Loeber et al., eds., *Regional Identity Under Soviet Rule: The Case of the Baltic States* (1990).

2. A photo of this "forest brother," August Sabe, taken by the KGB agents moments before trying to arrest him, is reproduced in Priit Vesilind, "The Baltic Nations," *National Geographic* 178:5 (November 1990), 2–27.

3. In my earlier indirect calculations based on the number of inhabited farms, I counted 60,000 deportees, whereas based on the amount of grain confiscated from the deportee farms, there was a minimum of 20,000; see Rein Taagepera, "Soviet Collectivization of Estonian Agriculture: The Deportation Phase," *Soviet Studies*, vol. 32 (1979), 379–397. Evald Laasi has recently worked on lists of deportees in several township archives and extrapolates to about 22,000 (personal communication), which is also the number Karotamm confidentially reported to Stalin. The number of railroad wagons used in the deportations of 1949 was double that of 1941; this also points to 20,000.

4. The best English-language book on the Estonian refugees is Karl Aun, *The Political Refugees: A History of the Estonians in Canada* (1985).

5. "A large part of it [*Gulag Archipelago*] was written in 1965–1966 in a couple of south Estonian farm houses" (Heli Susi, "Aleksandr Solženitsõn 70," *Looming*, December 1988, 1713–15). Heli Susi, daughter of Solzhenitsyn's aforementioned campmate Arnold Susi, helped Solzhenitsyn on weekends with food and checking the references.

6. Aleksandr I. Solzhenitsyn, *The Gulag Archipelago, 1918–1956* (New York: Harper & Row, 1974), 213–214.

7. My translation from Enn Uibo, "Norilski portree," *Memento* (Information Bulletin of the Estonian Union of the Illegally Repressed), no. 16 (January 1991). Uibo (1912–1965) was arrested in 1944, first by Germans, then by Soviets. Released in 1954, he was rearrested in 1957 and died in Dubrovlag, Mordvinia.

8. Ilmi Kolla, "Minu kallima auto" [My boyfriend's car], in *Luuletused* [Poems], Tallinn, 1957. This translation from I. Kolla, *Minu kevad* [My spring] (Tallinn: Eesti Raamat, 1983), 54.

9. Debora Vaarandi, "Uus paat" [New boat], in Paul Rummo, ed., *Eesti luule* [Estonian poetry] (Tallinn: Eesti Raamat, 1967), 664, originally published 1949. My translation.

10. For details of the Latvian purge, see Misiunas and Taagepera (1983), 134–141.

11. Betti Alver, "Sõnarine," *Looming*, November 1966, 1736–37. My translation.

12. Personal communication, during my visit to Narva, August 1989.

13. For detailed source references and comparisons with Latvia and Lithuania in the period 1968–1980, see Misiunas and Taagepera (1983), 195–259. See also Tõnu Parming and Elmar Järvesoo, eds., *A Case Study of a Soviet Republic: The Estonian SSR* (1978); and Sirje Sinilind [Juhan-Kristjan Talve], *Estonia in the Prison of Nations* (1984). See articles by Gregory (1987) and Bohnet and Penkaitis (1988) on relative living standards; Meissner (1987) and Dreifelds (1988) on social changes and inequality; and Uibopuu (1988) on the limited autonomy of the "republic" legislators.

14. Of all the features of Soviet Estonian life, this seemed to bewilder some of my California students most: "But what did they do with the bodies before that time?"

15. This was made public only much later, in *Rahva Hääl*, 13 November 1988, as referred to in Endel Pillau, *Eestimaa kuum suvi 1988* (1989), 215.

16. The memo was first published in *Baltic Events*, no. 46 (October 1974), a newsletter published by Rein Taagepera and Juris Dreifelds 1967–1975; also in *Documents from Estonia on the Violations of Human Rights* (Stockholm, 1977), 19–26; and Küng (1980), 260–267.

17. Full text in *Baltic Events*, no. 48/49 (February–April 1975), 2–3; also in *Documents from Estonia* (1977), 10–13.

18. Full text in Vardys (1981) and in "Samizdat Documents from the Period 1969–1987" (1988); see also commentary by Bungs (1988).

19. Detailed data on population changes up to 1979 are given in Taagepera (1982). Hints are given in Estonian Geographical Society (1984, 1988). On the Jewish minority, see Segal (1988).

20. The argument that Stalin regressed from capitalism to precapitalist feudal structures is made by Harry Paalberg, "On the Origins of Soviet Economic Mechanisms and the Need for Radical Reform—An Essay" (1989). See also Ruus and Usackas (1991).

21. For ecology, see Mare Taagepera, "Ecological Problems in Estonia" (1983).

FIVE

History Starts to Move

In 1980 and 1981, Estonian dissent and protest of various types suddenly reached unprecedented levels. One of its forms, inspired by the Polish Union Solidarity, had the potential to spread throughout the USSR and threaten the very existence of the regime, until Solidarity itself was crushed. The Soviet regime's softening without liberalization deepened: Lacking the will to carry out reforms, it also lacked the will to repress dissent decisively. A succession of moribund individuals at the helm did not help, and the first years of a healthy leader in Moscow changed little in Estonia. Economic stagnation deepened, but native Estonian communists made their first inroads into the ESSR top administration. The situation began to resemble another thaw, reminiscent of that of the mid-1950s, and those old enough to remember it also remembered its disappointing outcome. Then, in spring 1987, the threat of ecologically catastrophic phosphate mining forced the Estonians into a last-ditch resistance, and to their surprise, they won a reprieve. By August 1987, ecological protest spilled over into a political mass demonstration by thousands, led by the formerly isolated dissidents.

In May 1987, the Soviet authorities allowed me to visit Estonia—for the first time since 1944.[1] Upon my return from these five heady days, I made these observations in an article entitled "History Has Started to Move" (Taagepera 1987b:1–2):

> History in Eastern Europe has started to move much faster than we are used to. It may leap forward, and it may also suffer disastrous backlashes. . . . At the glacial pace under Brezhnev, it did not matter whether one was behind events by three months. Now it matters. . . . You go to Estonia and talk with people ranging from officials of the ESSR Academy of Sciences to people suffering from repression and to youths with shirts reading "Phosphate? No, thanks!" . . . You start worrying whether some things are changing too fast while most things do not change at all, so that a dangerous imbalance appears. . . . This must generate considerable stress and frustration for the reformers hoping for change and the bureaucrats doing outdated work—and the reformer and the bureaucrat are often housed within the same person.

In retrospect, the pace of history already had begun to quicken with the various forms of protest in 1980.

THE FALSE START, 1980–1981

Opposition to Soviet occupation of Estonia had never completely vanished. There was even some overlap between the fading guerrilla resistance and the rise of nonviolent dissent. The last known forest brother, August Sabe (1904–1978), drowned rather than surrender in 1978,[2] and the first known act of nonviolent dissent was biology student Mart Niklus sending abroad photos of Soviet Estonian everyday realities in 1956. However, the rise of the new dissent in Estonia (and Latvia) trailed that in Lithuania. There, the Catholic faith offered a support basis that the Estonian Lutheran Church, with its roots in German conquest, could not. The first Catholic mass petition in Lithuania, with 17,000 signatures, was organized in 1971, and *The Chronicle of the Lithuanian Catholic Church,* the most durable underground periodical throughout the Soviet empire, began publication in 1972. The massive religious protest offered some safety in numbers to the far smaller contingent of political dissenters, who seemed to be arrested only after considerable activity; in contrast, individual dissenters in Estonia were arrested in the 1970s at the first open sign of protest. Furthermore, the top administration in Lithuania was in the hands of native communists, who at least understood what the protest was about; the Russian-Latvian and -Estonian top administrators in the two other Baltic states did not understand even that much.[3]

In this atmosphere, several cultural establishment members in Lithuania voiced protest in the mid-1970s; they were demoted but also were allowed to emigrate. But the Estonian cultural elite did not produce any open protesters, one reason being that more so than in Lithuania, potential dissenters in Estonia were ferreted out before they even reached the cultural elite. For example, a young inquisitive historian, Tunne Kelam (1936–1990), saw his application to join the Communist Party rejected; he later lost his job at the Soviet Estonian Encyclopedia and became a night watchman (we shall hear more of him). Whatever their social status, the Estonian dissenters in the 1970s avoided signing their names to protest declarations. A change in this pattern came with the "Baltic charter" of 1979 that four Estonians and four Latvians signed, along with thirty-seven Lithuanians (discussed in the previous chapter). The ratio by nationality is notable. Changing regime attitudes are reflected in the fact that no arrests followed, whereas in 1974 the authors of the anonymous EDM/ENF memo to the United Nations were quickly identified and arrested.

All four Estonian signers of the Baltic charter had a long track record of minor dissent, turned into a lifelong vocation by imprisonment and subsequent employment below their capacities: Mart Niklus, first arrested and imprisoned in 1958, was released after eight years and taught foreign languages. Enn Tarto (b. 1938), arrested during the 1950s thaw for joining an unofficial student organization, had accumulated nine years in prison and then stoked coal into boilers of apartment houses. Endel Ratas and electrical engineer Erik Udam (1938–1990) had spent four and six years in prison, respectively.

Existence of underground publications in Estonia was reported in the early 1970s, but the major semiregular one was started in 1978, six years after the Lithuanian *Chronicle*. I cite this Estonian journal as *Lisandusi* (Contributions) as a short form of its lengthy full name (in English translated as *Contributions to Unimpeded Circulation of Ideas and News in Estonia*). Approximately three issues were published per year, typed with half a dozen carbon copies; these were then distributed to be copied again by the same procedure. The circulation perforce remained small, but copies were passed on and read by many people. Contents included programmatic and philosophical pieces, reports of harassment, and later, court proceedings.[4]

The Life and Death of Jüri Kukk

In January 1980, the Baltic dissidents signed letters protesting against Soviet aggression in Afghanistan.[5] The four Estonian signers of the Baltic charter were now joined in the Afghanistan protest by an ex-establishment member, Jüri Kukk (1940–1981), who had resigned from the Communist Party in 1978; he subsequently was fired from his post as associate professor of chemistry at Tartu University but was refused permission to emigrate. Niklus and Kukk took the documents to Moscow for transmittal to Brezhnev and the Western press. The militia (police) arrested Kukk on groundless and shifting charges and returned him to Estonia under escort three days later.

After nothing worse happened, a subsequent Estonian letter protesting the deportation of academician Andrei Sakharov collected as many as fifteen signatures, including those of two local Russians. In retrospect, the most prominent signatory was engineering technician Lagle Parek (b. 1941), daughter of an Estonian army captain who had been shot by the Soviets a few months after she was born. The family was deported to the Novosibirsk forests in 1949, and Lagle returned in 1955. Much of the informal organization of dissent centered at her office at the Tartu branch of the Institute of Cultural Monuments.

Discovering that the USSR had introduced direct telephone dialing from abroad to Tartu (but not in the reverse direction), the freedom workers quickly established connections with Estonian refugees in Sweden, pa-

Deported as a child and imprisoned 1983–1987, Lagle Parek became leader of the Estonian National Independence Party in 1989. Photo Kalju Suur, August 1990. Reprinted with permission.

tiently waiting for incoming calls at Kukk's telephone (no other dissident had one). They transmitted information about the fake nature of Soviet elections and the spontaneous demonstrations on Estonian Independence Day (24 February), which drew unprecedented numbers of people in 1980. KGB listeners needed up to thirty minutes to tap into incoming calls. (The KGB never solved this technical problem, and the USSR abolished direct dialing in 1982.) The Kukk telephone was repeatedly disconnected, but was reconnected after negative publicity abroad. Four KGB attempts to interrogate Kukk failed because he refused to be questioned, insisting on proper warrants. The KGB apparently was at a loss for what to do next in the face of such a peaceful but determined demand, activity of a type it had never encountered before.

The Soviet repression agency soon recovered from the initial shock. Kukk was arrested in March 1980 as he was on the point of handing in all the required emigration papers, and Niklus's turn came soon after. Twenty-one residents of Estonia signed a protest, along with fifteen Lithuanians, and other protests about the arrests followed. In September 1980, ten Lithuanians and ten Estonians signed a congratulatory telegram to Lech Walesa in Poland for Solidarity's success. The same month about 3,000 young people rioted in Tallinn when a pop concert was banned, and several hundred were arrested; youth protest spread to other cities. In an unprecedented response, the official press, in a terse forty-eight-word condemnation, acknowledged the existence of unrest. The occupation regime had lost the will to sweep unpleasant events completely under the rug. Early October 1980 brought the first industrial strike since 1940, and the strikers' demands about norms and premiums were satisfied. It happened just as workers were winning major concessions in Poland.

The violent repression of youth protest triggered what became known as the "Letter of Forty," addressed in late October 1980 to Estonian newspapers and also to *Pravda* (which did not publish it). Composed chiefly by poet Jaan Kaplinski, it explained in a calm, nonaccusatory tone how Russification looked from the Estonian side and how it provoked protest against the Soviet regime. The letter, which called for debate instead of repression, seemed to mark the beginnings of a moderate opposition aimed at gradual increase in autonomy, in contrast to the uncompromisingly independence-oriented demands of the radical freedom workers. Signers of the Letter of Forty included Marju Lauristin (b. 1940), the sociologist daughter of the first postannexation ESSR premier, and poet Paul-Eerik Rummo. Heino Kiik, author of *The Spook Hostel*, also signed. Repressive measures were very mild by Soviet standards,[6] though another three independence-minded dissidents were arrested in late 1980.

After psychiatric and chemical treatments failed to have an effect on Niklus and Kukk, both of whom were weak from hunger strikes, they were tried in farcical settings and sentenced. One of the low points was the appearance of telephone operators who reported listening in on private telephone calls, a practice explicitly forbidden by Soviet law—but neither defense lawyer dared to point it out. In contrast to earlier trials in which no information was leaked, the system now had become porous. A detailed resumé of charges and a long description of the trial were soon published in the underground *Lisandusi*. As a "recidivist," Niklus was sentenced to "ten-plus-five" years (ten in prison and five in exile, in some remote corner of the USSR); Kukk received two years, but within three months he was dead.

In contravention of Soviet law pertaining to short prison terms, Kukk was removed from Estonia, first to Murmansk and then toward the Urals. Weakened by a hunger strike, he died in unclear circumstances in Vologda, northern Russia (27 March 1981). In a new spirit of decency, officials notified his wife, who attended the funeral with some dissident friends. Then, lapsing into the old rut, the prison authorities forbade them to erect a cross as a grave marker and instead installed a nameless stake with Kukk's prisoner number. Photos were confiscated, but new ones were taken a few weeks later, and the nameless numbered stake made it into the world press. If the Soviet authorities had wanted to create bad press for themselves on purpose, they could not have proceeded any more effectively. The Estonian dissenters now had a martyr figure, whose death in many ways was similar to that of Steven Biko in South Africa a few years earlier.

During spring 1981, three more dissidents were sentenced to four years. The protest letter after Kukk's death still carried some twenty signatures; the small group was attracting as many new members as it lost to arrests. The new ones included three of the four EDM/ENF members sentenced in 1975 and recently released: Artjom Juskevitš, Mati Kiirend, and Kalju Mätik; the fourth, Sergei Soldatov, had been forced to emigrate soon after his release from prison.

An open letter on disarmament in October 1981 represented a new high in Baltic dissent.[7] Noteworthy was that the signers for the first time included more Latvians (fifteen) than Estonians or Lithuanians (thirteen and ten, respectively). More important, they expanded their demands into a new area that made eminent sense and could strike a responsive chord in outsiders who might consider demands of Soviet withdrawal from the Baltic states understandable but unrealistic. In the face of Soviet-supported efforts to create a north European nuclear-weapon-free zone, these Balts simply asked to be included. The nuclear-weapon-free zone, as proposed earlier, included neutral countries (Finland, Sweden) and NATO members (Norway, Denmark) but no Warsaw Pact territories; as such, it was imbalanced and unrealistic. The Baltic letter redressed the balance between the military blocs by proposing to include the Baltic countries.

The Silent Half Hour

The challenge potentially most serious to the Soviet regime, however, did not arise from the independence-oriented dissent or from the gradualist opposition (which did not follow up on the Letter of Forty) but from a completely new underground movement that surfaced in summer 1981: the Democratic People's Front of the Soviet Union (DPFSU), the center of which was in Estonia. It seemed to baffle both the KGB and the established dissenters. Organizers began circulating leaflets calling for a "silent half hour" from 10:00 to 10:30 A.M. on 1 December 1981 and during the same time every first working day of subsequent months in support of the following demands: call home the Soviet army from Afghanistan; halt interference in Poland; halt export of food; abolish special stores for party brass; free political prisoners; reduce military service; and respect human rights. The leaflets recommended that any expression of nationalism and any argument be avoided—just sit there in silence without trying to explain.

For the authorities, this would be awkwardly indistinguishable from the loafing they felt workers engaged in anyway. Any repression squads dispersed could reach only a limited number of workplaces before the thirty minutes were over. Once established, the monthly demonstration could take on a life of its own and continue even if the original promoters were arrested. In sum, the strategy seemed to be an extremely resilient way to build up mass protest against the totalitarian regime. The DPFSU could not expect a wide initial response but only hope for gradual propagation of a new line of peaceful passive resistance. In case of future crises, such as a major food shortage, the masses would be aware of an alternative tactic instead of the time-honored but futile rioting.

Leaflets circulated in Riga and Vilnius and as far as Moscow, but the center was in Tallinn. I have still not learned who masterminded the plan and what became of them. Both Russians and Estonians seemed to be involved. The established dissenters were not involved and, in fact, resented the new competition. The authorities were nervous and took no chances. Even before 1 December, a number of people were fired for distributing leaflets, but the depth of the underground structure seemed to foil the KGB. Unable to ferret out the real organizers, the KGB took it out on the established dissenters so as not to look idle. Scarce consumer goods suddenly were announced to be available in Tallinn, precisely on 1 December at 10:00 A.M. As the date arrived, foreign journalists observed silent groups of workers in some factory yards in Tallinn, but participation was visibly limited. Repression was not—at least 150 people were detained, and four were sentenced to one or two years in prison.

I still wonder whether the silent half hours might have accelerated the end of communism by some eight years had their proposed starting date been set a month earlier. Lack of massive participation on the first try was not critical; a gradual buildup was part of the plan. However, when the Polish Solidarity was crushed in December 1981, the entire psychological atmosphere changed. The January 1982 silent half hour fizzled, and calls for it ceased in February 1982. More than a year later, CPE chief Vaino admitted that the situation was critical and the authorities had to mobilize all their resources to defeat the new tactic. Great efforts had to be made to secure Soviet control, Vaino said. In Poland, Estonia, and elsewhere, 1980 and 1981 were a period of near-revolution—a false start.

THE PEAK OF STAGNATION, 1982–1986

Should the period 1982–1986 be called the peak or the end of stagnation? It was both. Dissent was crushed but not eliminated. Economic woes worsened. But imperceptibly, native communists began to take over some top administrative posts, a transition that may have been crucial for keeping subsequent history on a nonviolent path.[8]

Dissident statements continued, albeit at a reduced pace. In 1983, four more freedom workers were arrested, including Lagle Parek and Enn Tarto. At least in Tarto's case, the indictment considered the open letter on the nuclear-weapon-free zone a highly anti-Soviet piece of evidence on a par with the Baltic charter of 1979. Sentences ranged from five to ten-plus-five. Thereafter, the Estonian dissidents reverted to anonymous statements that often lacked a clear focus, and their Latvian and Lithuanian ties seemed interrupted. In December 1984, signatures reappeared (including those of Ratas and Udam) in a letter addressed to states in possession of nuclear weapons. It called for disarmament and legalization of nonviolent opposition: "In our view, no major state's political and social order is in such a weak condition that they should worry about their survival in case of a free competition of ideas."[9]

The last known arrest came in 1985, the year Mikhail Gorbachev assumed power in Moscow. Hundreds of Estonian and Russian youths clashed in Tartu during preparations for Soviet Constitution Day in fall 1985. The underground *Lisandusi* put out its twenty-third issue in 1986.

In early 1987, the atmosphere changed. A number of dissidents were released, some because the authorities decided to discover a procedural error, some after signing a recantation and promise of future good behavior. Niklus was briefly returned to Tallinn but refused to sign such a recantation and was shipped back to the Urals. Parek accepted, figuring she could do more good in Estonia. Although several freedom workers still were in prison, the underground and semiunderground dissent was reaching its end: It was becoming accepted by the authorities, though not formally legalized.

In the ESSR top administration, changes began in 1983 when home-grown agriculture specialist Arnold Rüütel (b. 1928) became the ESSR chairman, bumping Käbin into full retirement. Rüütel had joined the CPE quite late, at the age of thirty-six. As the topmost vice-premier of the ESSR, he was in line to become the next prime minister, but now he was elevated to a ceremonial post often occupied by retiring prime ministers. The move seemed to be another reverse for homegrown communists. During the coming changes, however, the ESSR chairman was to become a crucial player.

When Klauson retired from the ESSR premiership in January 1984, this position finally went to a native Estonian, Bruno Saul (b. 1932). Saul had married a Russian while studying electrical engineering in Leningrad, which must have made him more trustworthy to the Kremlin, yet he put his son into an Estonian-language school. While visiting the United States in 1969, he told me the following anecdote: The Czechs wanted to form a ministry for maritime affairs. When reminded that Czechoslovakia is landlocked, they replied: "So what? After all, Russia does have a ministry for cultural affairs!"[10]

Homegrown Estonians now occupied two of the three most important posts in the ESSR, posts the Russian-Estonians had monopolized ever

A relaxed Arnold Rüütel, head of state of the Estonian SSR 1983–1990 and of the Republic of Estonia thereafter, at a meeting of the Estonian Nature Preservation Society. Photo Kalju Suur, around 1988. Reprinted with permission.

since the 1950s. Both changes occurred during Yuri Andropov's rule in Moscow, but not too much should be read into that: Local politics played a major role because Russian-Estonians were a dying generation, also weakened by some corruption cases that led to quiet resignations when Moscow became aware of them. The most important post, that of CPE first secretary, remained in the hands of Russian-Estonian Vaino. He was a typical Brezhnev appointee: stable, unimaginative, and unproductive. The post of CPE second secretary, Moscow's main watchdog in the ESSR, remained in Russian hands when incumbents were replaced in 1982 and again in 1985.

Of the third-ranking CPE secretaries, two were native Estonians and one a Russian from 1984 on.

Economic growth was grinding to a halt. The reported annual growth rate of produced national income per capita averaged 2.3 percent for the 1980–1985 period, compared with 4.5 percent in the period 1970–1975. The corresponding figure for industrial growth was 1.8 percent, down from 6.1 percent a decade earlier. Given the Soviet tendency to overestimate such figures by about 2 percent, growth actually had ceased. The production of electricity (largely based on oil shale) peaked in 1979, decreasing 9 percent by 1985. Food became more available than it had been in the late 1970s. Gorbachev's clumsy and heavy-handed anti-alcohol measures caused grumbling and dislocations. Half-hearted attempts to increase workplace autonomy and allow rental farms began in 1980, but similar attempts had been made ever since the 1960s. The regime always had killed such projects when they threatened to succeed.

Continued Soviet aggression in Afghanistan took its toll on the Estonian conscripts (see Philips 1986), and the Chernobyl nuclear disaster affected Estonia in many ways. The vagaries of wind and rain seemed to cause a relatively high radioactive fallout over the country, compared with Latvia. Relocation of at least 3,000 Ukrainian and Belarusian refugees to Estonia displaced locals on the apartment waiting lists and added to the demographic Russification pressures. At the same time, 4,000 Estonians were conscripted to do decontamination work in Chernobyl, sometimes with only an hour's notice in the middle of the night in a procedure reminiscent of Stalin's deportations. In a first sign of media openness, a series of articles in *Noorte Hääl* (Voice of the Youth), the Estonian Komsomol newspaper, reported on the horrendous conditions of men shoveling radioactive dirt but wearing no protective gear. Three hundred Estonians went on strike when their Chernobyl stay was prolonged from two to six months. When this was reported, the article series was cut short.

Construction of a huge new Tallinn harbor twelve kilometers east of the old began in 1982 (see Ratnieks 1984). Estonian economists were never consulted, though economic considerations alone would have argued for a more southern location as a way to shorten transport time and avoid ice in the winter. However, the main rationale for the dinosaurian project was to increase colonization. As with previous such projects, the Estonian population and elites felt powerless to object without making things even worse. But then came the phosphate issue, and the reactions changed.

THE PHOSPHATE SPRING AND HIRVEPARK, 1987

Small-scale phosphorite mining to make phosphate fertilizers had been carried out since the 1920s at Maardu, ten kilometers east of Tallinn.

Open-pit mines introduced in the 1960s disrupted ecology, mainly because the low-quality oil shale lying above the phosphorite layer did not
fit the production plan of the Soviet mining agency and was simply
dumped. The trouble was that the shale was self-igniting upon contact
with air. Fires began in 1965. By 1987, some 50 million tons of this shale lay
in dumps, catching fire and polluting air and groundwater. Furthermore,
it was rich in what the Soviet censors allowed to be called only "heavy
metals"—radioactive thorium, uranium, and radium. In 1979, the director
of Soyuzgorkhimprom, the agency in charge of mining for fertilizers, dismissed a careful evaluation of Maardu with an anti-Estonian slur: The
study could not be taken seriously because it depended on materials by
Estonian authors and organizations only. A new technology, touted by the
Moscow agency to solve all ecological problems, proved worse. In 1985, a
team led by physicist Endel Lippmaa (b. 1930) was finally able to publish a
research paper on gamma ray radiation in Maardu Lake.[11]

Such was the sad record of Soviet inability and unwillingness to mine
phosphorite with even minimal ecological safeguards. The attitude of
Russian planners, managers, and even individual miners revealed this
tendency: Our country is vast; if we mess it up here, we can always go
somewhere else. But the Estonians' country was small; if they or anyone
else destroyed it, they could not move away and remain Estonians.

New phosphorite deposits were discovered in the 1970s around
Rakvere, halfway between Tallinn and Narva at the Russian border, and
the start-up of a trial mine was scheduled for 1987. Because it was located
on a watershed, it threatened to contaminate water supplies as far as Lake
Peipsi in the east and the Pärnu River in southwestern Estonia. Mining
was also another pretext for bringing in more colonists. An anonymous
group of Estonian scientists issued a protest against phosphorite mining
and also against the dinosaurian new port of Tallinn (March 1986). On the
official level, scientists published a thorough plan for the protection and
rational use of natural resources in the entire republic; it was ignored in
Moscow. A December 1986 meeting of the Estonian Writers Union raised
the phosphorite issue. Up to then, the occupation authorities had succeeded in keeping it a "merely technical" problem; now, under changing
conditions, it was becoming a political hot potato.

The Green Protest

Ill-advisedly, the director of Soyuzgorkhimprom gave an interview to
Juhan Aare (b. 1948) of Estonian Television just a few days before
Gorbachev was to visit Tallinn on 27 February 1987. The director was
blunt: Construction of mines had to begin immediately to meet the goal of
full industrial-scale capacity by the year 2000; over 10,000 workers would
be needed (and presumably imported from Russia). As for ecological

problems, the director pronounced them solvable. What had been only a rumor outside the specialized agencies now hit Estonians in their faces from their TV screens. The issue was raised with Gorbachev during his visit by a most unlikely person: chairman of the Writers Union Vladimir Beekman (b. 1929), who had been a docile prop of the Soviet regime. His involvement indicated the depth of national despair. Once Beekman's speech was heard by Gorbachev, it was hard for local administrators to block it from being published in *Sirp ja Vasar* (Hammer and Sickle), Estonia's main cultural weekly.

The mining officials in Moscow and their local acolytes maintained that environmental safeguards were sufficient and action must not be delayed, but the general meeting of the Estonian Naturalists Society argued that mining under existing conditions would contravene Soviet legislation on ecology. The first sign of governmental vacillation came on 30 March 1987: An ESSR government commission chaired by Prime Minister Saul said construction projects had been halted until further study. The hedged wording did not satisfy public opinion—yes, there suddenly was such opinion, for the first time in forty years! Komsomol protest at Tartu University was followed by a resolution of the University Council (24 April 1987) that accused the USSR Ministry of Fertilizers of a "narrowly sectoral attitude that ignores essential statewide interests" and puts a third of Estonia at risk. The resolution gave detailed environmental, social, cultural, and demographic objections. It also reported that an opinion survey (another novelty!) in the proposed mining region showed three-fourths of the population opposed to it.

The student First of May demonstrations had green banners instead of the habitual red. The censors impressed on the Tartu University weekly that "not a single word must be printed" about the demonstrations. The paper obliged—reproducing only a photo, but one with many antiphosphorite slogans clearly legible. By that time, few words were minced in the media. There was talk of "typical colonial exploitation" and a TV debate on whether to hold a referendum. The very word had been taboo—and for reason. During my first five days in Estonia since 1944 (May 1987), dissident Tunne Kelam told me with his characteristic smile: "Oh, we've got other things we'd like to put to referenda, too"—like independence.

Evidence about the economic inanity of the project mounted. By world standards, the phosphate content of Estonian phosphorite was unmarketably low. Indeed, the waste heaps of some depleted mines in the Soviet Far East were equally rich, but the ministry would not have reaped any credit for reworking its previous blunders. Calculations presented in *Eesti Loodus* (Estonian Nature) in August 1987 suggested that only 1 percent of the phosphate mined in Rakvere would actually be taken up usefully by

Student protest during the Phosphate Spring: Placards proclaim "But What About Public Opinion?" "Phosphorite of Virumaa: Glasnost! Public Opinion!" "Phosphate Powder: What For?" One sign shows the map of Estonia in balance with a pile of fertilizers. I obtained this photo from two students in the backyard of a house in Tallinn, May 1987.

plants, given the inevitable losses plus the ones specific to Soviet practices.

Victory came in the fall. At a 27 October 1987 meeting of the CPE Central Committee, ESSR Premier Saul reported that the USSR Council of Ministers had decided to stop projects for new phosphorite mines in Estonia and, consequently, the CPE Central Committee and the ESSR government had voided their earlier resolutions on the subject. Was it meant as merely a temporary subterfuge until the popular uproar abated? Maybe. But subsequent developments made the stoppage permanent.

The indirect results of the Phosphate Spring were as important as the ecological reprieve. People learned to organize. They learned how to test the unknown gray zone between the allowed and the forbidden in a way that allowed for tactical retreat but also unexpected advances. They practiced focusing on one specific issue at a time. They discovered that many others shared their secret yearnings, while outwardly all of them had gone through the same proregime motions. Above all, the mood of "It cannot be done" changed into "We'll do it anyway." All this new experience could be applied to other issues besides ecology.

This first phase of social awakening carried an ecological stamp throughout the Baltic states. Ecology was nonpolitical and hence the hardest to brand as nationalistic. (The Soviet authorities saw it as nationalistic anyway—why otherwise would anyone worry about the ecology of just that small corner of the huge USSR one happened to reside in?) The ecology issue reached a critical point first, maybe prematurely, in Lithuania, where several environmental inspectors were murdered in 1983 without much investigation undertaken by authorities. In retrospect, Latvians had the best timing. Their protest about a proposed hydroelectric station, which involved flooding large areas, began in October 1986, and by March 1987 the Latvian Council of Ministers advised Moscow to give up on the plan. One might think that the Latvian success would have been a major factor in encouraging the Estonians, but such was the degree of isolation of the various SSRs that I encountered no mention of Latvia during my visit. Rather than a chain reaction, the ecology revolts, first in Latvia and then Estonia, were separate events generated by similar conditions.

Protest Goes Political

Latvia preserved its head start from late 1986 to August 1987, a period that could well be called the "Latvian phase" of the reemergence of the Baltic states. Latvian action went political on 14 June 1987 with the commemoration of the 1940 deportations, but it could still be interpreted as protest against excesses of Stalinism within a Soviet Leninist context. The case was otherwise with the commemoration of the Molotov-Ribbentrop

Pact on 23 August 1987 because the demand for publication of the MRP secret protocols impinged on the very legality of the Soviet regime in the Baltic states.

The dissidents had remained on the sidelines in the ecological protest, which was advanced by establishment figures and organizations. The reverse was true for the MRP protest: It was a dissident initiative, and the establishment shied from such a direct challenge. Because the dissidents had an all-Baltic network long established, the action was coordinated in all three capitals. Latvia still led, if one judges by the number of participants in the Riga demonstrations (over 10,000). Estonia came next, with 2,000 to 5,000 participants, and the Lithuanian protest was a comparatively minor one (over 1,000).[12]

Hirvepark (Deer Park) near the Toompea (Dome Hill) castle in Tallinn was the site of the Estonian demonstration on 23 August 1987, and under this name it went into history. The protest was organized by longtime dissidents, some, such as Lagle Parek, recently released from detention. They asked for official permission to hold the meeting in the medieval City Hall Square, but city officials redirected them to Hirvepark, and the dissidents obliged. This tacit cooperation is noteworthy: Hirvepark was not an illegal meeting from the authorities' standpoint. The dissidents bothered to ask for permission, and the city officials gave it. The main speech presented the demand for publication of the MRP secret protocols and stressed the sovereignty of nationalities: "By national sovereignty, Soviet jurisprudence means a nationality's full authority, a genuine opportunity fully to determine its fate, and above all, ability of self-determination, including the ability to secede and form an independent state."[13] The speaker was Tiit Madison (b. 1950), a dissident imprisoned 1980–1984 who later had applied for an emigration visa; the Soviet authorities hastened to give it immediately after Hirvepark. (Pleased by the outcome, they subsequently expelled to the West several other dissidents who did not want to go.)

Hirvepark demonstrated that a public mention of the MRP was possible. Furthermore, signatures were collected during the meeting to start a new organization: MRP-AEG, the Molotov-Ribbentropi Pakti Avalikustamise Eesti Grupp (The Estonian Group for Making Public the MRP). The founding of MRP-AEG marked the end of the dissident phase of Estonian freedom work, because this quite public organization no longer was severely harassed. Many other organizations of varied types followed. If they applied for official registration, they were refused (and hence lacked certain advantages such as bank accounts), but they were not repressed by police action.

From February to August 1987, the atmosphere in Estonia changed more than it had during the previous thirty years. Repression of freedom to organize and express opinions faded. Public opinion and public action were born. History had indeed started to move.

NOTES

1. For discussion of a previous unsuccessful attempt I made to visit Estonia, see Rein Taagepera, "When a Visa Is Not a Permit to Enter," *Nationalities Papers* 6:2 (1978), 199–201. It was touch and go even in 1987—I was already in Estonia when the CPE ideology secretary told poet Jaan Kaplinski that I would "never be let in."

2. Romuald J. Misiunas and Rein Taagepera, *The Baltic States: Years of Dependence, 1940–1980* (1983), 240. See photo in Priit Vesilind (1990).

3. The section on the false start is based largely on Rein Taagepera, *Softening Without Liberalization in the Soviet Union: The Case of Jüri Kukk* (1984a), which has detailed references and full texts of various dissent statements.

4. The first nineteen issues have been subsequently printed in Sweden, in three volumes: *Lisandusi mõtete ja uudiste vabale levikule Eestis 1–19 (1978–1984)* (Stockholm: Relief Center for Estonian Prisoners of Conscience in the USSR, 1984–1986).

5. Full text in Taagepera (1984a), 62–63; and "Samizdat Documents" (1988), with comments in Bungs (1988).

6. An English translation of the Letter of Forty is given by Vardys (1981). A full account of the entire episode is given in Sirje Kiin, Rein Ruutsoo, and Andres Tarand, *40 Kirja lugu* [The story of the letter of forty] (Tallinn: Olion, 1990).

7. Full text in Taagepera (1985 and 1986a).

8. For details of the period of the peak of stagnation, see Romuald J. Misiunas and Rein Taagepera, "The Baltic States: Years of Dependence, 1980–1986" (1989). See also Jaanus (1989); Šilbajoris (1989); and Valgemäe (1989) on Estonian literature in the 1980s; and see Hilkes (1987) on school reforms.

9. Full text in *Vaba Eestlane* (Toronto), 24 December 1985; English-language overview in Taagepera (1986a).

10. Although the source is not identified, the joke is reported in *Estonian Events*, no. 15 (August 1969).

11. Mare Taagepera, "The Ecological and Political Problems of Phosphorite Mining in Estonia" (1989); Arthur H. Westing, "The Greening of Estonia" (1988).

12. "Glasnost in the Baltic: Summer Demonstrations," *Baltic Forum* 4:2 (Fall 1987), 1–29.

13. *Vaba Eestlane*, 6 October 1987.

• SIX •

The Quest for Autonomy

The period from September 1987 to September 1989 was characterized by active Estonian demands for autonomy within the Soviet framework. Of course, there were some people for whom autonomy was not an urgent matter and others who called not for autonomy but independence, as the organized dissidents had done ever since the early 1970s. However, for the majority, independence seemed either a pipe dream in 1987, or something one could think about only after meaningful autonomy was attained. During the Phosphate Spring, this majority shifted from "can't do" to spontaneous action on a single issue. In September 1987, a comprehensive economic autonomy proposal by four establishment members marked the beginnings of a concerted drive for autonomy.

As effective autonomy of press, political symbolism, and local administration (but not economy) was achieved in 1988, the mood increasingly shifted toward a focus on independence. The usual pattern of rising expectations during reforms was reinforced when the limitations of autonomy, as understood by the Kremlin, became apparent. Some major dates in that shift from quest for autonomy to quest for independence were October 1989, when the Popular Front spelled out independence as the end goal in its platform, and November 1989, when the ESSR Supreme Soviet declared that Estonia's annexation by the USSR amounted to a "military occupation" (see Chapter 7). Several more radical organizations of course reached that stage much earlier, but the CPE held out for autonomy until early 1990, when the economic autonomy promised by the Kremlin officially took effect. The niggardly way the Kremlin interpreted this "autonomy" sounded the death knell for any hopes of autonomy among the Estonians.[1]

Whereas Latvia had led the way during the ecological phase of Baltic self-assertion, the economic autonomy proposal in September 1987 ushered in an Estonian phase: During the next eighteen months, new developments came first in Estonia, then in Lithuania (with an average lag of 3.5 months) and Latvia (5 months).[2] In spring 1989, Lithuania began to lead.

THE ECONOMIC AUTONOMY DEBATE,
SEPTEMBER 1987–March 1988

The Hirvepark demonstration put the closet reformers in the Soviet Estonian establishment in a quandary. They had cautiously tested the waters, ever mindful not to provoke a backlash like the one in Latvia in 1959 that would leave Estonia even worse off than it was before. But now they realized they were losing initiative to more radical forces whose activities could trigger the very backlash they wanted to avoid. Thus, Hirvepark probably speeded up the publication of a plan for Estonia's economic autonomy that was slowly being drafted since spring 1987. Known as the "Four-Man Proposal" (although it had some ten authors collectively), it was published not in the media of the capital city but in *Edasi* (26 September 1987), the daily of the university city of Tartu, which had long been the most liberal newspaper in Estonia.[3]

The Four-Man Proposal

The proposal was bold. Indeed, four years later, after many breathtaking political changes, some of its parts (such as convertible currency) had not yet been implemented. The signers included Edgar Savisaar (b. 1950), a social philosophy graduate who had been director of long-term planning for the ESSR State Planning Committee but was being frozen out because of his activism; Siim Kallas (b. 1948), one of the editors of the Soviet Estonian main daily *Rahva Hääl* who had training in economics and finance; and Tiit Made (b. 1940), a political commentator on the state televison, who had spent some time at the Soviet consulate in Stockholm. Many of the ten collective authors desisted from signing, fearing heavy retribution, but a nonauthor of the basic draft who agreed to sign was gladly accepted, especially given his good contacts in Moscow: Mikk Titma (b. 1939), a sociologist at the ESSR Academy of Sciences and vice-president of the Soviet Sociology Association.

The Four-Man Proposal recommended that the existing factory-level autonomy principles be applied to Estonia as a whole, including self-financing, self-supplying, and self-administration. A territorial balanced budget implied that income and purchasing power of the population would depend "on the demand for our products in the all-Union and worldwide markets." Hungarian, Bulgarian, and the past Soviet *sovnarkhoz* precedents were mentioned, as were the Chinese special regions for export-oriented production of high-quality goods. The authors acknowledged their proposal was radical in Estonia but not out of line with the new thinking of Russian reformers such as Abel Aganbegian,

Tatiana Zaslavskaia, and Gavril Popov. The central points were the following:

1. Economic direction and planning shall be based on respect for the law of value determination and on commercial-financial relations.
2. Economic objects located in the territory of the Estonian SSR shall be subordinate to the Estonian SSR. This includes the railroads, merchant navy, and the enterprises presently subordinated to all-Union agencies. The economic structure shall be altered so as to ensure preferential development of those spheres which are based essentially on local resources, are economically profitable for us, are culturally acceptable, and agree with our traditions of management.
3. Trade with the other republics, krais [territories], and oblasts [regions] of the USSR as well as foreign countries shall take place through the marketplace and shall be based on direct ties between the producer and the consumer.
4. A convertible ruble shall be introduced, to be an internationally accepted medium of exchange. This shall also be the means for all exchanges with the agencies and enterprises in other regions of the USSR.
5. In its relations with the budget of the USSR, the republic shall act as an entity. The republic's contribution to the all-Union budget shall be determined by the USSR Supreme Soviet on the basis of long-term normatives. The Estonian SSR will share in the all-Union task specialization mainly as a booster of foreign currency profits. A separate taxation system shall be set up to establish the income for the budget of the Estonian SSR. The local budgets shall be separated from the republic budget.
6. Transition to complete self-management shall be effectuated throughout the territory and on all levels of economic command. The cooperation among the various regions, cities, and districts of the republic shall also be based on self-management relations.
7. Organizational plurality shall prevail in the economy, with all kinds of encouragement for the existence of enterprises competing for the customer. Cooperative production shall be extended, and a part of the enterprises shall be based on the principle of shareholding companies. To start and run enterprises, the financial resources of the inhabitants of the Estonian SSR will be tapped as well as foreign capital. Product quality shall be evaluated on the basis of international standards.
8. The movement of workforce between the republic which has shifted to self-management and the other parts of the USSR shall be regulated by a special regime of rational utilization of labor.
9. The direction shall be based on economic methods and independence of enterprises. Agencies not connected with planning and implementation of overall strategy of development shall be abolished. The planning organs shall deal only with the long-term planning of overall proportions.[4]

Throughout late 1987, the proposal was subjected to criticism by people close to the CPE top administrators and the ESSR Council of Ministers. Ironically, those who hoped to demonstrate that republic autonomy was impossible fell into the trap of documenting in great and petty detail the extent to which Estonia's economy was run from Moscow. Savisaar turned this argument on its head, using it as proof that overcentralization had reached absurd proportions. People from all walks of life participated in the debate. Few supported the status quo; for some radicals, the proposal did not go far enough and merely tried to reform an inherently flawed regime. On 26 February 1988, *Edasi* reported that five opposing articles but approximately 100 favorable articles and letters had been published in the Estonian press.

The debate exploded a number of myths. Despite the stipulations in the Soviet constitution, the republic government authorities were unveiled as passive subordinates to the Moscow command centers. The glorified Union-wide plan, supposedly designed with the best interests of the people in mind, appeared as a mere sum of bureaucratic compromises worked out among sectoral monopolies. And Estonia, the most developed part of the Soviet inner empire, learned how far behind Western Europe it really had fallen in its ability to compete. In fact, the Four-Man Proposal was far too optimistic in its hopes for foreign currency profits.

The opposition by the ESSR top brass began to weaken in December 1987. During all this time, Moscow's reaction was noncommittal. Even reformists such as Aganbegian and Zaslavskaia were skeptical about economic autonomy, afraid that it would spill over into political autonomy and then possibly to what they considered secession. In retrospect, political autonomy came anyway, and the absence of economic autonomy only fanned the demands for independence.

In April 1988, the Soviet Politburo agreed to turn seven economic sectors over to Estonia, ranging from industry and energy to forestry and environment. However, implementation was left to central bureaucrats who turned it into another stalling game. At the same time, all SSRs lost control of the construction materials industry. Although the direct results of the Four-Man Proposal were nil, its side benefits were considerable. It triggered the first informed debate on economic matters and mobilized the country's economists and sociologists into some three dozen independent task forces to study the issues. Indirectly, it also demonstrated the need for political autonomy.

Reconquest of History

Meanwhile, the media openness extended to history. Titma, one of the signers of the Four-Man Proposal, cast doubts on the wisdom of the

Molotov-Ribbentrop Pact, "one of the most disagreeable historical facts of our past foreign policy," and said it was "an indisputable historical fact" that the CPE could not have seized power in Estonia without the presence of the Soviet army. He was probably the first to mention the number of deportees and refugees in print:

> While for nearly the entire Soviet land Stalinist political regime was a matter of power, for the Estonians a national interpretation was added in 1940–1941 (which included the deportation of 10,000 people immediately prior to the Great Patriotic War). Hence the fairly extensive contribution from amongst the Estonians to the ranks of the army of the German conquerors, their historical enemy. One must view in the same context the extensive emigration of Estonians at the end of the war (70–80,000) and the guerrillas in Estonia.[5]

Titma also fairly transparently warned that the Russian colonists were already so numerous that they could be mobilized to quash demonstrations like that of Hirvepark, which thus could become counterproductive.

Historian Evald Laasi (b. 1931) followed up with detailed data on the 1941 deportations, arrests of Estonian army officers, the resulting massive surrender of the ex-Estonian army to the Germans, the postwar guerrilla activity, and the 1949 deportations:

> The damage this action [the deportation of 14 June 1941] caused to Soviet rule was certainly ten and possibly a hundred times greater than the limited gain from deportations. . . . On the basis of this event many made up their minds on whom to support in the coming war. Had there not been the deportations of June 1941, the choice would not have been hard for the overwhelming majority of Estonians, regardless of their political affinities, since the Germans, who had oppressed our people for 700 years, were very unpopular.
>
> People simply could not understand that such an action could be possible in the Twentieth Century. Therefore, the deportations of June 1941 came as a complete surprise to our nation. The last deportation in Estonia had taken place during the Nordic War when, in 1708, tsar Peter the First ordered all German inhabitants of Tartu (824 persons) expelled to Vologda.[6]

Vologda was also where Jüri Kukk had died in 1981. To appreciate the impact of the preceding statements, one has to keep in mind that every sentence of it would have been censored during the previous forty-three years, with dire consequences to the author. The attempt to silence comment was not quite ended even in 1987: Laasi was made to appear before an inquisitional body of scholars and Soviet army veterans and was accused of using the enemy's archival data, but he stood his ground and some scholars dared to side with him, breaking the Stalinist spell of unanimous condemnation.[7]

Many among the one and a half generations of Estonians who had learned falsified history during their entire schooling may have asked their parents and grandparents, upon reading Laasi: "Was it really like that?" And the answer may have been: "Yes, it was. But we never dared to tell you, because if you blurted it out in school, that would have been the end of us." A nation was recovering its history and, because of the intervening gap of silence, almost began to relive it. By 1988, I heard young people whose parents may have been born after 1939 talk of the MRP as if they had experienced this iniquity personally.

It again became acceptable to celebrate Christmas. A number of local organizations that had interacted for more than a year to clear overgrown churchyards and prepare for more extensive action combined officially on 12 December 1987 and formed the Estonian Heritage Society (EHS), chaired by Trivimi Velliste (b. 1947). In January 1988, a reactionary CPE ideology secretary was replaced by Indrek Toome (b. 1943), who established a dialogue with the reformists.

The reactionary communists counterattacked on 2 February 1988. An MRP-AEG demonstration in Tartu, held in commemoration of the Estonian-Soviet peace treaty of 1920, was brutally assaulted by the militia (police). In retrospect, this was the last major police brutality in Estonia, but at the time it brought a sharp disagreement over tactics between the radical ex-dissidents of MRP-AEG, who planned major demonstrations on Estonia's Independence Day (24 February), and the gradualist reformers, who advocated more measured approaches, fearing that confrontation could lead to a backlash. The latter published a call "To the Inhabitants of Estonia," recommending that the seventieth anniversary of the "declaration of statehood in Estonia" be marked by "scholarly conferences, respectful debates, and reflections in the press, without politicization and excessive security."[8] The forty-eight signers included the four proponents of economic autonomy, and writers Kross, Rummo, and Meri. Ironically, they had difficulties in publishing this appeal for calm: What the radicals considered a sellout was too radical for the Soviet authorities.

As the critical date arrived, about 10,000 people participated in the MRP-AEG demonstration in Tallinn, with several thousand siphoned off to the scholarly lectures organized by the gradualists. The Soviet police forces did not intervene. The radicals concluded that the gradualists had panicked for no reason, but the latter felt the event still had been too risky. To diffuse discontent, the ESSR authorities allowed the publication of some objective accounts of the events surrounding the birth of the Republic of Estonia in 1918.[9] (The official Soviet version had been that the newly independent democratic Estonia had been a "bourgeois dictatorship.") From then on, open praise of Estonia's period of independence was sanctioned (and at times lost its sense of perspective, especially about the authoritarian interlude).

THE SPRING OF THE FLAG,
APRIL–OCTOBER 1988

The public display of the prohibited national colors by the Estonian Heritage Society (in Tartu, 14–17 April) may not have been the most important event during spring 1988, but most Estonians remember it anyway as the Spring of the Blue-Black-White—the spring when display of the still-prohibited flag spread throughout the land and tens of thousands of people spent entire nights singing and waving flags. Some elderly Estonians declared they could now die in peace.

The flag apparently already had been displayed by the First Independent Youth Column, an unofficial group in the southern town of Võru, in late 1987. As for the EHS, it did not display the standard flag but rather three flags—one blue, one black, and one white. During the customary First of May demonstration in Tallinn, an MRP-AEG group marching among the environmentalist Green column briefly unfurled the national colors, causing the Greens to apologize to city authorities. However, by 20 May, the blue-black-white flags featured prominently in a photo on the front page of *Sirp ja Vasar* of the Tenth Rock Music Days in Tartu, and the chain reaction engulfed Tallinn. The presidium of the ESSR Supreme Soviet legalized the flag as the Estonian "national colors," distinct from the red ESSR "state flag," on 23 June 1988.

Founding of the Popular Front

Meanwhile, other major developments taking place were adding up to a multifaceted breakthrough. Indeed, the month of April alone featured highlight upon highlight. At a meeting of the leaderships of the creative unions (writers, artists, journalists, and so on) on 1–2 April 1988, the mood was extremely defiant. Economic autonomy was not making any headway, and a week earlier an anonymous Stalinist article had marked the anniversary of the 1949 deportations by maintaining that all deportees had deserved their lot. For the first time, a member of the establishment—Rein Veidemann (b. 1946), editor of the monthly *Vikerkaar* (*Raduga* in the Russian edition)—mentioned publicly the possibility of an Estonia outside the USSR, and his words were reported in the official press: "If self-management cannot be implemented within the framework of the existing legislation of the federal state, then the constitutional right of self-determination must be exerted so as to shift to self-management through this means" (*Sirp ja Vasar*, 15 April 1988).

The creative unions sent extensive proposals to the nineteenth CPSU conference to be held in June. Demands included clarification of the meaning of "republic sovereignty" in the Soviet constitution, establishment of a republic citizenship distinct from USSR citizenship, freedom to live abroad and return, freedom to nominate candidates in elections, the right to modify the republic electoral rules to suit the culture, openness of the courts, economic autonomy, and uninhibited use of one's native language in all spheres of life on one's national territory.[10] The meeting further adopted a letter to the ESSR authorities that expressed distrust of the two top CPE figures:

> Our nation expects more initiative and firmness of principles from the ESSR leadership, in the defense of the republic interests and constitutional rights. On this basis the plenary meeting expresses dissatisfaction with the present performance of the CPE CC First Secretary, K. Vaino, and the Chair of the ESSR Council of Ministers, B. Saul.[11]

All major ESSR government and CPE officials had been invited to the meeting, but only Toome showed up to give a noncommital talk. Media coverage was extensive. It could be argued that this was the birth of a new centrist force strongly opposed to the reactionary colonial administration but also clearly distinct from the radicals. The latter wanted to abolish the Soviet regime and restore the preoccupation Republic of Estonia, but the centrists found it more expedient to advance the national cause within the ESSR framework.

The Popular Front of Estonia (PFE) was the organized expression of this reformist political center. It was proposed by Savisaar in the midst of a brainstorming TV show on 13 April 1988, and the same night an initiative group was formed. The original name was Popular Front for the Support of Perestroika, a hook to a term floating around in Moscow. A proposal was submitted to the ESSR authorities; the CPE Central Committee approved it at a meeting First Secretary Vaino did not attend. As a safeguard against a reactionary takeover, the temporary bylaws of the PFE specified that no person could serve simultaneously in the PFE leadership and that of the ESSR government or CPE. In the PFE formulation, economic autonomy appeared under the acronym IME, for *isemajandav Eesti* (self-managing Estonia)—"*ime*" literally means "miracle"—and gained wide circulation during the rest of the year.[12]

At first, Gorbachev seemed delighted with such a reformist initiative from below, expecting it to be simply socioeconomic and democratic within the general framework of a Russian-speaking state, because this is how Gorbachev saw the USSR. He had shown his color blindness about the multinational character of the empire ever since he appointed a Russian to head the Communist Party of Kazakhstan, thus provoking the Alma-Ata uprising. By the time the Estonian national goals of the PFE became evident to Gorbachev, the organization had already struck deep roots. In early June 1988, the PFE claimed 40,000 members, one-third of them also CPE members. Given this overlap, it was a question of who was infiltrating whom. The leaders of each organization expected to subvert the other, using concessions and pressures. Slowly, the CPE began to crumble, and the PFE shifted toward ever more radical demands. An Estonian Green Movement closely allied with the PFE was founded in May, headed by Juhan Aare, who had helped to trigger the phosphorite debate. The EHS also voiced support for the PFE. The first major confrontation between the PFE and the CPE came in June 1988.

The Singing Revolution

CPE First Secretary Vaino was increasingly out of touch with the burgeoning popular movement of reform, especially because it used the Estonian language Vaino did not speak. Gradually, he became almost invisible in public life, leaving confrontations to his underlings (mainly Prime Minister Saul) but inciting articles against economic autonomy and sending secret complaints to Moscow. On 31 May 1988, Vaino decided simply to appoint the Estonian delegation to the upcoming nineteenth CPSU conference in Moscow without holding the multicandidate elections called for by the CPSU central leadership. A token Green (Juhan Aare) was included, but the PFE leaders were pointedly excluded. What Vaino did not expect was that the media would dare to protest. Among others, Estonia's English-language weekly *Homeland* described the pseudodemocratic procedure bluntly:

> A list of candidates to be voted on was hurriedly drawn up amid great controversy, since it excluded the most outspoken candidates. Though formally there were no irregularities in the voting procedure at the [CPE CC] plenum, there were no democratic elections either: The initial list of 77 [candidates] was reduced to just 32, the exact number of delegates Estonia can send to Moscow.[13]

Vaino and Saul were criticized in the press, and some local CP organizations called for elections of a new CPE Central Committee (CC). An attempt to remove Vaino failed, but the mood became extremely tense. Nearly 900 young people, representing at least a dozen extremely varied youth groups, came together and formed the Estonian Independent Youth

Forum (4 June 1988), ending the monopoly of the Komsomol in organizing youth. A long-scheduled festival, the Old Towne Days (11–14 June 1988) marked the breakthrough for the blue-black-white flag in Tallinn. An estimated 60,000 people participated in what became known as the Night Song Festival (11–12 June), during which masses of young people waved flags to the tune of rock music until dawn but maintained remarkable discipline. Cartoonist Heinz Valk (b. 1936) called it "The Singing Revolution" (*Sirp ja Vasar*, 17 June 1988), and as similar events occurred in the days that followed, this name came to characterize the summer of 1988. Vaino considered dispersing the youths by force of arms, but Toome and other cooler minds prevailed.[14]

On 14 June, the deportations of 1941 were commemorated. When the Popular Front called for a mass meeting on 17 June to meet the Estonian delegates to the CPSU conference, Vaino panicked, told Moscow that the situation was out of hand, and asked for military intervention. But CPE ideology secretary Toome intervened, presenting a more realistic picture. The Kremlin sensed that Vaino's alarmism was becoming dangerous and agreed to dismiss him on 16 June 1988.

The next day, 100,000–150,000 people came out to celebrate. Among the thirty-two delegates to the CPSU conference, only five showed up: Toome, Aare, Enn-Arno Sillari (b. 1944, one of the CPE third secretaries), Tiit Vähi (b. 1947, automotive manager of the town of Valga), and Mare Rossmann (b. 1939, a schoolteacher who had openly protested against the composition of the delegation). The demonstration also had implications for intra-Estonian politics. Up to then, the radicals of the MRP-AEG had taunted the autonomists as a bunch of intellectuals isolated from the people, touting that the radicals could get thousands of people out to demonstrate. Now the Popular Front had vastly outdone the radicals in ability to get the people into the streets. Between the CPE and the MRP-AEG, the PFE established itself at the center of gravity of popular opinion.

The new CPE first secretary was Vaino Väljas, the native Estonian over whom Karl Vaino had been chosen in 1978. Two other candidates (Toome and Sillari) quickly withdrew in his favor. Väljas was recalled from his ambassadorship in Nicaragua, learned of his new assignment only upon reaching Moscow, and reluctantly agreed to serve when Gorbachev insisted.[15] He was elected unanimously by the CPE CC bureau. At the CPSU conference, Väljas defended the Popular Front platform. Returning to unfinished business in Nicaragua, he did not settle in Estonia until 21 July 1988. He immediately introduced the use of either Estonian or Russian at the CPE bureau meetings, instead of obligatory Russian. Furthermore, simultaneous translation headphones were supplied only to the CPE second secretary as Moscow's official emissary: Väljas pointed out to the lo-

"Bureaucrats, surrender!" On the day after reactionary CPE First Secretary Karl Vaino was replaced by reformer Vaino Väljas, over 100,000 people came out to celebrate. It was among the highlights of the Singing Revolution. Photo Kalju Suur, 17 June 1988, Tallinn. Reprinted with permission.

cal Russian members of the CC that he likewise had to master Spanish quickly when sent to Latin America. The long process of the split of the CPE into Estonian and Russian factions can be traced to the return of Väljas.

On 9 September 1988, the CPE CC gave its backing to the longstanding demand that Estonian become the official language in Estonia. The purpose was not to prohibit Russian but to block its continuous de facto encroachment on the use of Estonian. By this time, the CPE leaders had fully endorsed the PFE platform for extensive autonomy. However, a gap persisted, because the PFE leadership itself had meanwhile moved on and called for a "transformation of the Soviet Union from a federal state into a confederation of states," with juridical guarantees and an established mechanism for leaving the union.[16]

In June 1988, the Heritage Society (at times in cooperation with the MRP-AEG) began to rededicate monuments to the war of independence (1918–1920) that had been hidden and saved when the Soviet regime ordered them destroyed. Clergy members and church choirs, previously restricted to officially registered church buildings, participated. So did Boy Scouts, who had been banned since 1940. As mentioned, the Presidium of the ESSR Supreme Soviet legitimized the blue-black-white as "national colors," distinct from the red "state flag" of the ESSR. It also returned the age-old name to the town of Kuressaare, which the occupation authorities had called "Kingissepa," based on the name of Estonian communist Kingissepp.[17] Dissident Mart Niklus was released from prison near the Urals in July 1988, leaving Enn Tarto the last clearly political prisoner.

The last taboos regarding "blank spots" in history (as they were called) crumbled in summer 1988. Laasi's documentation in November 1987 mainly addressed Stalinist excesses (such as deportations) in the vein of Khrushchevian denunciation of the "cult of personality." That means Laasi did not challenge the legitimacy of Soviet rule in Estonia directly. The praise of the independent Republic of Estonia since February 1988 had laid to rest the fiction of a popular Estonian Workers Commune being replaced in 1919 by an unpopular "bourgeois dictatorship," but it stopped short of tackling the events of 1940; thus it relegitimized the memory of the Republic of Estonia without delegitimizing the subsequent Soviet annexation. But the June 1988 issue of the cultural monthly *Looming* included a scathing description of Soviet occupation of Estonia:

> What happened was a peaceful but very resolute military entry, to the saturation point. A few days later, a little staged revolution was superimposed on it—a pretty clumsy and unconvincing one. . . . But didn't the Estonian people thereafter elect a new parliament, consisting of those who decided to liquidate Estonian sovereignty? Sure, given that at the so-called free elec-

Return of dissident Mart Niklus from Soviet prison camp where he spent sixteen years. He received a hero's welcome at Tartu railroad station despite the early hour (7:20 A.M.). Photo Heldur Napp, 13 July 1988. Reprinted with permission.

tions of July 1940 the candidates opposing those of the Working People's League were simply refused registration—and this was the entire election there was. . . . But enough said about this nice and bloodless revolution (we got blood and all that aplenty later on) and about this long-stale fairy tale of nations located in the midst of Twentieth-Century Europe—a whopping three of them at once!—who enthusiastically voted themselves free of the burden of sovereign statehood.[18]

A ditty in a terse style reminiscent of poet Hando Runnel had circulated among Estonian youth ever since the early 1980s and said it more laconically:

> Tell me 'bout the sun,
> tell me 'bout the moon.
> Tell me 'bout my home,
> tell about that June,
> about which a stupid
> legend travels wide,
> as if our death
> had been a suicide.[19]

In late 1988, the ditty finally saw print—under Runnel's name, sure enough.

Founding of ENIP and Intermovement

Finally, one year after MRP-AEG was formed, the secret protocols of the MRP were published in Estonia in the main daily *Rahva Hääl* (11 and 12 August 1988) that, as the official organ of the CPE, had until June been a last bastion of Stalinism. Having achieved its short-term goal, the MRP-AEG folded and reemerged on 20 August 1988 as the Estonian National Independence Party (ENIP).[20] Initiators included Lagle Parek and Lutheran clergyman Vello Salum (b. 1933). The "Political Declaration" of ENIP proposed to achieve independence by persuading Moscow that such a course was more advantageous to Russia as well as Estonia. At a press conference (17 October 1988), ENIP representatives said their goal was to use the appropriate article in the Soviet constitution (article 72) to take Estonia out of the USSR.[21] ENIP's relations with the PFE were tense because for ENIP any Communist Party members were suspect, and the PFE leaders in turn all too often called ENIP "extremist."

The Moscow CPSU conference (28 June–1 July 1988) offered an opportunity to clarify the Estonian position. Because the Communist parties of Latvia and Lithuania still maintained their stagnation-oriented first secretaries (who were replaced only in October 1988), the Estonians were the most vocal exponents of republic autonomy. The idea of a confederation based on a new union treaty was first aired. Apart from the replacement of Vaino with Väljas, the Estonian delegation remained the one appointed by Vaino. However, either from conviction or as yes-men to anyone who was the boss, they supported Väljas.

Soon after the conference, it was rumored that the Baltic republics, the Tatar ASSR, and the city of Moscow would switch to economic self-management on 1 January 1989. Nothing came of it, but being put on the same level with a city and an ASSR ("autonomous" SSR, one notch below the fictionally sovereign SSRs) indicated the limits of the degree of autonomy Gorbachev was toying with. Furthermore, the central ministries in Moscow were not prepared to yield any of their feudal prerogatives, regardless of what their suzerain might promise.

ESSR Prime Minister Saul gave lip service to Estonian interests but covertly played along with his fellow Brezhnevites in Moscow. In particular, a secret decree by the ESSR government (Decree No. 344–3, 18 July 1988) required Estonian housing cooperatives to give preferential treatment to newcomers who had worked ten years in the Soviet far north, thus discriminating against Estonians and other local residents. Although the initiative for the decree came from Moscow, Saul agreed to it without even informing the public. When the secret decree was published in *Edasi* (26 August 1988), the Green Movement called for Saul's resignation.

Meanwhile, the local forces of reaction were also mobilizing. The political developments had largely bypassed the Russian and Russified settlers in Estonia. Most of them had ignored the Estonian activism that began with the Phosphate Spring. When it snowballed a year later, it was incomprehensible and frightening to the colonists.

Later, Estonians reproached themselves for not informing and educating the local Russians sufficiently during that crucial period, but the task was inherently Herculean. No one's health in Estonia was threatened more by antiecological mining than that of the Russians, nearly half of whom lived close to the mining area; yet they completely disregarded the issue during the Phosphate Spring. It was not a matter of differing degrees of information but a question of how the Estonians and the colonists reacted emotionally. The colonists felt they could easily move away if they soiled their momentary nest excessively; the Estonians felt they could not. No amount of education could have surmounted that difference of attitudes if there was no self-education. And if the colonists could not be motivated about something that would benefit their own health, the task was even harder on matters on which they stood to lose—like the requirement of bilingualism for public servants instead of permitting them Russian-language privileges.

The colonist and the Estonian basic premises about Estonia differed in a fundamental and perhaps irreconcilable way. For Estonians, Estonia was a country. For most colonists, it was just another Russian province, in which the colonists still graciously allowed another language to coexist with Russian for the domestic purposes of the natives. Arguments based on such mutually exclusive premises were hard to settle. One might as well argue that the Algerians could have converted the mass of the French *pieds-noirs* to give up on the idea of *Algérie française* if they only had taken the time to inform and educate the colonists.

In this light, it is not surprising that a reactionary colonialist movement arose in Estonia. To the contrary, what is surprising and gratifying is that about one-third of the non-Estonians did show solidarity with the Estonians and another third remained neutral. Furthermore, even the confrontation with the imperialist wing of the colonists remained a nonviolent political struggle, to the credit of everyone involved.

In July 1988, the first demands were voiced by the colonial hardliners to separate Kohtla-Järve and Sillamäe from Estonia. An "International Movement" (soon shortened to "Intermovement") was founded in Tallinn after a couple of thousand people participated in a demonstration (19 July 1988) led by Evgeni Kogan (b. 1954), an engineer. Those who knew only one language (Russian) had the gall to call themselves "internationalists," whereas those they labeled "nationalists" usually could handle at least two languages (Estonian and Russian). To the Estonians, they sounded more "Inter-Nazi" than internationalist. On 9 August 1988, another colonialist demonstration included slogans "Down with the Estonian language!" according to a report on Estonian TV.[22] On the moderate side, a Forum of Estonia's Nationalities, led by Hagi Šein (b. 1945), brought together the representatives of seventeen minorities, ranging from Russians to Armenians to Jews (24 September 1988).

The numerous Estonian mass events during summer 1988 culminated with the demonstration Eestimaa Laul 1988 (The Song of Estonia 1988) on 11 September 1988. Organized by the Popular Front, it drew an estimated 250,000 to 300,000 people from all over Estonia, an all-time record not likely to be beaten soon because they accounted for 20 percent of the total population of Estonia and 30 percent of the Estonians. The Singing Revolution reached its grand finale.

Thereafter, even the formal founding congress of the PFE (1–2 October 1988) was anticlimatic. It represented a high point in PFE–Communist Party relations. CPE First Secretary Väljas gave a conciliatory talk, and CPSU Secretary Gorbachev sent his greetings. A charter, a program, and thirty separate resolutions were adopted.[23] The general program of the PFE called for "achieving factual independence of the Estonian SSR" by "turning the Soviet Union from a unitary state into a union of states on the principles of confederation." This was to be Gorbachev's program two years later, but at the time he ignored it. At the same time, the idea of a compromise based on a "new union treaty" was condemned by ENIP as a sellout.

Of the 3,071 delegates at the PFE congress, 22 percent were CPE members. However, only 5 percent of the delegates were non-Estonians. Although the organization pointedly called itself the "PF of Estonia," it turned out an "Estonian PF," in an ethnic sense. Efforts of the PFE to attract non-Estonians were hampered by the uncooperative attitude of the Russian-language newspapers in Estonia. PFE itself lacked the resources to establish its own daily or weekly, in any language. The seven-person directorate elected consisted of Estonians only (including Savisaar, Lauristin, Valk, and Veidemann), partly because of an ill-advised electoral rule that inadvertently worked not only against minorities but also against provincial Estonian leaders.

The first Estonian opinion poll on the popularity of public figures (mid-September 1988) showed that Savisaar (PFE), Aare (Greens), Made (Greens), Väljas (CPE), and Lauristin (PFE) ranked first in the opinion of the Estonians, all with approval rates of 88 percent and above. The most popular with the non-Estonians were Väljas, Tartu University economist Mihhail Bronštein (b. 1923, PFE), Lauristin, creative unions leader Enn

Heritage Society leader Trivimi Velliste talks of bears and honeybees at a podium decorated with the emblem of the Popular Front, which organized the Song of Estonia, the largest mass meeting of the Singing Revolution. A quarter million people sang and listened to speeches. Photo Kalju Suur, Tallinn, 11 September 1988. Reprinted with permission.

Põldroos (b. 1933, PFE), and on a par, Tallinn Technical Institute chancellor Boris Tamm (b. 1930), Savisaar, and Aare; however, the approval rate was only 66 percent for Väljas and as low as 34 percent for Savisaar.[24] There was considerable overlap at the top of the two lists. The highest approval by non-Estonians went to Estonian activists and Bronštein, who ranked ninth with the Estonians too. The ENIP leaders ranked low among the Estonians, and the Intermovement leaders ranked almost equally low among the non-Estonians. However, even the highest-approved public figures had quite low ratings among non-Estonians, who lacked any real heroes and frequently did not know any of the eighty names listed. Many of the non-Estonians were in the country but not of the country: Estonia's politics was of little interest to them.

When Enn Tarto, the last imprisoned nonviolent dissenter, returned home in October 1988, a dark era in Estonia's history closed. Equally symbolic was Estonia's decision to return to its proper time zone (the same as Finland's) instead of Moscow time that was imposed in 1940. The changes that took place in these six months, April–October 1988, were the fastest in Estonia's recent history. At no time was there more optimism than in fall 1988. It seemed that one-half of Estonian desiderata had been achieved in a breathtakingly short time, and the remaining did not seem any harder to achieve. It was not going to be that easy.

THE WINTER OF SOVEREIGNTY, NOVEMBER 1988–April 1989

During the heady days of the Spring of the Flag and the still headier summer of the Singing Revolution, the events in Estonia were largely internally driven. The empire was still there, of course, and exerted a braking power whenever it wished, but it desisted from doing so outside the economic sphere. The impulse for Moscow to dismiss Vaino came from events in Estonia, not vice versa. The creators of the Popular Front used a made-in-Moscow label, but reversed its meaning and chose the timing.[25] In Moscow, radical reformer Boris Yeltsin and reactionary Yegor Ligachev balanced each other out; Gorbachev was completely in charge, but his attention was focused on USSR-wide matters, not Estonia.

Likewise, Estonia received few impulses from Latvia or Lithuania because by fall 1987 it was ahead of them in practically everything: public discussion and concerted planning for economic self-management, end of repression of demonstrations, birth of the Popular Front, removal of the Brezhnevite CPE chief, legalization of national colors, declaring national language the state language—and also the birth of local colonialist organization.[26] By October 1988, Lithuania and Latvia began to catch up, a most welcome development, because being alone in the front had left Estonia overly exposed. The formal founding congresses of the Popular Front of Latvia and the Lithuanian Sajudis occurred only weeks after that of the PFE.

The next major step on the road of reform, however, did not come as a result of an Estonian initiative but was imposed by Moscow. Either by design or through wording insensitive to the needs of non-Russians, the changes in the Soviet constitution that Gorbachev wanted to ram through the USSR Supreme Soviet in November 1988 appeared to limit the rights of the SSRs. Estonians raised a number of objections to the proposed changes. In the existing constitution, article 72 read: "Each Union Republic shall retain the right freely to leave the USSR." Although article 72 was not abolished, an alteration in article 108 appeared to eviscerate it by granting the USSR Congress of People's Deputies the sole power to "take decisions on questions of the composition of the USSR." Was it to mean that the "Union" would have veto power over a republic's decision to leave the USSR? Estonians also felt that other proposed changes even further centralized power in Moscow more than was already the case and that SSR representation in the new Council of Nationalities of the USSR Supreme Soviet would fall in relation to that of the Russian SFSR.

The Sovereignty Declaration

The popular mood in Estonia (and the other Baltic states) favored invoking article 72 while the right to leave the USSR was still relatively unambiguous. An extraordinary session of the ESSR Supreme Soviet was convened on 16 November 1988.[27] Instead of the usual chair, Väljas was unanimously asked to chair the session. A report was heard that 861,000 persons (57 percent of Estonia's population!) had signed appeals to oppose the proposed changes in the Soviet constitution. Väljas guided the tense meeting to the adoption of a "Declaration About the Sovereignty of the Estonian SSR." The vote was 258 for, 1 opposed, and 5 neutral.

In view of numerous mistranslations, it is important to point out that the declaration was a clarification "about" a sovereignty already seen to exist in the Soviet constitution—not a declaration "of" sovereignty as something new. It did not imply that the Estonian SSR had decided to leave the USSR. The Soviet constitution was ambiguous, presenting the USSR as a "unitary federal" state, a contradiction in terms. It said the SSRs were sovereign (article 76), yet assigned indispensable attributes of sovereignty to the central government (e.g., articles 73–75, 77, 133, 134). In view of this ambiguity, the ESSR Supreme Soviet interpreted the Soviet constitution in the manner most favorable to Estonian autonomy. What was revolutionary was that an SSR dared to propose an interpretation of the constitution rather than meekly accept however Moscow chose to construe it.

The Estonian declaration set the precedent for later sovereignty declarations in many other corners of the empire.[28] It also foreshadowed the Union Treaty that Gorbachev began to promote in 1990 and 1991 (when his actions and delays already had tarnished the idea in the eyes of the Balts). Hence the full text is worth giving.

DECLARATION ABOUT THE SOVEREIGNTY OF THE ESTONIAN SSR

The Estonian people have been cultivating their land and developing their culture on the coast of the Baltic Sea for more than 5,000 years. In 1940 the ethnically homogenous and sovereign Republic of Estonia became a subpart of the Soviet Union. At that time, it was envisaged that the guarantees of its sovereignty would be retained and the nation would flourish. The domestic policy of the Stalinist and stagnation periods ignored these guarantees and positions. As a result, an unfavorable demographic situation has developed for the Estonians as the indigenous people; the natural environment in many parts of the republic is in a catastrophic state; the continuing destabilization of the economy has a negative impact on the living standard of the entire population of the republic.

To escape from this difficult situation, the Estonian SSR Supreme Soviet sees but one path—Estonia's further development must take place under conditions of sovereignty. The sovereignty of the Estonian SSR means that, through its highest organs of power, administration, and justice, it possesses the supreme power on its own territory. The sovereignty of the Estonian SSR is integral and indivisible. Accordingly, the future status of the republic within the Soviet Union should be determined by a Union Treaty.

The Estonian SSR Supreme Soviet does not agree with those alterations and amendments to the constitution of the USSR, submitted for discussion by the USSR Supreme Soviet Presidium, which preclude the constitutional right of the Estonian SSR to self-determination. Relying on the international covenants on economic, social, and cultural rights as well as on civil and political rights dating from 16 December 1966, which were ratified by the Soviet Union, and on other norms of international law, this supreme body representing people's power in the Estonian SSR, the Estonian SSR Supreme Soviet, declares the supremacy of its laws on the territory of the Estonian SSR.

Alterations and amendments to the USSR constitution shall henceforth come into force on the territory of the Estonian SSR upon their approval by the Estonian SSR Supreme Soviet and upon the introduction of corresponding alterations and amendments in the constitution of the Estonian SSR.

The Estonian SSR Supreme Soviet calls on all those who have tied their fate with Estonia to join together in order to build a democratic and socialist Estonian society. The realization of sovereignty, de jure and de facto, also means that in the future the people of Estonia will not agree to any law that would discriminate against members of whatever nationality living in the Estonian SSR.[29]

Changes in the constitution of the ESSR were also adopted; they legitimized private property and specified that the ESSR had sole ownership of Estonia's natural resources and basic means of production.[30] Proposals for changes in the USSR constitution were forwarded to the USSR Presidium, including the stipulation that alterations in the constitution of the USSR can take effect "only after they have been approved by all union republics."[31]

The wording of the declaration was an inevitably uneasy compromise between the major tenor of the rights of the "Estonians as the indigenous people" and those newcomers "who have tied their fate with Estonia." It was a successful compromise in that it got all Estonians and most of the non-Estonian members of the Supreme Soviet to vote in favor of the declaration. The basic demands of the Popular Front and the Greens were satisfied. The essentially prodeclaration stand by Nikolai Zahharov (b. 1941), CPE secretary of the city of Kohtla-Järve, is credited by some for tilting the opinion of many other Russian members.

One should keep in mind that the ESSR Supreme Soviet members had not been recently elected during the period of reforms but had been appointed through fake elections in 1985, presumably on the basis of their docility toward the Soviet regime. Thus, Gorbachev was not likely to get a better deal from any future genuinely elected Estonian representatives. However, neither were the Estonians likely to get a better deal from genuinely elected representatives of the colonists, compared with the existing group whose gut reaction was to follow the lead of the CPE first secretary. In view of its handpicked nature, the Supreme Soviet's claim to represent "people's power" was weak (to put it mildly), but at the moment most Estonians did not care to raise the issue, because the declaration met with wide approval.

From Sovereignty to Language Law

Gorbachev did not recognize what a remarkable opportunity he was offered when the ESSR Supreme Soviet asked for a new Union Treaty between the ESSR and the USSR. If implemented, it would have tied Estonia to the USSR, for the first time ever, in a legal and arguably voluntary way, in contrast to the extant forcible occupation and annexation. Later, when independence had replaced autonomy as the predominant goal, many Estonians shuddered at the thought that Gorbachev might have accepted the Estonian offer of November 1988. Actually, he did not even come close to accepting. It is one of those inexorable rules of revolutionary progressions that rulers usually agree to concessions only when it is too little, too late.

The Lithuanian Supreme Soviet met two days later (18 November). Sternly warned by Moscow, the Lithuanian Communist Party (LCP) desisted from following Estonia, over the objections of Sajudis. The result was that the relations of the LCP and the Sajudis were poisoned for a long time, and Estonia stood alone to face the Kremlin's wrath. (Once Lithuania capitulated, Latvia with its large Russian minority was bound to do the same.)

The Estonian leaders (and Presidium Chairman Rüütel in particular) had to withstand coarse verbal assaults from the Moscow leadership, echoed in the Soviet imperial press.[32] The Presidium of the USSR Supreme Soviet declared all significant parts of the Estonian sovereignty legislation unconstitutional (including the third and fourth paragraphs of the declaration). On 7 December 1988, the ESSR Supreme Soviet decided (with a majority of 200 for, 18 opposed, and 15 neutral) to acknowledge receipt of the Moscow pronouncement but express neither acquiescence nor rejection. The PFE considered this CPE-promoted response overly timid, and the relations between the two leaderships cooled. The constitutional issue remained unresolved between Estonia and Moscow.

Other changes proceeded apace. The discredited Bruno Saul resigned from the ESSR premiership and was replaced by Indrek Toome (16 November 1988). In the latter's place, Mikk Titma, one of the signers of the Four-Man Proposal, became ideology secretary of the CPE. These appointments largely completed the takeover of the ESSR leadership by the reform communists. A new colonist organization, claiming to be more moderate than Intermovement, was founded 30 November 1988: the Joint Council of Work Collectives (JCWC), led by Vladimir Jarovoi (b. 1943) and other managers of large military plants. The same evening, the Estonian managers responded by founding the Union of Work Collectives (UWC), headed by industrial manager Ülo Nugis (b. 1944) and physicist Endel Lippmaa.

A detailed language law was passed by the ESSR Supreme Soviet on 18 January 1989 (204 for, 50 against, 6 neutral). It owed much to linguist Mati Hint (b. 1937), a member of the PFE board, and attempted to draw a balance between the rights, needs, and claims of the indigenous population and the colonists. It confirmed Estonian as the state language but also gave even stronger guarantees for the use of Russian, and consequently many Estonians protested its ratification. At the same time, a number of colonists protested the requirement that within two to four years all officials and salespeople become sufficiently bilingual to give service both in Estonian and Russian. Previously, Russian was required, Estonian optional. Now the extremists among the colonists considered the new parity discriminatory. On behalf of the more moderate non-Estonians, Hagi Šein stressed that the Forum of Estonia's Nationalities supported the language law.[33]

Some leaders of the Popular Front of Estonia: Mati Hint, Rein Veidemann, future prime minister Edgar Savisaar, and Siim Kallas (in the rear) at the Song of Estonia gathering (11 September 1988). Photo Kalju Suur. Reprinted with permission.

Estonian Political Groupings and the USSR Elections

In early 1988, the Estonian political spectrum had been fairly simple: the reactionary CPE versus the radical MRP-AEG and in between these extremes the moderate reformers who eventually organized into the PFE, supported by the Greens and the Heritage Society. By early 1989, the spectrum had become much more complex. The colonists differed in their reactions to autonomy and language law. Estonians differed on the issue of autonomy (at least as a way station) versus independence—and even on the legal format of such independence (as explained shortly). The elections to the USSR Congress of People's Deputies (26 March 1989) brought these differences more sharply into the open. Before discussing these elections, I will briefly characterize the various groupings.

Table 6.1 shows levels of support for various groups in the first Estonian opinion poll on political preferences (April 1989, i.e., after the USSR elections). Among the Estonians, the PFE and its Green allies dominated the scene; among the non-Estonians, the CPE and the JCWC predominated in an appreciably more fragmented field. Only 10 percent

TABLE 6.1   Political Preferences of Inhabitants of Estonia, April 1989 (Percent)

Organizational Preference [a]	Estonians	Others	Percent of Total Population	Ratio of Estonians to Others
Intermovement	0.0	10.9	4.0	.00
Union of Work Collectives[b]	0.2	5.9	2.3	.03
Joint Council of Work Collectives	0.9	17.8	7.0	.05
Communist Party of Estonia	7.2	32.2	16.2	.2
No preference	3.4	6.8	4.7	.5
Estonian Green Movement	12.6	11.5	12.2	1.1
Rural Union	7.5	4.1	6.3	1.8
Estonian Christian Movement	2.4	0.6	1.7	4.0
Popular Front of Estonia	50.3	8.9	35.2	5.0
Estonian National Independence Party	9.6	0.9	6.4	10.0
Estonian Heritage Society	6.0	0.3	3.9	20.0

[a]Organizations are ordered according to increasing Estonian/Other support ratio.

[b]Union of Work Collectives was an Estonian countermove to Joint Council of Work Collectives, but, paradoxically, it received even less Estonian support than JCWC.

Sources: Iltasanomat (Helsinki), 2 May 1989; also *Homeland,* 17 May 1989; and *Vaba Maa* (Tallinn), no. 6, May 1989.

of the Estonians preferred the radical ENIP, and only 11 percent of the non-Estonians preferred Intermovement. In their statements and actions, however, little seemed to distinguish the JCWC from the reactionary Intermovement.

The CPE was badly split along national lines. Even so, the Russian CPE leaders were considered too soft on Estonian nationalism by Intermovement, and many Estonian CPE leaders were considered pro-Moscow by most Estonians. Väljas, Rüütel, and Toome remained popular, but the PFE suspected that the CPE tacitly helped to build up the reputation of Intermovement so as to balance off the PFE and put the CPE in a position of arbitrator between the two fronts. The Rural Union, created by kolkhoz and sovkhoz bosses, was a rural ally of the Estonian wing of the CPE. The Union of Work Collectives played the same role in regard to the industrial managers, but its direct competition with the JCWC for control of industrial workers put it closer to the PFE.

The Popular Front was the main centrist force both in its moderate reformist program and its extensive support (including a foothold among the non-Estonians). The Greens were the only group attracting an equal degree of support from Estonians and non-Estonians, but they suffered from internal power struggles. Closely aligned with PFE, they were more radical on ecological issues.

The remaining three groupings could be characterized as radical in that they refused to participate within the Soviet political framework even as a temporary expediency. The idea of using article 72 of the constitution, to which ENIP leaders had given some thought in more difficult times, became unacceptable to the radicals. Because the Soviet occupation and annexation in 1940 were illegal, the preoccupation Republic of Estonia continued to exist in a legal sense. Hence there was no question of Estonia leaving the USSR but only of Soviet occupation forces leaving the territory of the Republic of Estonia: "We cannot secede from the Soviet Union, because we never joined." From this viewpoint, it was also absurd to elect Estonian delegates "to the parliament of a neighboring country" (i.e., the USSR Congress of People's Deputies). Instead, the three groups joined in an effort to form citizens committees to register the citizens of the preoccupation Republic of Estonia. This action, which gathered steam in fall 1989, is discussed in the next section.

Of the three radical groupings, the Estonian Heritage Society was the most centrist and had collaborated with PFE. In February 1989, EHS leader Trivimi Velliste publicly proclaimed "the Hungarian path" as the immediate objective—a "socialist" Estonia outside the USSR. The EHS neither participated nor called for a boycott of the Soviet elections, and neither did the Estonian Christian Union (formally founded in December 1988), which was more radical than the EHS in its emphasis on religious rights. ENIP was the only group that called for a boycott of Soviet elections. They were right in legal terms; however, if the Estonians had heeded their call, Estonia would have been represented at an important forum only by Russian colonists.

Tensions between CPE and PFE as well as between PFE and the radicals fluctuated, as PFE seesawed between the commands of its head and its heart. CPE angered PFE by delaying the official registration of PFE until 2 February 1989. On 24 February, the Popular Front in turn angered the radicals by canceling at the last minute a planned joint mass rally and joining the CPE in replacing the red ESSR flag on the Toompea Castle (the seat of government) by the blue-black-white flag. The radicals felt it was a cheap trick by the communists. For opposite reasons, Intermovement and JCWC also protested the change of flag and, on 14 March 1989, succeeded in organizing their own first mass demonstration. It was held during working hours, and the imperialist factory managers commanded their workers to march; 40,000 people showed up and gradually dispersed. Ironically, Intermovement calls for resignation of the native CPE leaders increased their personal popularity, but that of the CPE as an organization nosedived.

152

For the first time in forty-five years, Estonia's flag flew again, from the medieval Tall Hermann tower (built 1370–1500) of Toompea castle, the seat of government, 24 February 1989. This date was the seventy-first anniversary of the country's declaration of independence in 1918. Photo Kalju Suur. Reprinted with permission.

In the elections to the USSR Congress of People's Deputies (26 March 1989), about 95 percent of Estonians and 75 percent of non-Estonians participated (despite the ENIP boycott call). Nominations and vote counting were basically fair. The candidates supported by PFE (who for tactical purposes included Väljas, Rüütel, and Toome) won twenty-seven out of the thirty-six seats. Intermovement and its allies won five seats. The second secretary of the CPE and the ESSR KGB chief—both non-Estonians—were shunned by both sides and lost badly. Voting generally followed nationality lines, and twenty-nine of the thirty-six seats went to Estonians. However, Leningrad-born economist Bronštein, who was endorsed by PFE, won handily in a heavily Estonian district. Estonian nationals also received eleven of the twelve seats allocated to the ESSR through various empirewide organizations.[34]

April 1989 brought increasing picketing of Soviet military commissariats by students, the Greens, and the Estonian Women's Organization making demands that, at the very least, Estonian conscripts into the occupation army be kept in Estonia. The Tbilisi massacre of unarmed Georgians by Soviet troops (9 April 1989) added urgency to the anticonscription drive and increased the Estonian desire to put more distance between Estonia and Moscow. Going along with a growing mood for independence, PFE adjusted its stated ultimate goal to be quite close to ENIP's (on 29 April 1989). Its earlier proposal of turning the USSR into a loose confederation (first voiced in August 1988) now was said to be possibly only a "transitional step" on the road to full independence. The PFE representative assembly recognized the preoccupation Republic of Estonia as the only legal Estonian state; however, the illegal ESSR structures were to be used as a tool in gradually abolishing the single-party monopoly and returning to independence through parliamentary means.

The warm breezes of spring and summer had changed in November 1988 into freezing winds that threatened to roll back even the formal sovereignty the ESSR had until then preserved. Estonia withstood the hard Winter of Sovereignty, but in spring 1989 the Estonian phase of Baltic activism was over. The initiative shifted to Lithuania as Estonia became increasingly weighed down by its large colonist "civilian garrison."

THE SUMMER OF THE MRP DEBATE, MAY–SEPTEMBER 1989

Summer 1989 was characterized by increasing Baltic cooperation. It reached its emotional high with a human chain of over one million people that ranged from Tallinn to Vilnius and received worldwide publicity. The establishment of a Baltic Council was as important as the Baltic Chain. A related focus of attention was the investigation Gorbachev instigated of

"Estonia Is in Danger"—from war and alcohol, among other things. The fence surrounds an excavation site in the medieval section of Tallinn, where houses were razed in a 1944 Soviet air raid and no reconstruction took place. Photo Kalju Suur, July 1989. Reprinted with permission.

the shadier parts of the Molotov-Ribbentrop Pact (MRP), an inquiry the Balts turned in a direction Gorbachev did not expect. Finally, Moscow formally accepted economic autonomy for the Baltic states, with a fixed date (1 January 1990), but public opinion in the Baltic was shifting decisively toward independence. In Estonia, initiative was passing from the Popular Front to new citizens committees organized by EHS and ENIP.

The speed of events and the isolation from each other in which the three Baltic states had been kept previously had worked to restrict information flow, not to mention common action, in 1988. The dissident Baltic charter of 1979 remained the major common declaration until the Baltic Assembly (13–14 May 1989) brought 300 leaders of Lithuania's Sajudis, the Popular Front of Latvia, and the PFE together in Tallinn. An appeal to the United Nations and the signatories of the 1975 Helsinki accord called for neutrality and demilitarization of the Baltic states; Baltic independence was hinted at. A consultative Baltic Council was formed, to meet periodically; it first met on 15 July 1989 in Pärnu, Estonia.[35]

In a different manner, the Baltic representatives at the USSR Congress of People's Deputies also began to mix.[36] Their interaction with the Soviet deputies clarified some misunderstandings about the Baltic situation. When Lithuania and Latvia issued sovereignty declarations (18 May and 27 July 1989, respectively) analogous to Estonia's, these caused hardly a ripple in Moscow. Furthermore, the Soviet Congress agreed in principle to the Baltic economic autonomy (27 July 1989), though leaving the enabling laws to be haggled out in fall 1989 with the various Soviet bureaucracies—and there was the rub. Savisaar became ESSR vice-premier in charge of economic reform and began to prepare for implementation of autonomy and movement toward a market economy. But the economic issues were overshadowed in the short run by the debate over the MRP, the fiftieth anniversary of which was approaching.

When the Soviet Congress convened in late May 1989, the Estonian representatives attempted to place the MRP debate on the agenda. (The ESSR Supreme Soviet had denounced the MRP on 18 May.) On 1 June, Gorbachev announced the imminent formation of a Soviet Congress commission to investigate the pact. He genuinely seemed to think that the MRP secret protocol was a falsification and wanted to put the matter to rest once and for all. The commission included Russians and other non-Balts, many of whom wanted to minimize the pact's historical significance, and Balts, who feverishly continued to discover new evidence on how the MRP had led to the occupation of the Baltic states. Physicist Lippmaa, in particular, scanned archives ranging from Moscow to Washington.

As the anniversary of the MRP approached, the members of the commission split; fourteen of its twenty-six members signed an assessment to the effect that the secret protocol to the pact was authentic and had infringed on the rights of third parties, including the Baltic states (20 July 1989). The fourteen members demanded that the USSR Supreme Soviet (a condensed version of the Congress) condemn the protocol and declare it invalid. On explicit orders from Gorbachev, Aleksandr Yakovlev, chair of the commission, refused to sign the assessment and, moreover, claimed the Pact had no connection with the incorporation of the Baltic states into the USSR. The Balts were disappointed and angry.

All this occurred against a backdrop of further Baltic moves favoring independence. The Popular Front of Latvia considered a referendum on "total political and economic independence," and the Lithuanian Komsomol severed its ties with the Soviet Komsomol in June 1989. The CPE came out in support of the PFE's earlier demand for a treaty of confederation between Estonia and the USSR, but the PFE simultaneously was moving further toward independence as the goal by asking that the ESSR Supreme Soviet declare Estonia's annexation by the USSR illegal and invalid.

Intermovement responded with a string of work stoppages in Tallinn, ordered by Russian factory managers. The longest of these lockouts, advertised as "strikes," lasted from 11 to 16 August 1989 and, at its peak, involved about 30,000 people (4 percent of the total workforce in Estonia). I

The Baltic Chain of more than one million people, on the fiftieth anniversary of the infamous Molotov-Ribbentrop Pact, by which Hitler gave Stalin a free hand in the Baltic area. Photo Kalju Suur, Tallinn, 23 August 1989. Reprinted with permission.

was in Tallinn at the time and felt less inconvenienced there than I was in Finland during the yearly season of labor contract renegotiations. The main target was a new Estonian local elections law with a two-year residency requirement in the district (or five years in Estonia), which was in line with democratic practices in many other countries. Indeed, many U.S. states have a one-year residency requirement. The main goal of the Estonian two years was to block local voting by Soviet army draftees stationed in Estonia. Under pressure from Moscow, Estonia later suspended the requirement.

The Baltic Chain

On the fiftieth anniversary of the MRP (23 August 1989), the Baltic popular fronts led the organization of a human chain of one to two million people, ranging from the Gulf of Finland to southern Lithuania—the Baltic Chain. It was an unforgettable day for me:

> Yes, the chain. Leaving Tallinn by car with some Estonian Popular Front leaders, we traced its route. We observed the Popular Front security patrols with their walkie-talkies, marking the positions on the western side of the road with chalk, and buses from the distant island of Hiiumaa arriving

early. In central Estonia we saw people starting to assemble in the road sections assigned to their particular locality, and in the southern reaches the roadsides were full. At a meeting in the townlet of Karksi-Nuia, I was recognized from previous TV appearances and was asked to give a speech. Further driving became slow. We sat on the windowsills of our "Volga" and waved to the thick band of people who waved back and shouted our names.

As the crucial moment approached, we joined the chain, clasping hands, packed side by side in a pine forest. Radios properly spaced transmitted the incantation, and the chain, standing on the western side of the road and facing east, repeated "We want freedom! Freedom! Freedom!"

We proceeded to the culminating meeting at the Latvian border. A field was full of Latvian and Estonian flags, intermixed as never before. As darkness fell, torches seemed to reach out to the horizon. . . . Along with a sentence-by-sentence translation into Latvian, I gave [my speech], sharing the podium with Dainis Ivans, leader of the Latvian Popular Front, and Edgar Savisaar, leader of the Estonian Popular Front. My opening sentences were broadcast on Estonian TV: "We do not just want a goodhearted estate owner but the dividing of the estate into family farms. We do not just want a good tsar but an end to tsardom and a beginning of the rule of law. We do not just want a good Soviet Union but also a Soviet Union that is a good neighbor for the Baltic states. Goodneighborly relations presume being neighbors."[37]

The Baltic Chain received first-page headlines and photos in the world press and put the Baltic states psychologically on the map. It contributed to intra-Baltic solidarity. It also was a training exercise in large-scale organization, communication, and transportation, the importance of which the work stoppages by colonial managers had accentuated. A joint statement of the three popular fronts, "The Baltic Way," condemned the MRP and the resulting occupation of the Baltic states, called for restoration of Baltic "statehood, " but refrained from using the buzzword "independence":

We remind all nations that under international law treaties of this kind [the MRP secret protocol] are criminal and unlawful from the very moment of signing. This knowledge, which the apologists of imperialism and red fascists have preferred to overlook, has supported and kept us alive despite the decades-long public terror and systematic genocide.

Stability on the shores of the Baltic must be built on a system of treaties, such as was in force before the deal of 1939 and stems from the peace treaties concluded between the Soviet Union and the Baltic states in 1920.

The BALTIC WAY is a parliamentary way for the peaceful restoration of our statehood.

The BALTIC WAY will guarantee social security, civil rights, and economic progress to all peoples in the Baltic republics regardless of their nationality.[38]

The imperial leadership responded with a CPSU Central Committee resolution "On the Situation in the Republics of the Soviet Baltic" (26 August 1989). The resolution condemned "the separatist line" and castigated "anticonstitutional acts that contradict the federal principles of the state and discriminate against the non-indigenous part of the population of these republics." The Central Committee statement then appeared to threaten with genocidal suppression:

> Things have gone far. A serious danger threatens the fate of the Baltic nations. People must know toward what kind of abyss nationalist leaders are pushing them. If they succeed in achieving their goals, the consequences could be catastrophic for their peoples. Their very viability could be called into question.[39]

The main target of Soviet recrimination seemed to be Lithuania, where a commission of the LiSSR Supreme Soviet had declared Soviet annexation illegal. However, the Kremlin tackled all three states together (in marked contrast to Stalin's one-by-one approach in 1939 and 1940). By so doing, it instigated consultations for the first time between the Communist Party leaderships of the three states and in general reinforced Baltic cooperation. The three popular fronts condemned the Soviet condemnation. Gorbachev met with Baltic party and government leaders on 13 September 1989 and toned down the Soviet threat. However, six days later, he publicly claimed that the Baltic republics had joined the USSR voluntarily. The Balts perceived it as blatant falsification of history.

Citizens Committees

Given the increasingly proindependence stance of the PFE, the gap between the Popular Front and the Estonian radicals should have decreased, but this was not the case. The reason was that, in principle, Baltic independence could be reestablished in two ways. One approach (that of the three popular fronts) rested on the factual existence of the Baltic SSRs and aimed at working through their political institutions toward gradual emancipation. The outcome of this approach could be genuine autonomy within the USSR, a treaty of confederation, or independent statehood outside the USSR, similar to the status of Hungary or Finland.

A second approach (that of the radicals) posited the continued legal existence of the preoccupation Republic of Estonia and the need to restore the effective rule of this republic (rather than create a new independent republic). As first outlined by EHS leader Velliste on 24 February 1989, the process was to be based on grassroots citizens committees somewhat reminiscent of the "committees of correspondence" that prepared the ground for independence in the American colonies. These committees would register citizens of the preoccupation republic (including offspring) as well as later immigrants who wished to be considered for citizenship in the restored independent republic. As soon as more than 550,000 people were registered (a majority of the population of the Republic of Estonia), an Estonian congress could be elected to enter into talks with Moscow regarding troop withdrawal.[40]

At first glance, this approach looked utopian: Why would Moscow wish to deal with representatives of a Republic of Estonia rather than those of an Estonian SSR? However, if and when Moscow became seriously interested in accepting Estonia's independence, the Republic of Estonia approach had advantages indeed. If an Estonian SSR were to leave the USSR, making use of article 72 of the Soviet constitution, this action would establish a precedent for all other SSRs. By contrast, a Soviet troop withdrawal from a Republic of Estonia unjustly occupied and annexed by Stalin would create no legal precedents for those SSRs that were part of the USSR before 1940.

The beginnings of the citizens committees were slow because the proponents of the idea (EHS, ENIP, and the Christian Union) insisted that the committees be formed locally and not by emissaries from Tallinn. The PFE voiced support for the initiative in March 1989 as a useful alternative option, but later became increasingly negative. However, the idea had popular appeal, and the number of local committees kept increasing. By September 1989, about 300,000 people had been registered, one-tenth of them postwar immigrants applying for Republic of Estonia citizenship. By giving such immigrants some peace of mind about their ability to stay in Estonia, the radicals, in fact, contributed to improving the ethnic relations.[41]

As ENIP assembled for its first congress (19 August 1989), one year after its foundation, I sensed a marked reversal in the moods of ENIP and PFE. In December 1988, the PFE leaders were self-confidently tolerant of divergent views, and the ENIP leaders were nervous and on the defensive. In August 1989, the PFE leaders were nervous and unsure of themselves, despite successes like the Baltic Chain, and the ENIP leaders were relaxed and confident about the future. Lagle Parek was elected chair of ENIP; Tunne Kelam emerged as an ideological leader.

The citizens committees movement was imitated in Latvia but not in Lithuania. Because Latvia and Estonia had large numbers of colonists, distinguishing between the preoccupation citizens and the colonists was felt to be more pressing than it was in Lithuania with its relatively few newcomers. Furthermore, Latvia and especially Estonia had lost territory to the Russian SFSR, and restoration of the status quo ante would mean regaining territory. In contrast, Lithuania had no desire to return to its borders of 1938, a time when Vilnius was held by Poland. Thus, the Lithuanians were more motivated to proceed from the factually existing SSR and create a new independent republic with symbolic ties to the preoccupation republic, whereas the Latvians and Estonians were split between this pragmatic approach (advocated by the popular fronts) and the restorationist approach of the citizens committees.

HOW MOSCOW MISSED THE TRAIN ON AUTONOMY

When I visited Estonia in December 1988, I was asked to give a talk at the Political Education Hall in Tallinn. My proposed title, "Is the Soviet Union to Become a Commonwealth?" was deemed too risky by the organizers, but they readily accepted and advertised "How Empires End." Although no U.S. publisher was interested at the time, my script may sound better with the benefit of four years' hindsight. The following section is a condensed version.

Is the Soviet Union to Become a Commonwealth?

Empires can end with a bang or a fizzle, or they can turn into elegant empty shells. The best contemporary example of an elegant shell is the British Empire, which became the British Commonwealth and then simply The Commonwealth. The existence of The Commonwealth is rarely noticed, because it imposes no restrictions on its member states. For this very reason it may keep going indefinitely.

Do these musings have anything to do with the Soviet Union? Multiethnicity combined with a large total population is a risky mix. The Soviet Union's multiethnicity is higher than Switzerland's but lower than that of Yugoslavia or the late Austria-Hungary. However, it has increased noticeably during the last thirty years because the share of the Russians has decreased. Under such conditions, there are two very different ways to hold the empire together: either an iron fist so that no one dares to complain, or such a degree of decentralization that no nation has reason to complain. The intermediary mixed policies are destabilizing, since they give both cause for protest and also opportunities for expressing it.

The iron-fist policy gained the empire some time for linguistic assimilation of non-Russians, but since 1960 it was more than canceled out by the declining birthrate of the Russians. Meanwhile, the iron-fist policy started increasingly to affect economic efficiency. The more the economy suffered, the less incentive the non-Russians had to belong to a system that the Russians had messed up. Therefore, the longer the iron fist ruled, the more indispensable it made itself in the multiethnic empire, but at the cost of wrecking the economy and also the people's psyche.

The linguistic assimilation policy has not worked sufficiently fast, and hence it has failed. This leaves Moscow only two political options with any hope of stability: full speed in reverse, back to the iron fist, or full speed ahead, toward a very loose confederation. Both options are disagreeable. Hence the likeliest outcome is marking time. However, this will not move the empire away from economic crisis. Radical decentralization looks almost unthinkable from the viewpoint of the Russians. The British once faced a similar shattering of their imperial dream. A federation model is inherently inapplicable to the Soviet Union where one republic yields an absolute majority, as long as Russia is not subdivided into separate republics of Siberia, Volga, etc.

That leaves only one stable solution for the Soviet Union: a confederation so loose that every republic would be effectively on its own. For some republics (such as the Central Asian), geography may dictate continuing tighter ties with Russia than most Commonwealth countries have with Britain. For some other republics, even a symbolic tie may feel excessive. This applies to the Baltic states, where people know that during their past independence they managed better than they do now under a Soviet rule imposed on them through a Stalin-Hitler pact. Ireland, too, left the Commonwealth, but this did not end its economic dependence on England. One does not escape geography.

The probability that Moscow would "ever" agree to a Commonwealthization of the Soviet Union seems low. The entire idea looks about as unrealistic as it would have been in 1955 to imagine that de Gaulle, that embodiment of *grandeur française*, would consent to liquidate the French overseas holdings. Yet it happened. There are indications that Moscow's "never," too, may not last much longer.

What is not feasible at once can be accomplished within several years. Often the dynamics is the following. At first those in power refuse to comment at all on a new proposal. Then they comment in order to say a categorical "no" without any discussion. Then they discuss why "no" is the proper answer—and then the real discussion starts.

I do not assert that things will inevitably go slowly but steadily in that direction. A partial or total counterthrust may take place, in the direction of the iron fist. But an iron fist could not last without leading to economic collapse. As a unitary state the Soviet Union has no future.

Independent Estonia's peace treaty with Lenin has not been voided. Maybe it would be best for all parties concerned if Estonia remained outside the Soviet Commonwealth even when the latter should materialize.[42]

A Thicker Broth at One Rim?

The thoughts condensed in the preceding section reflected the hesitations of December 1988. The cautious terminology of "statehood" heard in speeches given by moderates during such summer 1989 events as the Baltic Chain gave way to stronger language. By September 1989, the quest for autonomy was passé in Estonia (and the other Baltic states). The radicals never had agreed to it, but now the PFE centrists also presented au-

Indrek Toome, prime minister of the Estonian SSR, and Vaino Väljas, first secretary of the CPE, prepare to join the Baltic Chain. Their plans of autonomy began to lag behind events. Photo Kalju Suur, 23 August 1989. Reprinted with permission.

tonomy merely as a way station to ease the transition to independence, and the CPE was bound to shift in the same direction if it wanted to maintain any influence and support. The change owed much to Gorbachev's doings and dallyings.

Politics pushes nations apart, whereas economics often pushes them together. In western Europe, the European Coal and Steel Community evolved into a Common Market and only much later into a European Community with a political component. To try political unification before economic would have been hopeless (as the attempts by Charlemagne, Napoleon, and Hitler illustrated). In the Soviet-occupied Baltic states, Gorbachev delayed the implementation of economic autonomy to the point where political autonomy established itself first. The continuation of absurdly centralized economy, which performed worse year by year, made belonging to the empire increasingly intolerable, and decentralized politics enabled the Estonians to say so openly.

Gorbachev could block economic decentralization easily because most major economic objects in Estonia were controlled by agencies located in Moscow. In contrast, the political structure of the USSR always had been decentralized in principle; thus, political autonomy was inevitable once this structure began to be democratized. And Gorbachev could not avoid democratization because without it, any economic reforms were impossible, given the clout of the established economic interests.

Most likely, an early meaningful economic autonomy for Estonia would have been followed by demands for independence anyway, given Estonia's history and the sad record of the Soviet occupation. However, the pace would have been slower. The slogan "Let's first become wealthy, then independent!" that emerged in early 1988 among the autonomists would have carried considerable weight had Estonians felt they were profiting from a special status within the Soviet framework and able to keep the fruits of their efforts. There might have been economic motivation to delay independence by one year, then another, to the horror of those who wanted independence for its own sake. Instead, by December 1988 I heard: "You cannot cook a thicker broth at one rim of a large kettle."

In summer 1989, Moscow agreed to Baltic economic autonomy. Some enabling laws were hammered out in November, but various imperial bureaucracies took countermeasures to cancel out their effect. Consequently, when economic autonomy formally was instituted in January 1990, the Balts found themselves in many ways worse off than before. In particular, Baltic savings accounts were effectively confiscated when Soviet officials removed the money from local branches of the state banks to Moscow and made withdrawals by individual savers difficult. The lesson was that the broth could not be made thicker at one edge of the kettle, but it could be made more watery.

The question remains whether these countermeasures to economic autonomy were not provoked by the Balts moving too fast in proclaiming that autonomy would be only a stepping stone to independence. Tactically, should the Balts have delayed their independence calls until they had economic autonomy firmly in hand? The answer seems to be no, in view of Gorbachev's later treatment of republics like Belarus and Ukraine, where the demand for independence was muted until late 1991. The autonomy Gorbachev offered them in early 1991 under the label of the Treaty of Union still was a fake autonomy in which the purse strings were jealously concentrated in Moscow. Gorbachev was willing to yield on any symbolism of "autonomy," "sovereignty," and even "independence"—as long as these features did not change the actual centralized structure. Himself the product of a centralized system of government going back many centuries and reinforced during his lifetime, Gorbachev seemed unable to understand the very meaning of the term "autonomy," except that it sounded nice.

In sum, whatever tactics the Balts used in 1989 would probably not have advanced economic autonomy. Gorbachev missed the train on autonomy because he did not even know what it looked like.[43] In addition to inherent cultural and historical reasons, the Baltic demand for independence snowballed in late 1989 because it was already clear, two years after the Four-Man Proposal, that genuine autonomy was equally hard to squeeze out of Moscow. Hence, political independence came to be seen as a prerequisite for economic autonomy. The earlier slogan was reversed into "We can't become wealthy without becoming independent first." Few had illusions that Estonia could be economically independent in an autarkic sense. Cooking a thicker broth in an excessively small pot looked difficult. But doing it at the rim of the imperial kettle looked hopeless.

NOTES

1. For further details and Baltic comparisons for 1987–1989, see Walter C. Clemens, Jr., *Baltic Independence and Russian Empire* (1991), 74–176; Toivo Raun, *Estonia and the Estonians* (1991a), 222–229; Rein Taagepera, "Estonia in September 1988: Stalinists, Centrists, and Restorationists" (1989a); and Rein Taagepera, "Estonia's Road to Independence" (1989e). A number of Estonian official documents are translated in *Restoration of the Independence of the Republic of Estonia: Selection of Legal Acts (1988–1991)* compiled by Advig Kiris (1991). Biannual reports of events are given in *Baltic Forum*: "Glasnost in the Street," 5:1 (Spring 1988), 64–80; "The National Renaissance of 1988," 5:2 (Fall 1988), 1–21; "On the Road to Sovereignty," 6:1 (Spring 1989), 38–51; and "Goal: Independence," 6:2 (Fall 1989), 58–80. A compact week-to-week report of events is found in *Homeland,* the two-page English-language supplement of the Soviet Estonian weekly *Kodumaa,* which was specifically aimed at Estonians abroad. Possibly because the Russian-Estonian CPE leaders could not read English, *Homeland* was one of the first among the Soviet Estonian periodicals to transform itself from a propaganda rag into a balanced source of information. *Baltic Chronology 1989* by BATUN is very valuable, and so is the Estonian-language chronology for 1988 by Pillau (1989); see also *Documents from Estonia* compiled by Michael Tarm and Mari-Ann Rikken (1989) and the Estonian-language review of 1987–1991 by Raidla (1991).

2. See comparative table of Baltic dates in Taagepera (1989e).

3. For a thorough account of the proposal, its background, and the ensuing debate, see Toivo Miljan, "The Proposal to Establish Economic Autonomy in Estonia" (1989). Reprints of relevant press articles are reproduced in *Diskussioonid IME-projekti üle* [Discussions about the economic self-management project] by Liina Tõnisson and Erik Terk (1991). A related aspect is studied by Thomas Palm, "Perestroika in Estonia: The Cooperatives" (1989).

4. Siim Kallas, Tiit Made, Edgar Savisaar, Mikk Titma, "Ettepanek: kogu Eesti NSV täielikule isemajandamisele" [A proposal: Complete self-management for the entire Estonian SSR], *Edasi,* 26 September 1987, 3. My translation.

5. Mikk Titma, "Tänane poliitika ja eilsed kibestumused" [Today's politics and yesterday's embitterment], *Sirp ja Vasar,* 9 October 1987. My translation. Longer excerpts are translated in Rein Taagepera, "Estonia Under Gorbachev: Stalinists, Autonomists, and Nationalists" (1988).

6. Evald Laasi, "Mõnede lünkade täiteks" [To fill some gaps], *Sirp ja Vasar*, 27 November 1987. My translation.

7. Three years after his path-breaking articles, Laasi was dismissed from his permanent position at the History Institute of the Estonian Academy of Sciences (spring 1991) under circumstances that can be explained but still leave me very uneasy.

8. "Eestimaa elanikele!" [To the inhabitants of Estonia], *Sirp ja Vasar*, 19 February 1988, 5. Full translation in Taagepera (1988).

9. A major article was Küllo Arjakas, "Ühe riigi sünnist" [About the birth of a state], *Vikerkaar*, no. 2 (February 1988), 61–68.

10. *Homeland*, 29 April 1988, has full translation.

11. *Sirp ja Vasar*, 8 April 1988. Major parts of the letter are translated in Taagepera (1988).

12. The acronym IME seems to have been used first by Marju Lauristin at a 3 May 1988 meeting; see Endel Pillau, *Eestimaa kuum suvi 1988* [Estonia's hot summer of 1988] (1989), 66. Pillau's book is an excellent date-by-date chronicle of the entire year 1988.

13. *Homeland*, 8 June 1988.

14. Pillau (1989), 94.

15. Interview with Vaino Väljas, 15 September 1991.

16. "Rahvarinde Algatuskeskuse seisukoht enesemääramise kohta" [The position of Popular Front Initiative Center on self-determination], *Sirp ja Vasar*, 5 August 1988.

17. Except for Tallinn, practically all Estonian place names end with a vowel, the ending of the genitive case. Kuressaare/Kingissepa in the island Saaremaa should not be confused with the Russian town Iamburg/Kingissepp, east of Narva, also renamed for the same person.

18. Endel Nirk, "Juhuslikud eksitused?" [Accidental errors?], *Looming*, no. 6 (June 1988), 813–825.

19. My translation from Hando Runnel, *Laulud eestiaegsetele meestele* [Songs for men of the Estonian times] (Tallinn: Perioodika, 1988), 6.

20. The first proposal to form such a party was aired in January 1988. ENIP's name does not include the unambiguous term for "independence" (*iseseisvus*) but rather the fuzzier *sõltumatus*, translated as "independence; freedom; autarky" in Paul F. Saagpakk's *Estonian-English Dictionary* (1982). *Iseseisvus* would have been too provocative at the time, and the radicals also made concessions to reality.

21. *Õhtuleht*, 28 October 1988, as reported in Pillau (1989), 189.

22. Pillau (1989), 133.

23. *The Popular Front of Estonia: Charter, General Programme, Resolutions, Manifesto, adopted at the Congress of the Popular Front of Estonia on October 2, 1988* (1989). More detailed proceedings are available in Estonian and also Russian: *Narodnyi kongress: Sbornik materialov kongressa Narodnogo Fronta Estonii, 1–2 oktiabria 1988 g.* (1989).

24. Margo Veskimägi, "Poliitikute populaarsusest" [On the popularity of politicians], in EMOR, *Toimetised I: Eesti avalik arvamus 1990 poliitikast ja majandusest* [Publications I: Estonian public opinion 1990 on politics and economy] (1991), 49–59. It

lists the ten front-runners from polls conducted September 1988 to March 1991. Detailed lists were published in the daily press.

25. The Estonian radicals' claim that the founding of the PFE was orchestrated by Moscow is long on faith but short on evidence. If Gorbachev had wanted to initiate popular fronts, it would have been safer and more in line with his Russocentric thinking to do it first in a Russian oblast. It is likely, of course, that the founders of PFE tested the waters in Moscow so as to guard against a possible severe backlash against their initiative. The name itself harks back not only to the various communist fronts but also to the Popular Front for Implementation of the Constitution devised by Päts in 1937.

26. For comparative dates, see Taagepera (1989e).

27. *Eesti NSV üheteistkümnenda koosseisu erakorraline kaheksas istungjärk 16. novembril 1988—Stenogramm* [The extraordinary eighth session of the eleventh Supreme Soviet of the Estonian SSR, 16 November 1988—stenograph] (1989).

28. Soviet reactionary Colonel Viktor Alksnis claimed on 28 August 1991 at the USSR Supreme Soviet that the undoing of the Soviet Union began when the Estonians were not sanctioned for their declaration on sovereignty three years earlier (*Päevaleht*, 29 August 1991).

29. *Eesti NSV . . .* , 81–83, in Estonian and also Russian. The texts were first published in a joint special issue of *Rahva Hääl* and *Sovetskaia Estoniia*, 18 November 1988. Different English translations are given in *Homeland*, 23 November 1988; *Baltic Forum* 5:2 (Fall 1988), 74–79; and *Restoration of the Independence of the Republic of Estonia: Selection of Legal Acts (1988–1991)* (1991), 3–4. The present translation is mine.

30. "Law of the Estonian SSR on Making Changes and Amendments to the Constitution of the Estonian SSR," 16 November 1988; translation in *Restoration of the Independence* (1991), 4–7.

31. "Decree of the Estonian SSR Supreme Soviet with Proposals Regarding the Draft Laws on Changes and Additions to the USSR Constitution (Basic Law) and on Elections of the USSR People's Deputies," 16 November 1988; Estonian and Russian texts in the joint special issue of *Rahva Hääl* and *Sovetskaia Estoniia*, 18 November 1988.

32. Later (13 December 1990) I asked Rüütel about reports that Gorbachev had treated him in a crude style reminiscent of Khrushchev in late 1988. Rüütel became diffident, then said Gorbachev personally always had remained correct.

33. Full English translation of "Language Law of the Estonian SSR" is given in *Restoration of the Independence* (1991), 7–16. See comments by Riina Kionka, "Are the Baltic Laws Discriminatory?" *Report on the USSR* (Radio Liberty), 12 April 1991, 21–24. The atmosphere in Estonia in January 1989 is vividly presented in David K. Shipler, "A Reporter at Large: Symbols of Sovereignty" (1989).

34. For further details of groupings, campaigning, and results, see Rein Taagepera, "A Note on the March 1989 Elections in Estonia" (1990c). *Baltic Chronology: Estonia, Latvia, Lithuania 1989*, issued by BATUN (Baltic Appeal to the United Nations), no date, gives an excellent overview of the year and also describes the groupings.

35. *Baltic Assembly, Tallinn, May 13–14, 1989* (1989).

36. Igor Grazin, "On the Influence of Baltic Policy on the Process of Democratization in the USSR—The Ethical Aspect" (1991). Grazin was one of the Estonians elected to the USSR Congress.

37. Rein Taagepera, "The Chain and the Course" (1989f). I gave a longer version of my Baltic Chain address at the ENIP congress and, in English, at an MRP conference of the Latvian National Independence Movement in Riga: "On Goodneighborly Relations of Estonia and the Soviet Union" (Taagepera 1989c).

38. Full text in *Homeland,* 4 October 1989.

39. *Pravda* (Moscow), 27 August 1989. English translation in *Homeland,* 6 September 1989.

40. In an interview (*Postimees,* 19 July 1991), Trivimi Velliste says: "The thought of Citizens Committees came to me on a sleepless night in January 1989, inspired by Mr. Tillemann's idea to convoke a national congress and Mr. Taagepera's recommendation to set up a separate register of the citizens of the Republic of Estonia."

41. Having left Estonia after 1940, I qualified as a citizen of Estonia, and during my stay there in August 1989, I registered at a booth set up in front of what used to be my kindergarten. The person in line in front of me was a Russian who knew no Estonian; he received his card as a registered applicant for citizenship.

42. The script I followed on 22 December 1988 in Tallinn at a public meeting attended by nearly a thousand people was published in *Looming,* no. 3 (March 1989), 395–398, and a full English translation followed in *Homeland,* 12, 19, and 26 July 1989. The condensed version given here deletes much but does not add anything to what was said four years earlier.

43. Boris Yeltsin apparently urged Gorbachev to give the Baltic states extensive autonomy: "If they don't get autonomy, they'll start pressing for independence."

· SEVEN ·

The Quest for Independence

The Central-East European communist governments crumbled in late 1989. The events exhilarated the Balts but actually complicated their situation. The most painless way for the USSR to let the Baltic states go would have been to allow them to become communist-ruled countries outside the USSR—the "Hungarian path," as Trivimi Velliste had called it in February 1989. But now Hungary itself had escaped the Hungarian path, leaving Moscow with the knowledge that independent Baltic states would be noncommunist. The Balts felt they would have to act rapidly so as to become part of the Central European chain reaction before it petered out. Indeed, all signs in early 1990 indicated that the Soviets were prepared to cut their losses in the Baltic. However, when Lithuania declared its independence reestablished and Estonia and Latvia proclaimed they were in a transition phase toward the same goal, Mikhail Gorbachev reacted with everything short of military suppression in spring 1990.

By this time, new elections had resulted in popular front governments in all three Baltic states, breaking the Communist Party stranglehold on power. In this sense, the political occupation of the Baltic states ended in March 1990. What remained was military and economic occupation; in Latvia and Estonia, one could also talk of a demographic occupation in view of the extensive civilian garrison of colonists.

From August 1990 on, one or another Baltic state would repeatedly be invited to send a delegation to Moscow to talk about independence, but the moment the delegation arrived the Soviet side would ignore it or try disingenuously to turn independence talks into federation talks. This pattern left the Balts frustrated and distrustful of Gorbachev. The rise of Boris Yeltsin in Russia offered a counterweight that became crucial during Soviet attempts to topple the duly elected Baltic governments in early 1991. Russia, Moscow, and the Kremlin no longer could be used as synonyms. In the discussion that follows, "Moscow" refers to Gavril Popov's reformist city government, "Russia" to Yeltsin's government of the RSFSR, and

169

only "the Kremlin" (or "Soviet") stands for the Soviet imperial government headed by Gorbachev (although, admittedly, Yeltsin's headquarters also were physically located in the Kremlin).

A confusingly worded referendum was Gorbachev's next attempt to fabricate an empirewide consensus where none existed. The Baltic states responded with their own referendums on independence (February–March 1991), which the Kremlin refused to acknowledge.

A complex stalemate developed throughout the empire and also in Estonia in early 1991. The Kremlin and its local colonist supporters could block but not suppress the Estonians and their reformist supporters in Russia. Administrative powers of the Estonian government slowly increased, but the colonists developed their own administration in the Russian-dominated northeast. Tensions in Estonian internal politics also ran high, especially between two differently elected representative bodies, the Estonian Congress and the Supreme Council. Meanwhile, economic conditions worsened in Estonia and throughout the empire. The power to block action was widespread, but no one had the power to act. Then, in August 1991, history played deus ex machina and quickly solved Estonia's external problems.[1]

ESTONIAN CONGRESS AND SUPREME COUNCIL ELECTIONS, OCTOBER 1989–MARCH 1990

The major internal change in Estonian politics in late 1989 was the steady progress of the citizens committees. Their program of independence-through-restoration came from the Estonian National Independence Party (ENIP), while the numerous local branches of the Estonian Heritage Society (EHS) supplied a ready-made organizational network. When committees had been established in all the traditional parishes, a nationwide fifty-member General Committee of Citizens of Republic of Estonia was elected (11 November 1989), headed by Tunne Kelam, to prepare for elections of an Estonian Congress.[2] It was to be a national parliament untainted by any Soviet origins (as was the ESSR Supreme Soviet). The former radical fringe was becoming the mainstream.

My Independence Is Better Than Yours

Faced with this serious competition to their plans of gradual emancipation through the use of the existing Soviet structures, the Popular Front of Estonia (PFE) came out with a program that unambiguously set independence as the final goal (October 1989).[3] It specified a long sequence of intermediary steps, which I group here by their degree of success over the course of the following twenty months.

- Instituting democratic elections; specifying the present status of Estonia as an occupied territory; and formally abolishing the entity called the Estonian SSR—all this was achieved by May 1990.
- Convoking an Estonian Congress of all proindependence forces—here the PFE tried to steal the radicals' key term, emptying it of its original content; it did not succeed.
- Obtaining the Kremlin's approval for a referendum on independence in which only citizens of the preoccupation Republic of Estonia (including descendants) would take part—the referendum took place in March 1991, but over the Kremlin's objections and with all residents of Estonia participating.
- Concluding a temporary treaty of confederation with the USSR that would include a fixed date for independence; establishing a new Estonian citizenship (presumably available to postoccupation settlers); developing economic autonomy and diversified East-West ties; gradually demilitarizing Estonia; carrying out another referendum on a new Estonian constitution; and declaring an independent Republic of Estonia—on all this little progress was made during the following twenty months.

In contrast, the citizens committees led by ENIP/EHS opposed a referendum on independence, resting their case on the continued legal existence of the preoccupation Republic of Estonia, which the Soviet occupation forces should leave. For ENIP/EHS, many of the preparatory steps proposed by PFE looked pointless or impossible before withdrawal of the occupation forces.

The PFE platform also intimated that PFE would soon declare itself a Social Democratic Party. However, in January 1990, only a part of the PFE activists, headed by Marju Lauristin, formed an Estonian Social Democratic Independence Party. Some others began to establish a Liberal Democratic Party, while Edgar Savisaar and many others remained undifferentiated PFE members. As an umbrella organization, PFE continued to include Social Democrats and Liberals. Most PFE members who had belonged to the Communist Party of Estonia left it in early 1990.

Local elections were held in Estonia 10 December 1989. They served as a training ground for the ESSR Supreme Soviet elections to come in March 1990. Pressure by the Kremlin brought about removal of the two-year residency requirement for voters. For candidates, however, a ten-year residency requirement was maintained, and although Intermovement and its allies called for a boycott, electoral participation was over 70 percent nonetheless. In Tallinn, the partial boycott by the colonists assured a solid Estonian majority on the city council.

In the imperial center, meanwhile, advances toward economic decentralization were slow. A plan for economic autonomy proposed for all SSRs was so utterly devoid of any content that the Baltic deputies led a successful drive to defeat it. A week later, a special plan for the Baltic states alone was adopted by the USSR Supreme Soviet (27 November 1989). It allowed the Baltic republics to set up their own financial systems and issue their own currencies, share in the profits of Soviet-controlled factories on their territories, and determine the use of their natural resources. However, the autonomy law insisted on maintenance of existing economic relations with other Soviet regions, even when unfavorable to the Baltic states, and it affirmed the prerogatives of the republics as well as central ministries without specifying which side should yield in case of disagreement. The Soviet central agencies never honored most of the autonomy aspects of this package in practice. The USSR Finance Ministry, in particular, refused to acknowledge the decision of the Supreme Soviet and, in fact, tightened its hold. It removed all Baltic savings from the state bank branches in the Baltics and subjected direct contracts with foreign firms to a new time-consuming approval procedure. The Kremlin's notion of autonomy looked indistinguishable from extreme centralization.

The ESSR Supreme Soviet denounced the Soviet "aggression, military occupation, and annexation" of Estonia in 1940 and annulled the 1940 vote to join the USSR as illegal, but did not spell out the logical consequences of such an annulment (12 November 1989);[4] Lithuania and Latvia followed suit in February 1990. The Soviet reaction was mild, and on 24 December 1989, the Soviet Congress of People's Deputies condemned the Molotov-Ribbentrop Pact, saying it violated the sovereignty and independence of other nations. The MRP secret protocol that divided Central-East Europe into German and Soviet spheres of influence was declared legally untenable and invalid from the moment it was signed. Although the Soviet Congress had watered down the report of its special commission on the MRP, its condemnation of the pact still looked like a first step toward undoing the injustice involved—the annexation of the Baltic states, in particular.

If Gorbachev still harbored any illusions about the Baltic masses remaining pro-Soviet—or at least about his ability to talk them out of thoughts of independence—such illusions must have been dispelled during his visit to Lithuania (11 January 1990). In the streets of Vilnius, Gorbachev bluntly presented a falsified version of Baltic history, claiming no connection between the MRP deal and the incorporation of the Baltic states into the USSR. He received equally blunt replies about the vicious origins and the present unacceptability of Soviet occupation.

In a negative way, Gorbachev began to mention deannexation, threatening to demand huge compensations (for alleged Soviet investment

losses) and even territorial dismemberment in case of Baltic independence. It looked as if he were building a tough bargaining position. Meeting with six Baltic delegates to the USSR Congress of People's Deputies
(27 February 1990), he left the impression that he had agreed to open negotiations on independence. The Baltic deputies announced that henceforth they would act only as observers at the USSR Congress. The Balts
also began to compile counterlists of damages they had suffered under Soviet occupation.

The Soviet atmosphere at the time should be kept in mind. The USSR
abolished the special privileged constitutional status of the Communist
Party in early February 1990. (Lithuania and Latvia earlier had taken similar action, but Estonia, ironically, lagged behind the USSR.) Thus, the expected noncommunist nature of the independent Baltic states had become
less of a problem for the Kremlin. Through economic autonomy decisions
for the Baltic states only, the USSR Supreme Soviet acknowledged that the
Baltic republics were special, and its denunciation of the MRP explained
why.

By early February 1990, Baltic independence looked imminent not only
to the Balts themselves but also to Washington. In Estonia, it became a race
of who would formally have the honor to go and bring the cookies home.

Endel Lippmaa and Ülo Nugis of the Union of Work Collectives were
instrumental in convoking a General Assembly (2 February 1990) that
somewhat incongruously consisted of over 3,000 winners of the recent
multicandidate local elections, the 284 quasi-appointed members of the
ESSR Supreme Soviet, and the 48 competitively elected Estonian delegates to the USSR Congress. The assembly called for negotiations leading
to restoration of independence on the basis of the 1920 Estonian-Soviet
Tartu Peace Treaty (concluded exactly seventy years earlier).[5] About one-
half of the qualified Russian delegates participated, and one-half of these
voted for the resolution. The assembly was marred by the shouting-down
of a Russian delegate who, apparently in a conciliatory vein, tried to explain some of the concerns of the immigrants.

The demands of the General Assembly were so close to those of the
planned Estonian Congress that the citizens committees suspected it of at-
tempting a preemptive step for scuttling the Congress elections. PFE, previously critical of the restorationist goals of the Estonian Congress, reversed its stance and hurriedly began searching in all quarters for
candidates for the Congress elections. The ESSR Supreme Soviet jumped
on the Tartu Peace Treaty bandwagon one day before the elections and
called for immediate independence negotiations.[6] Those Estonian communists, such as Prime Minister Toome, for whom PFE had been too radical, suddenly advertised themselves as the "Free Estonia" grouping. It
was not just that everyone was for independence as such; there was a re-

markable stampede to the restorationist version of it, grounded in the Tartu Peace Treaty. The slow construction of a new independent state through a new referendum, as proposed in the PFE platform, suddenly looked timid and even sacrilegious.

Elections for the Estonian Congress

Among the many odd happenings in Eastern Europe around 1990, the elections of the Estonian Congress (24 February 1990 and several following days) ranked among the strangest. Here was a country the Kremlin still considered a part of the USSR, yet its brash citizens committees carried out full-fledged general elections that bypassed the entire Soviet administrative structure. The Soviet leadership, with 50,000 to 150,000 troops stationed in Estonia, let open preparations proceed unhindered. The Estonian communist authorities first tried silence, then blistering attacks. The citizens committees circumvented an information blockade in the official media by person-to-person contacts. They weathered doubts and criticism by PFE, which put up candidates only at the last moment when it became clear that the Congress would be elected anyway. The approach was amazingly successful in that genuine countrywide elections materialized—perhaps the only privately organized general elections in world history.[7]

Of an estimated 910,000 residents of Estonia who qualified as Republic of Estonia citizens, 845,000 registered (including children registered by their parents). The turnout in the election was 590,000—98 percent of adults who registered and 91 percent of all adults who qualified. At stake were 464 seats, complemented by 35 filled by Estonian refugee organizations in the West. Postoccupation immigrants voted separately, electing 43 advisory representatives. About 34,000 participated, or about 8 percent of the adult immigrants. The logistical difficulties were considerable. Much was improvised, but there were no charges of intentional irregularities. The polling went peaceably even in colonist-dominated areas. Only in Sillamäe in the northeast did the Russian city authorities refuse to supply rooms—polling took place inside a bus.[8]

About 1,300 candidates vied for the 464 seats. They included sympathizers of all political currents found among Estonians, including local CPE functionaries. The major groups among winners were PFE (about 107), EHS (104), ENIP (70), and the CPE members (39), along with many independents and quite a few overlapping cases. For the advisory immigrant seats, the number of candidates barely surpassed the number of seats.

The high point of the Estonian Congress was its election. When it convened (11–12 March 1990), it was an "idyllic event," as a well-meaning observer from North America put it—that is, a political flop. The Congress wasted a precious "window of opportunity." It faced a lame-duck ESSR Supreme Soviet, appointed through choiceless elections several years earlier and hence in a very weak moral position compared with the freshly elected Congress. However, on 18 March 1990, competitive elections for a new Supreme Soviet were scheduled. Despite colonist participation and the illegitimate origin of the assembly itself, the new Supreme Soviet would enjoy the legitimacy of a genuinely elected body—like the Estonian Congress—plus administrative power and ability to appoint a government the Kremlin would have to recognize. The only chance the Congress had was to use immediately its extensive network of local citizens committees and persuade the local administrations to submit themselves to the Congress, thus creating a chain reaction at the end of which the ESSR government too would feel obliged to ask the Congress for permission to continue in office. The Supreme Soviet could then be downgraded to an advisory second chamber, before its election. It was a high-stakes path, but without it, having a Congress was pointless.[9]

The Congress desisted from adding radical action to radical verbiage. The members grandly authorized the ESSR government to continue in office without asking anything concrete in return; they might as well have bestowed their unsolicited authorization on the government of Sweden. In other words, Congress leaders failed to convert their enormous popular support into tangible assets. Lippmaa was dispatched to Moscow with the Congress resolution on independence talks, but the Kremlin ignored it.

The Congress majority of EHS, ENIP, and their allies elected Tunne Kelam chair of the Congress. They also could not forget previous slights by PFE; Lauristin in particular was submitted to quite unfair demagogy. The elections to the Congress had used a proportional-representation rule in multiseat districts, but when the Congress elected a smaller Estonian Committee (seventy-one members, plus seven advisory immigrants), it used a majoritarian formula that kept the representation of PFE low. This would have been a clever political ploy by ENIP/EHS had the Congress been the only game in town, but it wasn't, and thus it was counterproductive not to give PFE a stake in the Estonian Committee. Because PFE candidates had entered the Congress elections much too late, their share of seats fell short of their popular support. When underrepresented in the Estonian Committee too, PFE had little motivation to strengthen this body against the Supreme Soviet, once PFE gained a comfortable share in it.

Elections for the Supreme Council

What began as elections for the ESSR Supreme Soviet effectively produced the functioning parliament of a still-occupied Republic of Estonia—

the Supreme Council.[10] The assembly size was reduced from the previous 284 to 101 regular seats, plus 4 seats filled by Soviet occupation troops. Allocating them special seats prevented the soldiers' votes being thrown in at will in selected districts to secure election of Intermovement candidates (as had happened in the elections for the Soviet Congress a year earlier). The special seats also highlighted the incongruity of electoral participation by foreign troops.[11]

The primary cleavage ran between the overwhelmingly proindependence Estonians (62 percent of the population) and the partly antiindependence Russian colonists (30 percent). The remaining population (8 percent) was split, as were the Russians. Among the winning candidates, 76 percent were Estonians, partly because of the geographical dispersal of non-Estonians among the electoral districts but partly also because many non-Estonians voted for Estonian candidates. Party or group affiliations of candidates did not appear on the ballot at the insistence of the CPE leaders, whose personal name recognition surpassed the popularity of their party.

As the numerous independents chose sides, the following blocs emerged in the Supreme Council. The PFE could count on 41 to 45 deputies—the largest bloc but not an absolute majority. The reform communist Free Estonia group and its rural allies had 25 to 29. The colonist antiindependence Joint Council of Work Collectives and its military allies had 26 or 27. This left a floating remainder of some 10 deputies, some of them more radical than PFE members. The most important implication of these results was that the antiindependence colonists fell short of obtaining the needed one-third of assembly seats (35) that under the Soviet procedural rules would have given them veto power over major decisions. As long as the Estonians stuck together, proindependence legislation could be enacted.

When the Supreme Council (Soviet) convened, it immediately confirmed the status of Estonia as an occupied country and proclaimed the state authority of the USSR in Estonia unlawful (30 March 1990).[12] Mindful of the harsh Soviet response to Lithuania's affirmation of independence (11 March), the Estonian Supreme Council did not declare independence reestablished but said Estonia had entered a "period of transition" leading to restoration of the Republic of Estonia. The colonist representatives boycotted the vote.

The Estonian Communist Party began to split openly into two separate organizations on the issue of independence. Of the 441 Estonian delegates at the crucial meeting (25 March 1990), 432 voted to leave the CPSU (as the Lithuanian Communist Party had previously done 22 December 1989). The 250 non-Estonian delegates refused to vote and split, in turn, into two factions. The Latvian Communists also split on independence (7 April 1990).

The absence of a colonist minority veto in the Supreme Council added to the redundance of the Estonian Congress. The Supreme Council pledged cooperation with the Congress, recognizing it as "the restorer of independence." Satisfied with this compliment, the Estonian Committee (the permanent body of the Congress) in turn voted to hand over temporary authority to the Supreme Council. The representation of ENIP and EHS in the Supreme Council was woefully low, lower than their popular support, because they had made a mistake akin to the one PFE made in the Congress elections: They failed to present candidates.[13] Because the Supreme Council eventually evolved into the body of action, the ENIP/ EHS leaders had excluded themselves from the hub of constructive activity. Public opinion, which had briefly swung from PFE to national radicals in early 1990, gave up on the latter. Preference percentages (for the Estonian population only) varied as follows toward the end of the months shown:[14]

	Popular Front	National Radicals
December 1989	31	19
January 1990	25	28
February 1990	30	25
March 1990	21	42
May 1990	36	10

Estonian politics during the rest of the year became somewhat schizophrenic between the PFE-dominated Supreme Council and the ENIP-dominated Congress. Most Estonians supported cooperation between the two bodies, but little of it materialized.

FROM ESSR TO OCCUPIED REPUBLIC OF ESTONIA, APRIL–DECEMBER 1990

During the nine months that followed the Supreme Council elections, most of the Soviet symbolism was eliminated in Estonia. Some steps were made toward abolishing the Soviet political and economic structures, but advances were limited. Most important, no further progress was made toward Soviet acceptance of Baltic independence. The Lithuanian context of Estonian and Latvian developments during that time should be taken into account.

Lithuanian Supreme Soviet elections (24 February 1990, second round 4–10 March) preceded those in Estonia (18 March) and Latvia (18 March, second round 25 March and 1 April). Gorbachev had proposed new antiseparation legislation to the USSR Congress of People's Deputies. It was formally presented as a procedure by which the famous article 72 of the Soviet constitution could be implemented, but the extremely cumbersome process actually subjected a republic's leaving the USSR to a minority veto by local Russians and also a final veto by the Kremlin. These vetoes and various other maneuverings made it effectively an antiseparation law. Under comparable "orderly procedure," the United States could never have seceded from the British empire.[15]

The Lithuanian Supreme Council decided to avoid the new complications and declared Lithuania's independence restored (11 March 1990) before the USSR Congress met. Gorbachev continued to emit mixed signals (to put it mildly). He agreed to independence talks in a discussion with the ESSR chair Arnold Rüütel, but on the same day (12 March 1990) told the USSR Congress that such talks were out of question. The next day, he again guaranteed independence negotiations to Latvian deputies, whose votes he needed for his candidacy as USSR president. Two days later, the USSR Congress declared Lithuania's independence illegal.

Abolition of ESSR

By the time the Estonian Supreme Council met, Soviet troops had begun to maneuver and seize buildings in Lithuania—hence the more cautious wording about Estonia being an illegally occupied country "in transition" toward independence (30 March 1990). Four days later, the USSR Congress passed Gorbachev's antiseparation law, and Gorbachev demanded immediate retraction of the Estonian declaration. The Kremlin soon (18 April 1990) began an economic blockade of Lithuania, which Boris Yeltsin called a violation of human rights. Threats against Estonia and Latvia increased. In Latvia, the Supreme Council did not meet until 4 May 1990 because of delays in completing the elections.[16] Despite Gorbachev's threats, the Latvian Supreme Council voted to reestablish the independent Republic of Latvia through negotiations with the USSR.

In some ways, the Latvian declaration was a degree more cautious than Estonia's in that no immediate start of a transition period was proclaimed. However, in introducing the preoccupation state symbols, Latvia went as far as Lithuania and further than Estonia. Instead of "Estonian SSR," simply "Estonia" was used in April 1990—not yet "Republic of Estonia." The Estonian Supreme Council caught up with its neighbors on 8 May 1990: The preoccupation name "Republic of Estonia" and its state symbols were reinstated, and those of ESSR and USSR were eliminated.[17] In the colonist-dominated northeast, some cities continued to use ESSR flags. Elsewhere, the changes in official seals and stationery proceeded slowly because of a dearth of materials and printing facilities.

The new Estonian Supreme Council, by a bare majority, replaced Indrek Toome as prime minister by PFE leader Edgar Savisaar. The Supreme Council then insisted on approving each minister separately, choosing them (apart from the premier) from outside the Supreme Council as a reaction to the Soviet accumulation of legislative and executive posts by the same people. Thus, defeated Supreme Council candidates qualified as ministers, but winners did not, and the appointment process lasted a full month. Writer Lennart Meri became minister of foreign affairs, and Endel Lippmaa became a special minister for relations with the USSR—the overlap between the two jobs was bound to create friction. Only four of the more than twenty ministers were CPE members, but about one-half were recent ex-members. Many but not all had PFE connections. Four ministers were retained from the previous Toome cabinet. Arnold Rüütel was reconfirmed as chair of the Supreme Council Presidium and hence head of state. For practical conduct of the council sessions, a separate speaker was elected, Ülo Nugis. Marju Lauristin and Viktor Andrejev (b. 1948), a Russian moderate, were elected vice-speakers. The new leadership soon encountered its first test of strength.

Gorbachev pronounced the Estonian and Latvian decisions null and void; and one day later (on 15 May 1990), his colonialist supporters tried to storm the parliament buildings in Riga and Tallinn but were repulsed. In Tallinn, up to 5,000 colonists assembled in front of Toompea Castle, the seat of the Supreme Council and government. Egged on by some Russian Supreme Council members watching at the windows, the mob forced its way to the internal courtyard, from where the broad doors of the parliament wing were easy to enter. However, the enclosed courtyard felt too much like a trap, and the mob hesitated for a crucial moment. Meanwhile, Estonians began to respond to a radio call by Premier Savisaar, and eventually about 15,000 arrived. The colonists were forced to withdraw through a narrow passage in the Estonian crowd that fortunately kept its collective temper.[18]

It should be noted that in a city of approximately 250,000 Estonians and 250,000 non-Estonians, several times more Estonians could be mobilized on short notice than the colonists' side could assemble at a time of their own choice. Clearly, only a small fraction of non-Estonians supported the antiindependence activities. In reaction to the riot, the Estonian government established an unarmed Home Guard of volunteers.

Already on 12 April 1990, the Baltic prime ministers had signed a Baltic common market agreement, but in practice Latvia and Estonia could give the blockaded Lithuania only limited help. Compared with blockades of unoccupied countries that have control of their borders and ports, the Soviet blockade of Lithuania was especially vicious because Soviet troops occupied all points of access inside the country itself. It was akin to "blockading" a prisoner, refusing him food and taunting him to get it elsewhere, yet keeping the door locked. Nevertheless, the Muscovites felt the loss of Lithuanian agricultural products, and it was not clear who was hurt more. On 29 June 1990, the Lithuanian Supreme Council offered a 100-day moratorium on the declaration of independence, effective only when independence negotiations with the Kremlin began. Gorbachev seized the occasion to lift the blockade, although negotiations did not start and hence the Lithuanian moratorium never went into effect.

Gorbachev's rigidity on Baltic independence came as a surprise—and not only to the Balts. "I thought you very astutely laid the predicate for accepting Lithuanian independence when you unearthed the infamous von Ribbentrop-Molotov Pact and denounced it," former U.S. Secretary of State George P. Shultz wrote in a public letter to Gorbachev. "Knowing you are a lawyer, I thought you were laying the groundwork for their realization of independence and also differentiating the Baltic states from the other republics in the USSR."[19] On one hand, Gorbachev missed this opportunity; on the other, he also avoided the use of massive military force after his initial testing of Baltic resolve indicated that use of local colonist mobs interspersed with a few soldiers would not do. The negative reaction in the West, on which the USSR increasingly depended economically, exerted a restrictive hand.

The latter half of 1990 saw an uneasy stalemate in the Baltic states and, indeed, throughout the Soviet empire. Gorbachev seemed intent on upstaging Hamlet. Twice he shrunk from decisive economic reform (in June and September 1990), even as the command economy continued to crumble and a market economy was shackled by the old rules. Gorbachev was equally indecisive in Baltic matters. At first, the Kremlin insisted on talks with Lithuania alone. The Baltic governments, now all led by popular fronts, proposed a "three-plus-one" formula (three Baltic states plus the USSR) and a preset agenda on restoration of independence. However, when the Kremlin offered independence talks to Estonia alone, it could not resist the temptation and abandoned the agreed formula. The talks opened on 23 August 1990, but when the Soviet side in early September shifted its position to discussing merely an improved "federation," the Estonian delegation left Moscow. In October 1990, the meetings resumed and fizzled again. Lithuanian-Soviet talks were repeatedly in the air but never materialized.

At the same time, Boris Yeltsin, the new head of the Russian SFSR, played a game of his own. He met the Baltic leaders in Jurmala, Latvia (August 1990), but delayed formal treaties that would recognize their independence. The term "sovereignty" was on everyone's lips, but its meaning became ever hazier. A monkey wrench was thrown into Estonian-Russian negotiations when some Estonian radicals began to erect markers at the preoccupation Estonian border, east of that imposed by Stalin and hence inside the RSFSR of 1990. A draft accord (2 October 1990) declared mutual acceptance of the Russian declaration of sovereignty (12 June 1990) and the Estonian declaration of 30 March 1990 about transition toward independence. The border issue was sidestepped with an agreement to solve it through later negotiations. Yeltsin rushed to Tallinn to sign the accord in the midst of the January 1991 crisis (discussed in the next section), but it still was not ratified by the Russian Supreme Soviet when the game was changed in August 1991.

Army and Police

One tangible achievement by the Estonians in 1990 was to halt the conscription of Balts into the occupation army. Popular protest against it had begun in April 1989 (see previous chapter). It evolved into the "Geneva 49" movement based on article 49 of the Geneva Convention, which provides that inhabitants of occupied territories cannot be conscripted into the occupying army. Occasional conscription resistance in 1989 snowballed in spring 1990 and was facilitated when the Baltic governments began to offer alternative service in the Baltic civilian sector. Soviet army spokespersons denounced the alternative service laws and said only 10 percent of youths in Estonia responded to the Soviet army call in spring 1990; the Estonian war commissar put it at 29 percent.[20] Either way, it was clear that not only Estonians but also an appreciable proportion of non-Estonians refused Soviet conscription. Military training at Baltic universities was halted. On 25 December 1990, the Kremlin retaliated in a rather welcome way: Because Estonia had failed to supply troops for the Soviet military, the USSR Interior Ministry stopped guarding prisons in Estonia. The short notice presented temporary difficulties, but another institution passed into Estonian hands.

The shift in internal policing was a longer saga. Soviet police forces in Estonia consisted of the large, poorly trained and paid militia and the elite KGB for political and serious criminal matters. Both were effectively subject to Moscow control and, especially in northern Estonia, were predominantly staffed by Russian colonists. To these forces, one should add border guards and military police. Under conditions like the 15 May storming of Toompea, it was not at all clear how the heavily Russian militia of Tallinn would behave. The Estonian government began immediate steps to shift from a Soviet militia to a Western-style police. USSR Interior Minister Vadim Bakatin signed in August 1990 an agreement to turn all law enforcement over to Estonia, but the KGB remained under dual control, and the radicals pointed out the incongruity of a "KGB of the Republic of Estonia." An Estonian police school was opened. A further agreement in November 1990 set a timetable for transfer from militia to police. Before Bakatin could work out similar deals with the other Baltic states, Gorbachev replaced him with a hardliner. But the earlier Estonian agreement was respected, and an Estonian police with Finnish-inspired uniforms took over formally on 1 March 1991. The actual transfer was much more gradual. The requirement that police officers speak both Estonian and Russian weeded out many former Russian militia members, although the expected extent of Estonian spoken was minimal.

The continued presence of the KGB (under an Estonian who reported to the Kremlin) remained a sore spot. At least equally important was the Soviet stranglehold on the western border. Entry and exit through the Tallinn harbor and airport (newly opened to international traffic in 1990) remained completely outside the Estonian government's control. Even government members as well as the ENIP radicals had to secure Soviet travel documents, and when Westerners (including Estonian refugees) were refused Soviet visas, without explanation, the Estonian minister of foreign affairs said he was unable to do anything about it.[21] Soviet control of exports and imports impeded economic reform severely.

Besides the nascent police, the Estonian public-order forces included Kodukaitse (Home Guard) of unarmed volunteers. When Estonia established an "economic border" against Russia and Latvia (22 October 1990) to limit exports of scarce goods, unarmed border guards began to be trained in customs procedures, and they gradually staffed the twenty-eight export-control checkpoints. A private Kaitseliit (Defense League), using the name of the preoccupation national guard, was formed in spring 1990 by radicals close to ENIP. The colonists formed their own paramilitary. They had few arms, but the good contacts the colonists had with some Soviet army units made them dangerous. Meanwhile, discipline of Soviet troops crumbled, and their efficiency was uncertain.[22]

Economy

The economy became even more of a sore spot than it already had been. The Estonian Supreme Council guaranteed private property rights in principle (13 June 1990),[23] but it later restricted transfers of state property because too much of it threatened to end up in the hands of present Russian managers, almost cost-free. (This reminds me of how the last Grand Master of the Catholic Livonian Order almost overnight became the Protestant Duke of Courland!) The political issue of whether to return to old independence or advance to a new one had its analogue in privatization: Should one return preoccupation private property or allow for formation of new wealth? For instance, to what extent should farms be returned to the Canadian-born grandchildren of their legal owners rather than be distributed to those who had tilled them for the last decades and intended to stay on the farm?

This multifaceted issue bedeviled all countries in East Central Europe. (Ironically, Russia seemed to be spared because of the longer communist rule there, which destroyed and dispersed the property owners more thoroughly.) The Estonian Supreme Council finally decided in December 1990 that all claimants to property should register within one year. Meanwhile, little could be sold to would-be new owners for fear of encroaching on old claims. Returning preoccupation private property became a severe brake on efficient privatization. Legality collided with rapid introduction of free enterprise, delaying it for at least two years.

Meanwhile, the socialist economic structure crumbled and shortages multiplied. Estonia was hemmed in by Soviet restrictions that could be disregarded only at the cost of losing supplies from habitual sources, but alternate sources could not be developed because the USSR prevented direct trade with the West. Russian managers of major factories in Tallinn and the northeast often ignored the Estonian government and laws. Private barter deals with individual Soviet republics, oblasts, cities, and factories became widespread and eased some of the shortages. However, the fact that an Estonian newspaper had to scavenge for Estonian pork to barter against Karelian printing paper was a far cry from a market economy or, indeed, any money-based economy. Various trade and cooperation treaties (Ukrainian-Estonian, Georgian-Estonian) had limited effect. A coordinating committee for bilateral relations formed in Tallinn (28 September 1990) at Estonian initiative attracted representatives of the Baltic states, Russia, five SSRs, and the Leningrad city council. It offered economic advantages and an alternative to Gorbachev's plans for a centralized Union Treaty, but in its own way it blurred the difference between the Baltic states and the various Soviet subunits.

In October 1990, the Estonian government implemented a risky price increase, doubling and tripling some prices. The Kremlin and the local colonists opposed any such deviation from USSR-wide policies, and the popular reaction was unpredictable and certainly not happy. Later, in January 1991, the Lithuanian government fell because of such price increases, but in Estonia the population accepted them, grumbling but remaining calm. The price rise alleviated shortages only marginally because even the new prices often were too low to offer producers sufficient incentives. Clothes and textiles, which for decades had been available in sufficient quantities, vanished by the end of 1990; it was not a matter of lack of choice but absolutely bare shelves.

184

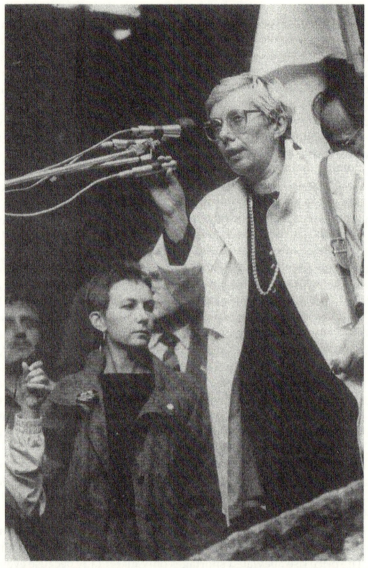

Social Democrat leader Marju Lauristin at protest meeting on the fifty-first anniversary of the MRP (23 August 1990). Next to her is Eve Pärnaste of the Estonian National Independence Party. Photo Kalju Suur. Reprinted with permission.

Internal Politics

Politics within Estonia was marked by two cleavages: colonists versus Estonians, and the Congress versus the Supreme Council. Because the colonists had not boycotted the Supreme Council elections (as they had done for some local ones), the avenues of parliamentary action were open to them.[24] The non-Estonian Council members were quite fractionalized, but tended to close ranks in matters of language, citizenship, and anything they did not quite understand. Although given a podium, they were outvoted on matters on which the Estonians agreed among themselves. The most reactionary colonists began to build up a regional power base in the northeast where the immigrants had surpassed the Estonians in numbers. This meant a shift in tactics, compared with 1989, when their efforts concentrated on Tallinn and the northeast was relatively quiet.

Eleven days after the unsuccessful storming of Toompea, an Interregional Council was formed in Kohtla-Järve to "defend Soviet power in Estonia" (26 May 1990). Most delegates were locally elected officials; a quarter were appointed by managers of Soviet-controlled enterprises. Soviet soldiers prevented proindependence Russian delegates from attending the meeting. Formally led by Estonian Supreme Council member Vladimir Lebedev (b. 1952) and obviously receiving guidance from the Kremlin, this council voted to ignore Estonian law and remained a constant threat to Estonia's territorial integrity because the council could count on Soviet army support in case of a confrontation.

At the same time, there was never-ending jousting between the Estonian Congress and the Supreme Council. Most Estonians felt both assemblies were legitimate, the Congress reflecting the national goals and the Council the political realities. In this unintentional two-chamber setup, the Congress increasingly looked like a powerless Chamber of Lords. It convened two more times in May and October 1990. The Congress leadership condemned the Supreme Council as a Soviet creature that still was in cahoots with the Kremlin (as supposedly proved by the Council's failure to get the occupation army out) and yet demanded that this body allocate funds for the functioning of the Congress. At the October 1990 Congress, an attempt was made to replace Kelam as chair by former political prisoner Enn Tarto, who took an equally dim view of the Supreme Council but also refused to join ENIP.[25] Kelam won the election, 60 to 40.

Intra-Estonian politics reached a low in October 1990 when fractures developed in the Supreme Council leadership and the government. Stonewalling by the Kremlin motivated Lippmaa, the special minister for eastern affairs, to turn his activities to the West, where he inevitably stepped on the toes of Foreign Affairs Minister Meri. Head of state Rüütel developed his own foreign policy contacts, and Premier Savisaar did not always inform Meri of his foreign travels. Estonian Congress leaders also traveled widely in the West, and it seemed to become a contest of who among Kelam, Savisaar, and Rüütel would be the first to be received by U.S. President George Bush. The Lithuanian and Latvian prime ministers had been received in May and July 1990, respectively. Savisaar made it in October 1990, Rüütel in March 1991, and Kelam was not received.

The rifts in the Estonian establishment were actually not as deep as in Lithuania, where the prime minister was replaced in January 1991, but they were less well hidden from the outside world because they dealt with foreign policy. Some U.S. officials signaled that the Estonians better get their program organized if they wanted to be taken seriously.

This is the context in which some of the reform communist Free Estonia leaders (notably Toome) and some of the radicals (notably Kelam) joined forces against the Savisaar government in the so-called Eight-Person Proposal (4 November 1990). It was a clever move by the communists but frivolous on the part of the radicals. In the Supreme Council, the Estonian communists were squeezed between the Russians (communist or not) and the Popular Front, and they were carrying the guilt of the treasonous past of the CPE toward Estonia. Now the radicals, those self-appointed guardians of national purity for whom PFE was too communist, were willing to absolve Free Estonia and help its adherents out of the political doghouse. Of course, Toome would agree, even if the chances of toppling the government were minimal.

The radicals had everything to lose. They never had been considered skilled politicians by the average Estonian, but were given credit for steadfastly promoting the goal of independence at a time when others were still denying any such thoughts. The radicals were felt to be the conscience of the nation, those who could say "We never played games." After November 1990, they no longer could. If PFE was seen as overly communist-ridden, then a deal with the communists themselves amounted to an unholy alliance. Such alliances are frequent in politics, but in this case the radicals paid with the only capital they had: their reputation for not playing games. Further, they demonstrated again their clumsiness at the political game because the Savisaar government survived.[26]

Popularity polls in August and November 1990 reflected the general reaction. Savisaar's approval dropped by a few percent (to 76 percent), but approval of all those connected with the Eight-Person Proposal nosedived. Toome dropped from 79 to 57 percent and Kelam went from 45 to 27 percent, ranking fifty-fifth among eighty Estonian and non-Estonian public figures on the list.[27]

By early December 1990, internal politics calmed down. During the year, Estonia had made considerable progress in building internal democracy. For the first time in fifty years, it had an elected parliament, which, after fumbling around for a while in procedural issues, had began to work rather efficiently. The colonist minority's participation in the Supreme Council was objectionable on legalistic grounds, but it also gave the group a chance to talk issues out instead of taking other action. The party system had not yet coalesced.

Political Freedom, Military Occupation

The Republic of Estonia still was a militarily occupied country, reminiscent of 1943 Denmark, where free elections also had taken place despite German military occupation. Estonia had succeeded in drawing some symbolic lines of demarcation between itself and the USSR. In July 1990, the chairmen of the Supreme Councils of all three Baltic countries withdrew from the USSR presidential council meetings. Echoing the reason ENIP gave for boycotting the Soviet Congress elections in March 1989, Arnold Rüütel said that "representatives of occupied countries have no business in the state organs of occupying countries."[28] The Baltic members of the USSR Congress and Supreme Soviet had withdrawn even earlier. This withdrawal weakened the reformist forces in these assemblies, and some Russian reformers thought the Balts had miscalculated because only a victory of democracy throughout the USSR could assure Baltic freedom. However, many a self-styled reformer in Moscow still thought in imperial terms and took the Balts' support for granted without listening to them, thus contributing to the Baltic exit.

In some other respects, especially economic, interaction could not be reduced easily, even when the Soviet bureaucrats treated the Estonian government officials condescendingly. When Tunne Kelam criticized the Supreme Council leaders for excessive compliance in March 1990, Arnold Rüütel told him: "Come with us to Moscow, and you'll see how tough it is."

The Baltic states had achieved considerable international visibility, and support for their quest for independence had grown, especially in northern Europe. The French government invited the Baltic foreign ministers as its guests to the Conference on Security and Cooperation in Europe (CSCE) in Paris, but Soviet objections blocked their entry at the last moment (18 November 1990). The Balts were foiled, but the USSR looked like an international bully. Another regional meeting of government representatives took place in Tallinn in December 1990, the third since September 1990, and this time it included not only the Baltic states and a widening circle of Soviet republics but also some Scandinavian diplomats and representatives of Central European governments.

In the touchy areas of language, citizenship, and immigration, little progress was made. An immigration law was passed.[29] The official figures showed an outflow toward Russia that exceeded the influx, but illegal immigration remained a big question mark. For 1991, the immigration quota was set at 2,290, or about one-third of the net immigration in the early 1980s. The law on citizenship was delayed because the colonists insisted on both automatic Estonian citizenship and retention of their USSR citizenship, but the Estonian Congress and a large part of Estonian public opinion felt the present Supreme Council, itself partly elected by colonists, had no business deciding on citizenship. The first deadlines for bilingualism of public servants and sales personnel, stipulated in the language law of January 1989, were approaching, and the eagerness of Russians to learn basic Estonian varied by individual and locality.

As I arrived in Estonia for a month's visit in late November 1990, ethnic relations seemed less tense than they looked from afar. In the company of the Estonian Committee leaders, I visited Sillamäe, a colonist stronghold, and we had an orderly public meeting. In Tallinn, I crisscrossed through a rather passive crowd of 4,000 at a protest meeting of the colonist JCWC (16 December 1990); when I was addressed by the colonist paramilitary, I responded in Estonian with no undue consequences.[30]

However, signs of new pressures by the Kremlin were appearing, prompting the Lithuanian government to convoke a joint meeting of the three Baltic Supreme Councils (Vilnius, 1 December 1990). A joint commission of five members from each country was formed, a potential seed of a common Baltic parliament. In mid-December 1990, Gorbachev convened the USSR Congress of People's Deputies; and one of the main issues was the draft of a new Union Treaty. It ostensibly offered wide autonomy to the members of the proposed confederation, but made such broad exceptions in economy, finances, and many other fields that all effective power would remain centralized. The Baltic states refused to discuss this sham, pointing out again that they never had legally joined the USSR. The Lithuanians did not attend the USSR Congress; the Latvian and Estonian leaders did, after lengthy debates of pros and cons, but only to declare their status as outside observers. The Baltic response obviously hardened the stance of the prewar SSRs such as Ukraine and contributed to the stalemate at this Congress.

If by blocking Baltic independence in early 1990 Gorbachev intended to prevent a domino effect, he miscalculated and boosted it. If the Baltic states were no longer in the USSR, the prewar SSRs might have accepted the new Union Treaty in December 1990. But when the Baltic leaders were forced to voice their resounding no, resistance throughout the USSR was stiffened. What had been called the Soviet Union unveiled itself as the Soviet Disunion the moment repression was removed.

The year that had started with so much promise ended in a stalemate. Although Gorbachev had thwarted the restoration of Baltic independence, reasonably free elections had established the legitimacy of noncommunist Baltic parliaments and governments that began to be taken increasingly seriously by the Nordic countries and the rest of the world. Lithuanian Premier Kazimiera Prunskiene's meeting with U.S. President George Bush in May 1990 looked like an exception, in the face of a general reluctance of the U.S. administration to deal with the Baltic governments. However, by the end of 1990, such encounters had become rather commonplace. The democratic legitimacy of the new Baltic governments made it increasingly more expensive for the Kremlin to crush them. At the same time, Estonia and the other Baltic states remained completely at the mercy of the occupation forces and any calculations (or miscalculations) made in the Kremlin.

INDEPENDENCE REFERENDUM, JANUARY–JUNE 1991

The central events in the first half of 1991 were first the Kremlin's efforts to topple the elected Baltic governments by hidden use of force, then a struggle of referendums. In spring, attention focused on Kremlin attempts to establish an oxymoronic "Union of Sovereign States." The Baltic states refused to participate in these negotiations, but the Baltic-Soviet negotiations were on hold while the future of the empire's core was debated.

The Kremlin Tries Force

The imperial forces began a major attack in the Baltic states in January 1991 while world attention was riveted on the Persian Gulf. However, in line with Gorbachev's general indecisiveness, the offensive was far from the sharp blow the USSR dealt to Hungary during the Suez war in 1956 or to Afghanistan during the Iranian hostage crisis in 1979. Action was slow and gradual, giving world opinion time to respond, despite the Gulf war, and enabling the Balts to improve their defensive positions. Gorbachev seemingly left much initiative to the military in an attempt to escape blame for bloodshed. By so doing, however, he reinforced the impression that no one was any longer in charge.

When the United Nations gave Iraq an ultimatum to withdraw from Kuwait by 15 January 1991, Soviet provocations in the Baltics began to multiply. USSR Defense Minister Dimitri Yazov ordered Soviet military commanders to eliminate allegedly fascist monuments erected in the Baltic states, and Gorbachev issued a decree to "protect" the rights of Soviet soldiers in the non-Russian "republics" (27 November 1990). USSR Interior Minister Vadim Bakatin was replaced by hardliner Boris Pugo, a Russian Latvian who had been KGB chief, then Communist Party first secretary in Latvia (2 December 1990). Soon two Estonian cemeteries for war dead were desecrated and a memorial to Stalin's civilian victims was blown up in the middle of the night; similar acts occurred in Latvia. Yazov's night shift appeared unable to tell democrats and fascists apart. USSR Foreign Minister Eduard Shevardnadze, the ranking non-Russian in the imperial leadership, resigned. The occupation forces established a mail blockade of the Baltic states.

The occupation troops began to seize key buildings in Latvia and Lithuania (but not Estonia). The USSR Defense Ministry announced on 7 January 1991 that paratroopers would be sent into the Baltic states and elsewhere, ostensibly as press gangs to hunt down conscription-age men. During the Soviet fall 1990 call-up, only 25 percent of conscripts showed up in Latvia and Estonia, and 12 percent in Lithuania. Savisaar obtained a promise from Yazov that paratroopers would not be sent to Estonia while a joint commission studied the issue. At the same time, PFE gave citizens detailed instructions for peaceful resistance in case of attack. The Russian Supreme Soviet declared the use of military force in the Baltics unacceptable, and Estonia and RSFSR signed the aforementioned bilateral accord, recognizing mutual sovereignty (12 January 1991).

Subsequent violent aggression concentrated on Vilnius, Lithuania, where thirteen unarmed civilians were killed in a Soviet tank attack on 13 January 1991—several days before the deadline issued to Saddam Hussein as a result of events in the Gulf. Yet the Soviet troops first went for secondary targets, thus alerting the population, who surrounded the parliament building and made a subsequent attack on the parliament impossible without major bloodshed. Invited by Savisaar, Yeltsin rushed to Tallinn and signed joint statements of mutual recognition with all three Baltic states. He also appealed to Russian soldiers to think of their own families and refuse to fire on civilians. The colonist members of the Estonian Supreme Council demanded government resignation, threatening strikes and other unspecified measures. Yeltsin's appeal thwarted these self-styled defenders of Russia, and they were so angry at him that Yeltsin did not dare to fly back from the colonist-ridden Tallinn airport but took the train. The colonist radio, broadcasting from Soviet navy premises, blared that the moment for the final battle had arrived and urged formation of antiindependence paramilitary units. The Estonian government erected barricades at Toompea.

The Gulf war began on 16 January 1991, and on 20 January the Soviet Black Beret special troops went on attack in Riga, Latvia, killing four people. Thereafter, military activity faded rather unexpectedly. Protest against the aggression slowly built up in Russia, the rest of the Soviet Disunion, East Central Europe, and the West. Even more important, there was also dissension among the imperialists themselves. In retrospect, the fate of not only the Baltic states but the entire empire hinged on the outcome in

After the Soviet tank attack in Vilnius, Lithuania (January 1991), all access roads to Toompea, the seat of Estonia's government and parliament, were blocked. The rocks remained in place in readiness until October 1991. Photo Kalju Suur, January 1991. Reprinted with permission.

Vilnius on that 13 January. Why did the Soviet forces choose to attack in Lithuania, where the colonist civilian garrison was less numerous than in Estonia and Latvia? And why didn't they attack the parliament building first? The likeliest explanation is the following, at least according to what was known prior to August 1991.

Gorbachev and the reactionary "Black Colonels" (antidemocratic Soviet junior officers) had reached an agreement to quash Baltic democracy by creating ethnic disturbances that would give Gorbachev an excuse for introducing direct presidential rule. The main thrust was to be in Latvia because it had the largest Russian population. To minimize international attention, attack was to start after the Gulf war had begun. However, when the Prunskiene government resigned in a dispute over prices (8 January 1991), Lithuania seemed in such disarray that the colonels thought the opportunity too good to pass up. They genuinely seemed to think that not only the Russian and Polish minorities but also the Lithuanian working class had become disaffected from the national leadership and that only a spark was needed to activate the masses. Without waiting for the Gulf war or even consulting with Gorbachev, they went ahead, using a minimal number of troops to supply that spark.

They certainly "activated the masses"—but in a direction unexpected by the colonels: Forgetting the price squabble, Lithuanians rallied around their parliament. By the time the colonels realized they had misread the mood in Lithuania, the uproar had become so strong that it was too late to inject more military muscle unless presidential rule was invoked. Sensitive to reactions abroad and appalled by the colonels' poor sense of timing and coordination, Gorbachev refused to proclaim presidential rule and distanced himself from the mess. The colonels in turn felt Gorbachev had lost his nerve and betrayed them, and soon they said so openly.[31] The subsequent action in Latvia came at the preagreed time and place, but world opinion was on alert, the Latvians had time to build barricades, and above all, the mutual trust between Gorbachev and the Black Colonels was destroyed. What began with an ill-advised timing for a Lithuanian cabinet crisis may have had far-reaching and unanticipated consequences.

Estonia played a secondary role compared with Latvia and Lithuania, both in imperialist plans and actual attacks. Savisaar's rapid invitation to Yeltsin and his contacts with Yazov and the local Soviet commanders played a role in delaying bloodshed until the danger passed.

Baltic Independence Referendums

Gorbachev's shift away from the military hardliners did not mean that he had given up on the empire. The pressure for a Treaty of Union now focused on a Disunion-wide referendum with a confused and convoluted wording. Referendums have been strongmen's favorite form of ballot ever since Napoleon, as long as they can set the rules and manipulate the question to be asked. For his referendum, Gorbachev arbitrarily set the acceptance level at merely 50 percent of actual participants, but he required two-thirds of all those entitled to vote in the case of a separation from the empire. The Baltic parliaments firmly opposed any Soviet referendum in the occupied Baltic states. There never had been a Baltic referendum on whether to join the USSR; in his hurry to annex, Stalin had neglected such formalities. Thus, the reasonable referendum question would be whether to join the empire, not whether to leave it or refurbish it.

Taunted by Gorbachev, who said the Baltic Supreme Councils were afraid of a popular verdict, the Lithuanian and then the Estonian and Latvian Supreme Councils decided to have their own preventive referendums. The wordings varied from country to country and, in Estonia, led to a heated internal debate. The question that finally appeared on the Estonian ballot was "Do you want restoration of the independence of the Republic of Estonia?"

From the legal viewpoint, "restoration" was a risky term, because it might imply that independence had been interrupted not only factually but also legally. In contrast, the proempire colonists would have wanted something like "Do you want a sovereign Estonia preserved in the USSR?" The inherent problem with any referendum is that a genuinely neutral wording often is impossible. At the very least, the Estonian question was short, direct, and about as unambiguous as humanly possible. (It certainly beat Gorbachev's referendum wording on all those counts.)

Colonist participation in the Baltic referendums was also legally debatable. Appreciable German settlement was undertaken in Poland's Poznan area during World War II. Should there later have been a referendum, with colonists participating, on whether Poznan should return to Poland? And if the Nazis instead of Communists had won the war, would a fifty-year occupation make any recent German colonist a legal inhabitant? Different people may give different answers. In the Baltic referendums, even the most recent colonists could participate. Because the outcome in all three countries was an overwhelming "yes" for independence, the colonist participation did not matter in retrospect. In fact, it made the outcome that much more unassailable. But if the results had been less clear-cut, they could have poisoned Baltic relations with the colonists.

The results of the Baltic independence referendums are shown in Table 7.1, in which the countries are arranged in decreasing order of percent share of native inhabitants. The bottom line shows that far more than two-thirds of those who cared to vote preferred independence.

The table includes various categories as percentages of the total adult population; hence these percentages add up to 100. As one might expect,

TABLE 7.1   Baltic Independence Referendums (early 1991)

	Lithuania	Estonia	Latvia
Non-Baltic population (percent)	20	39	48
Referendum date	9 February	3 March	3 March
Voting results (percent)			
Vote "yes"	76.4	64.5	64.6
Desist from voting	15.3	17.1	12.4
Invalid ballots	2.7	0.6	1.4
Vote "no"	5.5	17.7	21.6
Total	100	100	100
Ratio of percent "no" to percent non-Baltic population	.28	.45	.45
"Yes" votes as percentage of voters	90.2	77.8	73.7

Note: Countries are arranged by increasing non-Baltic population share (which includes the small number of Balts in a Baltic country not their own).

Source: BATUN, *Baltic Chronology,* February 1991, p. 2, and March 1991, p. 1.

the share of explicit "no" votes increases with the share of non-Balts in the population. However, even assuming that 100 percent of the Balts turned out and voted "yes," the figures imply that, at most, 28 percent of non-Lithuanians in Lithuania came out and registered a "no" to independence; the corresponding figures in Latvia and Estonia were at most 45 percent. The actual non-Balt opposition to independence was much lower because a few Balts also must have voted "no," and many more failed to turn out for various practical reasons. The extent of the proindependence vote by non-Latvians in Latvia was especially striking, and the imperialist aggression in January 1991 actually contributed to it. In popular opinion polls, support for the Latvian government among the non-Latvians skyrocketed from 43 percent on 12–13 January 1991 (before the attack) to 62 percent on 21 January (after the attack).[32]

Regional data not shown in Table 7.1 suggest that in Estonia, approximately 30 percent of the non-Estonians voted for independence, another 30 percent did not bother to participate and can be counted as neutral, and 40 percent voted against independence. In the border city of Narva, where Estonians had been reduced to 4 percent of the population, 17 percent voted for independence, 52 percent voted against, and 30 percent abstained. In view of imperialist control of the Russian-language press and city government, the results reflected a fairly strong proindependence beachhead even among the non-Estonians in Narva.

Gorbachev held his referendum on 17 March 1991. The Estonian Supreme Council refused to have anything to do with it, but private commissions of Soviet citizens were not prevented from organizing polling stations. The latter reported a civilian turnout of 250,000 (22 percent of the

TABLE 7.2   Political Preferences of Inhabitants of Estonia, February 1991 and
April 1989 (percent)

| Groupings | February 1991 | | | April 1989 |
	Estonians	Others	Total	Total
Antiindependence groups	0	29	11	11
No preference	2	13	6	5
Reform communists	11	17	12	22
Popular Front of Estonia	30	6	21	35
Estonian Social Democratic Party	9	8	8	–
Other PFE allies	13	11	12	14
Non-PFE center-right	25	14	21	–
National radicals	8	3	8	12

Source: Public opinion poll, 20 February 1991, by EMOR; also published in BATUN, *Baltic Chronology,* April 1991, p. 7. April 1989 figures are based on Table 6.1.

voting population), with 95 percent saying "yes" to whatever the muddled question meant. Military and civilian votes were not clearly distinguished, and multiple voting was easy: Several journalists had themselves photographed casting bogus votes at half a dozen different locations.

In sum, Gorbachev's referendum in Estonia was a failure and a fraud. Estonia's referendum satisfied Western observers, and its messsage was clear, though Gorbachev declared it invalid. A few months earlier, he had taunted the Baltic governments of being afraid of a referendum, but now Gorbachev himself was afraid of the referendum results.

Estonia's Political Groupings in Early 1991

The political preferences of inhabitants of Estonia in February 1991 are shown in Table 7.2. The categories are arranged in descending order from the most reactionary groups to the most radical. For comparison, the figures for April 1989 are also given (from Table 6.1); this comparison is imperfect because the identity and attitudes of some groupings changed in the interim.[33]

Antiindependence groups. These groups had no support among the Estonians. Among the non-Estonians, more than one quarter favored them. The most popular was the Joint Council of Work Collectives (JCWC), with 16 percent support among non-Estonians. The anti-independence branch of the communists, CPE on the Platform of CPSU—later abbreviated as CPE-CPSU—had a token Estonian as its leader and representative at the CPSU Politburo (an institution that had lost much of its former importance); it was supported by 9 percent of non-Estonians. Intermovement was a discredited label even among the colonists and attracted only 4 percent support among non-Estonians. Compared with April 1989, support for reactionary groups remained the same: about 11 percent of the total population. Previously opposed to autonomy, they had now shifted to supporting its Gorbachevian version. In their strongholds in the northeast, they flew the old red flag of the ESSR and refused to apply the laws adopted by the Estonian Supreme Council in which they were represented. Their dream of detaching the northeast from Estonia was shared neither by Russian President Yeltsin nor by the mayor of Leningrad, Anatoli Sobchak, so that attachment to Russia's Leningrad region was problematic even if detachment from Estonia were to make headway.

The no-preference people. Those who voiced no preference in the opinion poll amounted to 11 percent among the non-Estonians (plus 2 percent preference for groups not listed in the poll). These people (who appear in the table between the antiindependence and proindependence groups) either felt they were not part of Estonia or distrusted the pollsters. This indifferent category was minimal among Estonians.

Reform communists. Despite its declared proindependence stand, CPE attracted only 1 percent support among the Estonians under its own label; but under the lofty label of Free Estonia, the communists netted another 10 percent. For non-Estonians, both labels were equally attractive. Although CPE had declared itself independent of the CPSU, it maintained a representative in the CPSU Politburo so as not to abandon this field to the reactionary CPE-CPSU. As a result, two Estonians now sat in a body where none had ever been during the Politburo's days of glory. Free Estonia, chaired by former prime minister Indrek Toome, was a grouping that avoided becoming a party. As such, it included CPE members as well as those who had left CPE—and those whose status was not publicly known. Their program was equally unclear; their approach was to wait in the wings and suggest they had more managerial expertise than PFE and could obtain a better deal for Estonia from the Kremlin.

Popular Front of Estonia. Compared to two years earlier, support for the core PFE showed a marked decrease, but part of it was only realignment within the broader PFE coalition after the founding of new parties within it. Like Free Estonia, PFE refused to become a formal party. As such, it continued to house members of Social Democrat, Liberal, and Rural Center parties; but in a narrower sense, PFE was the only political home for many others, such as Prime Minister Savisaar. In the Supreme Council, this PFE core formed a distinct Popular Center faction, but talks about forming a corresponding party made no headway from late 1990 to mid-1991, largely because Savisaar was concerned about losing support from allied parties if he created his own. Meanwhile, frictions between the PFE as an alliance and the PFE core continued. The Estonian government was a PFE cabinet only in the broad sense of the term. Its policy reflected no clear ideological focus but pragmatic muddling through in the direction of decreased effective dependence on the USSR and increased private enterprise. PFE support among non-Estonians remained comparatively small.

Estonian Social Democratic Party (ESDP). Among the PFE-spawned political parties, the Social Democrats, chaired by Marju Lauristin, enjoyed
the most support among Estonians and also had some success among the
non-Estonians. The ESDP was patterned after the Nordic Social Democrats, who encouraged the fusion of the earlier Estonian and Russian Social Democrat groups. Like all proindependence groups (including the
CPE), ESDP supported extensive reprivatization under the existing conditions of tight state control. The ESDP Supreme Council faction was solidly
behind the Savisaar government.

Other members of the PFE alliance. Because of its support among the Estonians (8 percent), the Estonian Liberal Democratic Party, chaired by Paul-
Eerik Rummo, was notable, but it had only 1 percent support among non-
Estonians. Its mirror image was the Russian-led Estonian Democratic
Party, with 8 percent support among non-Estonians but none among Estonians—and no representatives in the Supreme Council. The Liberal Democrats often sympathized with the national radicals, but their Supreme
Council faction maintained support for the government with some hesitations. The Rural Center Party enjoyed little support in February 1991 (2
percent among Estonians) but formed a stable faction in the Supreme
Council, where it followed the Liberal Democrat pattern. The Green
Movement (2 percent support among Estonians and others) represented a
splinter of the once-prominent ecological organization.

Non-PFE center-right. Although it did not seem to seek electoral representation, the Estonian Women's Union was included in the poll and obtained close to 8 percent support both among Estonians and the others.
The Estonian Entrepreneurial Party was very much a one-man show by
Tiit Made, a populist ex-Green. Its popularity shot up in February 1991 (11
percent among Estonians, 3 percent among others), but fell to 3 percent
among Estonians in March. The Green Party, another splinter group resulting from the Green infighting, had some 3 percent support. The Estonian Royalist Party (1 percent support) distinguished itself by its humor
and playfulness in an otherwise sullen field. There was no common de-
nominator among all these disparate groups, except that they were
nonsocialist and not part of the PFE coalition (although many were neutral).

National radicals. These groupings predominated in the leadership of
the Estonian Congress and Committee and had considerable visibility in
Estonian politics, but their combined support in the opinion poll was only
8 percent among Estonians. The most prominent was the Estonian National Independence Party, which drew a fairly steady 4 percent of the Estonian preferences. One of its members, Tunne Kelam, headed the Estonian Committee, but ENIP was unrepresented in the Supreme Council.
The Estonian Christian Union and the Republican Coalition Party each

had 2 percent support, and they did have some articulate members in the Supreme Council. Three other parties had even less support. As for the Estonian Heritage Society, it had reverted to nonpolitical activities, and some of its leaders (including Velliste) joined the Christians. The radicals started out strongly opposed to communism, then fixated on PFE as being soft on communism and eventually came to dislike PFE, and Savisaar in particular, even more than they disliked CPE.

Clearly, the political spectrum was splintered and unsettled. Moreover, the factions in the Supreme Council did not always correspond to the party labels. Popularity of individuals often had little to do with their affiliation (and vice versa). As of March 1991, Estonians gave the highest approval ratings to the following public figures:[34]

Person and affiliation	Approval percent
1. Arnold Rüütel (head of state)	94
2. Marju Lauristin (Social Democrat leader)	86
3. Ülo Nugis (speaker of the Supreme Council)	85
4. Endel Lippmaa (minister for eastern affairs)	83
5. Heinz Valk (Liberal Supreme Council member)	79
6. Rein Taagepera (professor, University of California at Irvine)	78
7. Edgar Savisaar (prime minister)	78

No national radical made it into the top thirty. Rüütel, Lippmaa, and Taagepera (b. 1933) were not affiliated with any grouping, while Nugis belonged to the tiny Republican Coalition Party. Among the non-Estonians, no public figure received wide approval:

Person and affiliation	Approval percent
1. Arnold Rüütel (unaffiliated)	52
2. Indrek Toome (Free Estonia)	39
3. Vaino Väljas (independent CPE)	38
4. Vladimir Malkovski (CPE-CPSU)	33
5. Igor Šepelevitš (JCWC)	32
6. Edgar Savisaar (prime minister)	32
7. Vladimir Lebedev (JCWC)	31

All the individuals in the latter list were members of the Supreme Council. Lauristin ranked twelfth (28 percent) in the opinion of non-Estonians, Nugis thirteenth (26 percent), Lippmaa seventeenth (22 percent), and Valk and Taagepera about thirty-fifth (about 13 percent). In the opinion of Estonians, Toome ranked twenty-eighth (56 percent) and Väljas twenty-third (59 percent). Imperial activists like Malkovski (b. 1951), Šepelevitš (b.

1945), and Lebedev were very near the bottom in the Estonians' opinion, but their popularity among non-Estonians was also limited to about one-third. Another third of the non-Estonians seemed to share the Estonian pattern, and another third did not recognize most of the names on the list, Russian or Estonian. Thus, ethnic polarization between the Estonians and the colonists was not extreme.

The Estonian Congress, the object of such high expectations a year earlier, continued its slide toward negativism. Its standing Estonian Committee declared the Estonian treaty with Yeltsin's Russia, as signed on 12 January 1991, "devoid of legality and invalid," because it did not sufficiently stress Estonia's status as an occupied country and "threatened the territorial integrity of the Republic of Estonia" by leaving the borders issue open.[35] When no blood was shed in Estonia in January 1991, in contrast to Lithuania and Latvia, some national radicals wondered what secret concessions Savisaar must have made as a price for the relative quiet. The Estonian Committee's first reaction to the independence referendum was a call for boycott. A week later (7 February 1991), the committee reconsidered, but ENIP still insisted on a boycott and probably reduced Estonian participation by a couple percent. Ultrapatriotism began to border on the opposite stance in view of the disastrous consequences a wider Estonian nonparticipation could have brought.[36] The Estonian Congress met for its fifth and sixth times in March and May 1991. The PFE representatives stopped attending, which led to quorum difficulties.

As for the Supreme Council, it ran into increasing deadlocks. Ministers for industry and for eastern affairs resigned over policy differences, but the council refused to accept their resignations. In the latter case, the issue was the prime minister's proposal for a free-trade zone in Narva, provided that the colonist city government began to respect Estonian laws. Public reaction of Estonians was predominantly negative; they saw special status as a first step toward legal separation of Narva from Estonia. Savisaar argued that Estonia no longer had effective control over Narva and the deal was the only way to bring the city back into the fold. The Supreme Council tabled the issue until fall 1991—as it did with much other legislation.

May 1991 saw an escalation of terrorist attacks against first Lithuanian, then also Latvian and Estonian border customs posts by Soviet Interior Ministry Black Beret troops. The Kremlin denied any knowledge of the attacks, asserted the troops were acting on their own, but refused to condemn the attacks. Estonia added armed police to the previously unarmed customs posts.

The Baltic states resisted pressures and threats of economic retaliation by the Kremlin in case they did not join the so-called Union Treaty proposed by Gorbachev. Meanwhile, their diplomatic relations expanded. In

A different "Song of Estonia": When you finally locate gasoline, you really tank up. Photo Kalju Suur, summer 1991. Reprinted with permission.

particular, the president of Lithuania and the prime ministers of Latvia and Estonia were received by U.S. President George Bush (9 May 1991).

INDEPENDENCE REGAINED, JULY–SEPTEMBER 1991

Despite the unusually sunny skies, July 1991 was gloomy in Estonia. The Estonian government ceased attempts at independence talks with the Kremlin because Gorbachev visibly wanted to get the so-called Union Treaty signed by the most pliant Soviet republics before dealing with the more recalcitrant. The threat was palpable that the Baltic states might be left twisting slowly in a twilight zone, having neither independence nor even the limited autonomy yielded by the Union Treaty. In particular, they might be forced to sell their products for rubles while required to pay in hard currency for Soviet imports such as oil, which was in short supply. Soviet terrorist attacks on Baltic customs posts forced the unarmed Estonian border guards to retreat from Narva (18 July 1991). A bomb blast gutted the headquarters of the Estonian Home Defense next to Toompea (9 July).

The Estonian government and Supreme Council seemed unable to solve any issues, not even those in which the Kremlin did not interfere. An attempt to topple the government narrowly failed in the Supreme Council, but the joint effort by national radicals, reform communists, and antiindependence colonists bode ill for the future. Prices were up 170 percent compared with a year before. Industrial production was down by 6.8 percent (*Päevaleht*, 27 July 1991). Speculation and shady deals left people disgusted with nascent private enterprise and doubtful about democracy and even the moral qualities of the nation. The headline "The National Feeling Called Shame" (*Eesti Aeg*, 16 July 1991) captured the widespread mood. Could the national will, frayed by several years of rapid changes, collapse under the stress of political stalemate and economic disruption?

Such was the mood when, within a short week in August 1991, at first everything seemed lost, and then everything seemed won. A reactionary coup in Moscow (19 August 1991) toppled Gorbachev, met determined resistance by Yeltsin, collapsed on its third day, and brought results exactly opposite to those intended by the plotters.

The Resolution on Immediate Independence, 20 August 1991

The Soviet military commander of the Baltic district openly joined the reactionary coup, but the commander of the Soviet Baltic fleet refused to do so. Unsure of the reaction of the local garrisons, who had long been in peaceful contact with the population, the rebels ordered some eighty tanks in Pskov (in Russia, near the southeastern corner of Estonia) to roll to Tallinn. Unaware that the coup was unraveling in Moscow, the Soviet troops occupied parts of the Tallinn television tower in the early hours of 21 August, but no bloodshed occurred. At the same time, some issues of the democratic *Moscow News*, banned by the Moscow coup leaders, were printed in Tallinn.[37]

Meanwhile, on the second day of the coup, with the outcome utterly unclear, the Estonian Supreme Council adopted a "Resolution on the National Independence of Estonia":

> Proceeding from the continuity of the Republic of Estonia as a subject of international law,
>
> Relying upon the strength of the Estonian population's clear expression of will in the 3 March 1991 referendum to restore the national independence of the Republic of Estonia,
>
> Taking into account the 30 March 1990 Resolution of the Supreme Soviet of the Estonian SSR "On the Status of Estonia" and the Declaration of the Supreme Soviet of the Estonian SSR "On Cooperation Between the Supreme Soviet of the Estonian SSR and the Congress of Estonia,"
>
> Observing that the coup d'état in the USSR seriously imperils the democratic processes in Estonia and that it has made it impossible to restore the national independence of the Republic of Estonia through bilateral negotiations with the USSR,
>
> The Supreme Council of the Republic of Estonia resolves:

1. To affirm the national independence of the Republic of Estonia and to seek restoration of the diplomatic relations of the Republic of Estonia.

2. To form a Constitutional Assembly, whose composition shall be delegated by the highest legislative organ of state power, the Supreme Council of the Republic of Estonia, and by the representative body of the citizens of the Republic of Estonia, the Congress of Estonia, for the purpose of drafting the Constitution of the Republic of Estonia, to be submitted to popular referendum.

3. To hold new Republic of Estonia parliamentary elections during 1992, on the basis of the new Constitution of the Republic of Estonia.[38]

This resolution represented a truce between the Supreme Council and the Estonian Congress. On one hand, it carefully avoided being a new declaration of independence by stressing the continuation of the independence declared in 1918; on the other, it implied an end to the period of "transition to independence" proclaimed on 30 March 1990. It was meant to erect a frail juridical barrier between Estonia and the USSR in case the reactionary coup succeeded. When the coup failed, the resolution became a signal for immediate determined action within Estonia and beyond its confines.

Latvia proclaimed its immediate independence one day later. Thus, Estonia and Latvia caught up with Lithuania's declaration of March 1990 in symbolic terms. Yeltsin, who commanded enormous respect during this crucial week, not only recognized Estonia's independence on behalf of Russia but also urged the USSR and the world to follow suit (24 August 1991). In contrast to the cool international reception of Lithuania's proclamation of independence in 1990, the world now responded with a veritable stampede to recognize Baltic independence: By the end of August, some forty states had done so, Iceland being the first (on 22 August). The first foreign embassy in Tallinn, that of Sweden, opened on 29 August 1991.

In the wake of the collapse of the coup, the Estonian and Latvian proclamations unleashed a chain reaction within the USSR. By the end of August, six prewar SSRs declared their independence, although the implications regarding separation from the USSR were not always clear. It could be argued that Gorbachev's refusal to accede to Baltic independence in 1990 speeded up the collapse and fragmentation of the USSR one year later.

The Estonian border guards took back their positions on the Narva River, and the Estonian Supreme Council ordered new city council elections in northeast Estonia where the existing imperialist-dominated councils had flirted with the coup leaders in Moscow. The Soviet Communist Party was declared illegal on grounds of its being a part of another country's political system; the proindependence Estonian Communist Party

Lenin stood here. Four days after Estonia's decision of immediate resumption of independence, the monument in front of the nine-floor headquarters of the Communist Party of Estonia was dismantled. Photo Kalju Suur, 24 August 1991. Reprinted with permission.

continued to operate freely. The last statue of Lenin was toppled in Tallinn. Top leaders of the colonist paramilitary were arrested. Colonist leader Jarovoi was fired from his position as director of a major military factory and fled to Moscow. All organized Russian factions in the Estonian Supreme Council collapsed, and eleven relatively moderate Russians formed a new faction in support of Estonia's independence, to which even the most reactionary members of the council now paid lip service. A broad Russian Democratic Movement was formed (30 August 1991) to protect the ethnic Russian interests within the framework of an independent Estonia; however, its future was uncertain.

Joint control of the western sea border by Soviet and Estonian guards was agreed upon by the Soviet Baltic border guards commander with the blessing of the Russian and the newly revamped Soviet governments.[39] As August ended, independence had acquired some reality.

International Recognition

The United States recognized the Baltic governments on 2 September 1991, after forty other states had already done so. Washington stressed that it never had accepted the Soviet annexation of the Baltic states in a legal sense. The U.S. recognition was preannounced, but it was supposed to take effect only after the expected recognition of Baltic independence by the Soviet Congress when it met on 31 August. Delays in Soviet action put the United States on the spot. The United States finally announced that the USSR had until 1 September if it wanted to be the first of the two to extend recognition. When the USSR continued to temporize, the United States followed through with its decision.

The European Community recognized the Baltic states in late August and mentioned possible associate status. When the Baltic states made an actual request (6 September 1991), a decision was delayed until their economies stabilized; however, they became members of the CSCE immediately.

A new Soviet State Council, arguably expressly created for the purpose, accepted Baltic independence on 6 September 1991. Recovering rapidly from the effects of the coup, the Soviet reactionaries reasserted themselves in the Soviet People's Congress, and a two-thirds majority in favor of Baltic independence was uncertain in that body. Rather than risk defeat, Yeltsin and Gorbachev circumvented the congress by setting up the new State Council in which the SSRs had equal representation. Remarkably, the USSR still refused to acknowledge the illegality of its annexation of the Baltic states in 1940 and treated the Baltic separation as that of any Union republic, thus creating a precedent for all the SSRs. From the viewpoint of preserving the USSR, this approach was ill-advised. However, it should be kept in mind that the new council was dominated by SSRs that pre-

U.S. Secretary of State James Baker and Estonia's Prime Minister Edgar Savisaar at press conference in Tallinn, twelve days after the United States recognized the resumption of Estonian independence. Photo Kalju Suur, 14 September 1991. Reprinted with permission.

cisely might wish to have a precedent they could later turn to their advantage.

Negotiations about detailed transfer of authority were slow. Some Soviet agencies, especially the Ministry of Finance, temporized. In other cases, Estonia lacked the personnel for effective takeover. When I left Estonia on 19 September 1991, the Estonian presence at the Tallinn airport was limited to one symbolic sentry, but the entire passport control was still in the hands of Soviet personnel. The withdrawal of Soviet special forces and the KGB was fairly rapid in some cases but was expected to take many months in others; such a case was prison guards, for whom Estonia had to train replacements. Withdrawal of regular army units was scheduled to begin in October 1991 and take several years.

In domestic politics, a major new development was that the core of the Popular Front finally declared itself a People's Center Party (4 September 1991). It included Prime Minister Edgar Savisaar, whose prestige obviously had profited from the recent events. With the formation of the People's Center, Estonia seemed to move from a politics of movements to a more stable politics of parties. Only Free Estonia, unsure of what to do with its Communist Party core, remained a nonparty.

As foreseen in the proclamation of 20 August, a Constitutional Assembly was formed, with thirty members elected by the Supreme Council from among its members and another thirty elected similarly by the Estonian Congress (which met briefly on 7 September 1991). Centrist lists carried about twenty seats, another twenty could be counted as national radicals, and some thirteen were various Estonian moderates and reform communists. The seven Russians in the assembly ranged from moderates to imperialists who had rather transparently supported the reactionary coup in Moscow. The first meeting of the assembly (13 September 1991), well prepared through informal negotiations, was marked by a remarkable spirit of cooperation.

For forty-six years, Estonia, Latvia, and Lithuania had been the only former members of the interwar League of Nations to lack United Nations membership. This nefarious legacy of World War II was finally erased—and with unexpected suddenness. Less than a month after the attempted coup in Moscow, the United Nations accepted the Baltic states as members (17 September 1991). Estonia, Latvia, and Lithuania were again on the international map.

The Song of Freedom

These were heady days for Estonia. However, the mood was not what one might expect. Good news flew in at such a rate that there was no time to savor the information. Items that would have made banner headlines a month earlier were now relegated to the column of brief news—"another dozen countries recognized us yesterday" and similar short comments. More important, exhilaration was mixed with postcombat fatigue. Ever since February 1990, independence had been so tantalizingly close, and the frustrating delay had left people emotionally drained.

The entry of the massive tank column on 20 August 1991 was the last straw. People joked about it in late August, but in early September they broke down in a delayed reaction and began to tell about their despair. A widespread rumor said that an order for 240,000 handcuffs had been placed at a factory in Pskov, the city from which the tanks came to Estonia. True or not, the story's circulation was indicative of the mood. Ever since the mass deportations of 1941 and 1949, the Estonians knew it could happen. Even in September 1991, the Soviet armed forces still remained in the country; so did the KGB, barely beneath the surface, although it was officially being dismantled.

The Song of Freedom celebration, Tallinn, 8 September 1991. Some 100,000 people gathered to sing and listen to speeches, including an address by me. In this photo, my wife and I are in the third row, center right, marked with "x." Photo by Kalju Suur. Reprinted with permission.

To the continuing worry about the terrors they knew, the Estonians added new fears about the new unknowns. Would this or that political grouping try to seize power, now that the Soviets no longer kept them in check? From the street to the galleries of the Supreme Council, the wildest rumors flew.

The government officials were too busy to celebrate. Prime Minister Savisaar realized that anything that could be accomplished within days in September might take months if delayed until October. The international scene was uniquely propitious, but it need not last—and reactionary forces in Russia were recovering rapidly.

As the Constitutional Assembly opened, I could not help wondering about my own indifference. Here I was, the only assembly member residing in the Western Hemisphere, sitting at my desk in the second row of the parliament hall, listening to head of state Arnold Rüütel give the opening speech. It was an eminently historical moment—and yet it felt like business as usual. I merely waited for my turn to expound in a scholarly way the differences between majoritarian and consensus democracies and warn about excessive presidentialism.

Still, there was a day of exhilaration, the event called the Song of Freedom (8 September 1991), a more modest repeat of the Song of Estonia exactly three years earlier that 250,000 attended. Now the crowd was around 100,000. In the intermittent rain showers we sang the unaccustomed words "jää vabaks, Eesti pind!" (stay free, soil of Estonia), whereas for most of the last fifty years, it had been a hushed "saa vabaks, Eesti pind!" (be free again, soil of Estonia).

That feeling I cannot convey. We all knew that the most difficult times still lay ahead, especially regarding the economy. But at least Estonians were moderately free to make their own mess—or success—out of it. The Song of Freedom.

WHY INDEPENDENCE WAS RECOVERED

Again, the question of why independence became reality may sound naive and the answer self-evident. Independence was regained because it was regained. Was it regained because of the persistent efforts of Estonians? Or was it because of the internal collapse of the Soviet Disunion, so that sooner or later Estonians would have become independent by default even without much effort on their part? But didn't Estonians contribute appreciably to that collapse? On the other hand, could a reconsolidation in the Minsk-Moscow-Kazan basin draw the Estonians in again, even despite their efforts to avoid it?

Even if one should agree that independence had to come because Estonia was long prepared for it (see end of Chapter 2), that the flaws that ended independence in the 1940s had been eliminated (end of Chapter 3), that Sovietization had failed (end of Chapter 4), and that autonomy had become a nonsolution (end of Chapter 6), at least one question is left: Why independence in 1991 rather than 1971 or 2011? The answer has less to do with Estonia than with the empire. Estonia was ready for independence all the time, when given the least opportunity for it. But why did the empire begin to crumble in the 1980s rather than earlier or later?

If I had to hazard a guess, it would be that after seventy years the last material and human reserves of the pre-Soviet society finally were depleted. The regime survived as long as some pre-Soviet facilities—and above all, work and play habits—survived. When the last tsarist railroad cross ties finally rotted and the last *homo ludens* (playful human) left the field all clear to the *homo sovieticus*, the Marxist-Leninist regime was doomed, just as Gomorrah was after the exit of the last person that did not fit in. The Balts, having been subjected to the process for only forty-five years, were able to go their own way.

However, an explanation in terms of empirewide processes takes us back to that nagging thought: Is independence now more irreversible than it turned out to be in 1940? It will depend largely on what will happen in the Russias.

Will Russia Last?

A wider question overshadows the Estonian: Is the Russian-Tatar plain a more natural center for an empire than, say, the British islands or the Danube basin? Was the USSR a historical anomaly, an old-fashioned empire that should have begun to break apart in the early 1900s but was temporarily given a boost by a new ideology that itself now seems an anomaly? Or was the USSR a mere phase in a relentless state-building like the one that began with the Hsia dynasty in the Yellow River valley and expanded despite major periods of political fractionalization?

As this is being written (late 1991) the new Slavic-Turkic commonwealth is making headlines. This entity is unlike the ex-British Commonwealth in that it intends to preserve a common currency and nuclear weaponry. By the time this book reaches the reader, will the new commonwealth still exist? Will it become a genuine empty shell (see end of Chapter 6), shedding its communality of rubles and rockets? Or will it be another sham confederation like Lenin's, a device to recentralize the empire?

I submit that the commonwealth format proposed in December 1991 is flawed because the Russian component is too large and too disparate internally. Any structure in which one component represents more than one-half of the total is unstable. Within the former Russian SFSR, the centrifugal forces that destroyed the USSR continue to act. Tatarstan is unlikely to settle for a lesser status than Tajikistan has. The Far East and eastern Siberia are attracted to the Korean-Japanese well-being and are more distant from Moscow than the thirteen American colonies were from London, a common language notwithstanding. The ancient state of Novgorod now centered on St. Petersburg has no reason to have itself represented in Minsk through the intermediary of Moscow. Either the former Russian SFSR breaks up and joins the wider commonwealth in a dozen separate pieces, or else the commonwealth will not last.

The USSR composed one-half of the socialist camp it tried to keep together. The alliance had to remain a sham, because the USSR could not tolerate any liberalization in the other countries for fear (a well-founded one) that the spread of liberalization to the USSR would blow it apart. Gorbachev was willing to let the outer empire go, but refused to decentralize within the borders of the USSR. The results we know.

On a smaller scale, Yeltsin is likely to repeat Gorbachev's pattern. He is willing to let the former SSRs go, but refuses to decentralize within the former Russian SFSR as adamantly as Gorbachev did regarding the USSR. Yeltsin is likely to be replaced either by those who are willing to let Tatarstan, Siberia, and Novgorod–St.Petersburg go their separate ways, or by some others who will try to keep the various Russias together by force and also reconquer some previous SSRs. A steady state is far from being reached, and its eventual nature is uncertain.

Will Estonia Last?

By their cultural tradition, the Baltic states belong to the Catholic-Protestant Western Europe rather than the Orthodox Eastern Europe. By their geography, they belong to an ambiguous zone: part of the Baltic littoral when ships prevail but part of Eurasia when horses or tanks prevail. Estonia will last, if culture and ships prevail over tanks.

In principle, two supranational patterns of consolidation can take shape in Europe. The European Community (EC) can prove so successful that it attracts and is willing to accept ever-widening circles in south and east. If so, the Baltic states would join it soon after Hungary does and possibly before Poland, followed by Ukraine, Novgorod, Belarus, and Muscovy. Also possible is that a separate consolidation area prevails in the former USSR, either through force or economic pressures. The use of force against Estonia remains a possibility, although its UN membership establishes a fragile barrier, especially in view of the precedent in Kuwait. The economic pressures are not to be underestimated if Estonia should find a market for its goods in the East but not in the West.

Much will depend on Scandinavia. Will the Nordic countries recognize Estonia and Latvia as natural parts of the culturally Lutheran realm? Will they be willing to play a role faintly similar to that of West Germany toward East Germany, establishing a special relationship? Or will they shrug their shoulders as Estonia reluctantly is drawn back into an eastern economic orbit? How will they see their short-term and long-term interests?

I do not think Estonia can survive as a nation with its own language and culture if it is drawn back into an eastern confederation (under whatever label); its population is too small. Within the European Community, it can survive, given the EC's record of respect for small nations.

My detailed historical account ends with the Estonian accession to the United Nations. This was the peak but hardly the end of the long process of implementing independence. The next chapter presents the problems and prospects the next few years may pose; my perspective is based on how events looked in early 1992.

NOTES

1. Toivo Raun, "The Re-Establishment of Estonian Independence" (1991b), surveys the events from 1987 to September 1991. Romuald Misiunas and Rein Taagepera, *The Baltic States: The Years of Dependence, 1940–1990* (in press), stop with the declarations of March to May 1990; Walter C. Clemens, Jr., *Baltic Independence*

and Russian Empire (1991), reaches September 1990; Toivo Raun, *Estonia and the Estonians* (1991a), goes up to March 1991. The democratization process in 1990 is discussed by Toivo Miljan, "Democratization in Estonia" (1991); Jurij Ruus and Vygaudas Usackas, "The Transition to Polyarchy in Lithuania and Estonia" (1991); and Cynthia Kaplan, "Estonia: A Plural Society on the Road to Independence" (1992a), and "New Forms of Political Participation" (1992b). For comparative analysis of the 1990 Baltic elections, see Rein Taagepera, "The Baltic States," in a special issue of *Electoral Studies* (1990d); and Cynthia Kaplan, "Elections in Estonia" (1992c). For the internal functioning of the Supreme Council, see Rein Taagepera, "Building Democracy in Estonia" (1991). The political scene at the time of the 1991 referendum is described in Rein Taagepera, "Ethnic Relations in Estonia" (1992). An excellent detailed chronicle of events is given in BATUN, *Baltic Chronology: Estonia, Latvia, Lithuania, 1989, 1990,* and separate monthly issues in 1991. Superbly compact week-to-week events and analysis are found in *Homeland,* which became a separate newspaper in 1990 under the title *The Estonian Independent* and expanded its coverage in 1991 as *The Baltic Independent.* A number of official Estonian documents are translated in *Restoration of the Independence of the Republic of Estonia: Selection of Legal Acts (1988–1991),* compiled by Advig Kiris (1991); and in *World War II and Soviet Occupation in Estonia: A Damages Report,* edited by Juhan Kahk (1991). See also Michael Tarm and Mari-Ann Rikken, eds., *Documents from Estonia, II* (1990); and *Eesti Komitee ja juhatuse materjalid* [Materials of the Estonian Committee and its board] (1991).

2. As stated in the Preface, I always translate *Eesti* in front of a noun as "Estonian" and *Eestimaa* as "of Estonia" for post-1980 names. Accordingly, *Eesti Kongress* is rendered as "Estonian Congress," although this body itself preferred the form "Congress of Estonia."

3. Full text in *Noorte Hääl* (Tallinn), 17 October 1989; English overview in *Homeland,* 25 October 1989.

4. "Resolution of the Supreme Soviet of the Estonian SSR on the Historical and Juridical Evaluation of the Events of 1940 in Estonia" (12 November 1989), in *Restoration of the Independence* (1991), 17–18. A different translation is given in *World War II and Soviet Occupation in Estonia: A Damages Report* (1991), 25–26, which also contains various Estonian reports on 1940, dated from 12 September 1989 to 21 February 1990, as well as the USSR Congress Commission report of September 1989 and the USSR Congress resolution on the MRP (24 December 1989). The main part of the book consists of a sixty-page damages report on Estonia's losses under Soviet occupation in all its aspects, completed on 21 February 1990.

5. "Declaration on the National Independence of Estonia" (2 February 1990), in *Restoration of the Independence* (1991), 18–21. A different translation is given in *World War II and Soviet Occupation* (1991), 87–89.

6. "Resolution of the Supreme Soviet of the Estonian SSR on Preparations for the National Independence of Estonia" (23 February 1990), in *Restoration of the Independence* (1991), 21–22. A different translation is given in *World War II and Soviet Occupation* (1991), 90–91.

7. Rein Taagepera, "A Brash Nation Awaits Do-It-Yourself Election," *Los Angeles Times,* 22 February 1990, B11.

8. Riina Kionka, "The Congress of Estonia: Day One," Radio Free Europe commentary, 12 March 1990.

9. These comments are not Monday-morning quarterbacking. As a duly elected member of the General Committee of Citizens of Republic of Estonia, I transmitted detailed recommendations to this effect to Trivimi Velliste, vice-chair of the committee, in mid-February. They were published in Estonia eight days before the Congress convened in Rein Taagepera, "Ülemnõukogu äralõpetamisest" [On how to terminate the Supreme Soviet], *Eesti Ekspress*, 2 March 1990, with a follow-up on 9 March 1990. I also urged co-option of all establishment members willing to shift to the Congress and recommended immediate citizenship for those 10 percent of immigrants who had registered with the citizens committees as applicants.

10. The following terminological distinction occurs in English but not in Estonian: The Russian word *soviet*, which means "council," was never adopted into the Baltic languages as it has been into English, which uses the term in referring to the institutions of the USSR only. Therefore, I translate *ENSV Ülemnõukogu* as "ESSR Supreme Soviet" but *Eesti Vabariigi Ülemnõukogu* as "Supreme Council of the Republic of Estonia." To complicate the terminology even further, *Eesti Komitee* (Estonian Committee) decided to present itself in English as "The Council of Estonia." I'll stick here to translating *Komitee* as "committee"!

11. For details of electoral rules, the campaign, the outcomes, and Latvian and Lithuanian comparisons, see Taagepera (1990d) and Kaplan (1992c).

12. "Resolution of the Supreme Soviet of the Estonian SSR on the State Status of Estonia" (30 March 1990), in *Restoration of the Independence* (1991), 22–23.

13. When I later asked a top leader of the citizens committees why he had not run for the Supreme Council too, he said he thought the Supreme Council would no longer matter once the Estonian Congress was elected. When I wondered how they imagined the Supreme Council would fall without being pushed, he added that the citizens committees were so busy with the logistics of the Congress elections that they were exhausted and made few plans for what came thereafter. The ENIP was prohibited from nominating candidates to Supreme Council elections, but its members could have run as independents.

14. Ahto Lobjakas, "Eestlaste toetus poliitilistele jõududele 1989–1991" [Estonian support for political forces, 1989–1991], *Postimees*, 19 April 1991.

15. Jaak Treiman, "The Soviet Secession Law Is a Sham," *Wall Street Journal* (European edition), 3 July 1990; Rein Taagepera, "In 1776, George III Made Unbearable Demands," *Los Angeles Times*, 12 April 1990, B9.

16. Lithuania and Latvia maintained the standard Soviet electoral rules: one-seat districts, 50 percent participation required, and the requirement that the winner receive 50 percent of all votes (including those cast against all candidates). These rules often require runoffs between the two top candidates, or even new elections with completely new candidates, if all the existing candidates in the given district fail because of the unreasonably rigid requirements. These new elections were required in only a few districts in Lithuania, but so many were needed in Latvia that the assembly convocation had to wait. In contrast, Estonia shifted to multiseat districts with Irish-style ranking of candidates on the ballot (single transferable vote), so that elections were completed in a single day. See Taagepera (1990d).

17. "Law of the Estonian SSR on Estonia's Symbols" (8 May 1990) and "Law of the Republic of Estonia on the Principles of the Provisional Rule of Government in Estonia" (16 May 1990), in *Restoration of the Independence* (1991), 23–26.

18. The national radicals later tried to minimize the danger on 15 May 1991, suggesting that Savisaar either overreacted, calculatedly used the attack for a publicity stunt, or even arranged for a fake attack for this purpose. Having seen videotapes and heard various witnesses' accounts, I find such charges unfounded. The danger of a takeover was real, and so was the danger of a bloody clash once the Estonians arrived.

19. George P. Shultz, "What I'd Tell Mikhail Sergeyevich," *Wall Street Journal*, 9 April 1990.

20. BATUN, *Baltic Chronology: 1990*, 12–14.

21. The KGB demanded my expulsion from my native country in late August 1989, but the Estonian authorities blocked it. After I left in September 1989, CPE ideology secretary Titma said I was on a USSR blacklist that the Estonian authorities had no power to modify. After I was elected to the Estonian Congress from my native Tartu, the Soviet authorities repeatedly denied me a visa. I finally received it in November 1990, when the prohibition list apparently was shortened in preparation for Gorbachev's Nobel Peace Prize.

22. I accompanied former political prisoner Mart Niklus as he conversed with and distributed leaflets to soldiers of the Tartu air base (2 December 1990). Niklus had told me soldiers would poke a hole in the surrounding fence to leave the base, the officers would plug it, then the soldiers would open it again. By the time of my visit, the decay had deepened: A political officer used the hole to come and warn the soldiers talking with us and returned, making no effort to have the fence repaired. Soldiers belonged mainly to construction battalions—no weapons training, no milk or milk products in their diet, and not a single ruble earned paid out until the end of the draft period. Responses to Niklus ranged from cautious to "When will you set up your own state, so that we can go home?"

23. "Property Law of the Republic of Estonia" (13 June 1990) and "Law of the Republic of Estonia on the Principles of Property Reform" (13 June 1991), in *Restoration of the Independence* (1991), 30–43 and 55–72.

24. See Taagepera (1991).

25. When Enn Tarto returned from a Soviet prison camp, the last Estonian political prisoner released, ENIP members expected him to join them, using the following procedure: Two existing members had to write recommendations, and he would be a candidate member for one year before achieving full membership—the exact rules used by the CPSU, Tarto commented to me (28 November 1990, in Tartu).

26. Kelam and three other radicals signed the joint declaration with four reform communists personally, without consulting with their organizations. Privately, many of their fellow radicals were aghast, realizing the blunder it was. Publicly, they distanced themselves from the deal without condemning the signers.

27. Rain Rosimannus and Margo Veskimägi, "Keda rahvas toetab" [Whom do the people support?], *Rahva Hääl*, 19 November 1990.

28. BATUN, *Baltic Chronology: 1990*, 15.

29. "Immigration Law of the Republic of Estonia" (26 June 1990), in *Restoration of the Independence* (1991), 43–53.

30. Taagepera (1992).

31. *Boston Globe,* 12 January 1991; *Die Zeit,* 25 January 1991; *Argumenty i Fakty,* no. 1, 1991. See general chronology in BATUN, *Baltic Chronology: January 1991.*

32. BATUN, *Baltic Chronology: January 1991,* 6 and 9.

33. Public opinion poll, 20 February 1991, by EMOR, a private market research corporation. Detailed results are reproduced in BATUN, *Baltic Chronology: April 1991,* 7, and are discussed in Taagepera (1992). For Estonian respondents only, graphs of support from April 1989 to March 1991 are given in Ahto Lobjakas, "Eestlaste toetus poliitilistele jõududele 1989–1991" [Estonian support for political forces, 1989–1991], *Postimees,* 19 April 1991.

34. Public opinion poll by EMOR, 12–18 March 1991, as reported in *Vaba Eestlane,* 24 April 1991; also in EMOR, *Toimetised I* [Publications I] (1991), 54–55.

35. *Eesti Komitee ja juhatuse materjalid* [Materials of the Estonian Committee and its board] (1991), 27.

36. Many other people were unhappy with the wording and the circumstances of the Estonian referendum but realized that abstention would only make matters worse. I proposed (in *Postimees,* 31 January 1991) the following wording: "Should the Republic of Estonia belong to the USSR?"

37. Vera Tolz, "The Soviet Media and the Failed Coup," *Soviet/East European Report,* no. 44 (15 September 1991).

38. Based on the Estonian text and the English translation in *BATUN News—The Soviet Coup: August 19–22, 1991,* undated [early September 1991].

39. I may have been the first person to enter Estonia openly without presenting a Soviet visa. Instead, I offered at the Tallinn airport my faxed invitation by the Estonian government (25 August 1991). When the Soviet border control threatened, through an interpreter, to send me back to Stockholm, I stepped over the barrier past the control booth and got my way.

EIGHT

Independence in an Interdependent World

Estonia will never be independent again to the degree it was in 1938—no country will regain such status.[1] We live in an interdependent world. Indeed, one of the major tasks Estonia faced after the Soviet-imposed isolation from most of the world was to become more interdependent. From the vantage point of very early 1992, I have identified some of the key issues: My focus emphasizes ethnic issues because they could decimate Estonia, but I'll address economic woes first and close with discussion of various other issues.

ECONOMY

Escape from the economic doldrums certainly was an urgent need. The probability of eventual success was high, but it was not expected to come quickly and easily. Living conditions were bound to worsen during 1992 as Estonia reorganized, but by 1993 the worst might be over. Much would depend on developments in Russia, a region with which Estonia would have to work out new trade relationships while simultaneously seeking new, more diverse markets elsewhere. If Russia collapsed, Estonia would face major difficulties in obtaining oil, selling its products, and coping with a possible influx of refugees.

Private enterprise had begun to sprout in Estonia mainly in the service and trade sector; its more forceful extension to industry and agriculture was urgent. This was easier said than done—increased numbers of private restaurants would not boost exportable production. In tourism, Estonia could capitalize on the unique medieval old-town portion of Tallinn and grotesquely fascinating displays of Stalinist art and architecture. Estonia could also have a role as an intermediary between Russia and the West, but there was no future in buying Russian electric motors at cheap prices and melting them down for scrap copper to be sold in the West, as an Estonian enterprise was doing in 1991. Estonia had to find ways to add to rather than subtract from the transit goods. As for Western foreign aid, it was likely to be limited, as would Estonia's capacity to absorb it. However, an initial well-placed Western boost between 1992 and 1994 could make a major difference.

Reestablishing a work ethic was imperative, but could not be done by government decrees. As of 1991, almost everything in Estonia got done in an almost but not quite Western way. The last extra bit of effort and care in workmanship, quality control, and politeness of service was missing. It affected even some of the new private enterprises. Restaurants might close during the hours of peak demand because the owners felt they deserved a rest at the same time as other people, and they might reject customers without advance reservations on principle, although tables were empty. The Soviet habit of mistreating customers still at times overrode the profit motive. It would take meaningful competition to weed out such attitudes.

Much would also depend on the extent to which investment prevailed over instant gratification among a population deprived of so much of what they continuously saw on Finnish TV channels. Frugality now for the sake of future well-being was a notion discredited by decades of Soviet empty promises; yet so much depended on domestic investment. In unsettled times, conspicuous consumption might be more attractive than long-term investment to those who could afford it, but in the long run, was a Mercedes car a sign of success or foolishness?

Further social and political issues that have impacts on the economy are discussed in later sections. Despite all the problems, chances were good that Estonia would privatize, improve quality, and reinvest at a rate sufficient to start catching up with other Nordic countries. Within a few years, it was likely to become an associate member of the European Community, with full membership possible by the year 2000. An alternative possibility was that Estonia would be drawn back into a Russian orbit, but this was unlikely, given the basic attractiveness of Western Europe. Within the European Community, German predominance might become a problem for Estonia, among other countries. Hence Estonia might well become an early advocate of Russian ties to the European Community as a means of counterbalancing Germany.

ETHNIC RELATIONS

Ethnic relations were equally important and interacted with economic issues. Privatization would bring some job losses, and equal unemployment among Estonians and the colonists working in the same fields was likely to be decried as "discrimination" by the latter because they were accustomed to pervasive though low-quality social security. Moreover, many non-Estonians worked in obsolete industrial plants and were the group most likely to face unemployment. Thus, ethnic relations could be even more important than the economy if mishandled. They inevitably looked quite different from the Estonian and the colonist viewpoints. I try here to give both perspectives, but the situation was inherently asymmetrical.[2]

The Estonian Perception

I shall begin with a double portrait that is fairly typical of the Estonian view. Henn, a friend of long standing, is almost exactly two years older than I, and he never has dabbled in politics. Together we herded cows one summer. Together we built a masterpiece of a sleighway on the slope in his backyard. He is now a grandfather and recently retired from his job as an athletic coach. He and his wife, Eike, live in Lasnamäe, a high-rise suburb of Tallinn inhabited overwhelmingly by Russian colonists. They do not complain about the neighborhood. They own a car with a windshield coarsely glued on because the original one was stolen. Fortunately, the present one is cracked, which discouraged thieves who partly cut it out before noticing the flaw. The couple's flat was broken into and every piece of silver was located and stolen. They have a small summer cottage with a sauna bath in southern Estonia, and the adjoining garden and greenhouse give them some security against completely running out of food. However, the gasoline shortage may make it hard to reach the cottage.

Henn's sister, nicknamed Nann, is a grandmother and has been a widow since street thugs murdered her aging husband just for cheap thrills. She has a third-floor apartment on a street in Tartu where all the other houses are one-floor wooden buildings dating from the beginning of the century. In her youth, Nann was a ballet dancer in the troupe of Vanemuine theater. I have visited Nann and Henn repeatedly since 1988. Their mother, my godmother, died some ten years ago; her children, both of them quiet citizens, are typical Estonians of their generation.

But up to 1988, Henn did not dare to send me his address. He notified me of his mother's death by a postcard mailed in Lithuania. There was a time when he was prevented from entering college because his father had died in prison camp and his mother was in prison. He went into physical education because all other career paths were blocked. Before joining the ballet troupe, Nann was, at seventeen, a lonely deportee laborer in an artillery shell factory in Novosibirsk, Siberia, after deportation and separation from her parents in 1941. She eventually made her way back to Estonia through Central Asia, but when all ex-deportees were ordered rearrested in 1950, she escaped through a back window, hurriedly left Estonia, and went to Tashkent, Uzbekistan, in a kind of preemptive self-deportation.

Henn was not home when his parents and Nann were deported in 1941; he was subsequently raised by his grandmother. There was a time, shortly after the deportation of his family, when Henn and I were crouching in the rye with my parents, and a Russian officer, who had just burned down the village home for the aged, ordered us to come out or his soldiers would burn the farm. My parents told the children to stay put and went out; they were saved from execution because the Russian troops hastily retreated in the face of the German advance. Henn's mother, after being deported to Siberia, was arrested there for standing up for her fellow deportees and spent fifteen years in prison. Henn's father, a bank teller and part-time Estonian national guard officer, was sent to prison camp directly from Estonia. Most of his fellow prisoners died during the first winter, but he survived. When Soviet higher officials found out about it in spring, they were surprised and shocked—this was not the way it was meant to be. They had the survivors shot immediately.

In all these respects, too, Henn and Nann are as typical of Estonians as any. Subtract deportees' children or kin of deportees and prisoners, and few Estonians would be left. And this was done to Estonians by Russians, not by some faceless "Soviets"—unless one were also willing to claim that the Jewish Holocaust was Nazi and hence not German. Russian colonists took the place of Estonians who fled or were deported. Forgive? Yes. Forget? No. Accept colonial settlers refusing to learn Estonian as normal substitutes for Estonians killed and Estonian children forced to remain unborn? Take a guess at the answer.

As I rang Nann's doorbell in August 1989, I was met by a couple who could not speak a single word of Estonian. What was going on? With difficulty, I figured out that Nann was away and these were some of her friends from Tashkent. Nann later told me these were the people who had given shelter to the lonely girl from the Baltic when she escaped to Tashkent forty years earlier. They were Russian colonists who now were trying to leave Uzbekistan, and I could visualize Nann helping them stay in Estonia. (They eventually found they were highly welcome in a depopulated kolkhoz near Novgorod, northern Russia, and settled there.) On that individual human level, many broad generalizations fail.

Still, these generalizations must be made. The survival of a language and culture is at stake. In our increasingly homogenized biosphere, a variety of languages and cultures may turn out to be as essential as is the survival of varieties of wild wheat.

The Russian Colonist Perception

I'll start with another portrait. Forced to flee his home during the war, this boy eventually ended up in a country with a strange language and culture but ruled by people more akin to him. The colonists and the colonized lived very much apart, and he was automatically part of the colonist society. He was not expected to learn the country's language. In fact, it was not made easy, and after a few half-hearted attempts he gave up and became used to intermingling with people with whom he could not communicate unless they knew the language of the colonists. He left a few years before the country regained its independence, but under slightly different circumstances he could have found himself stuck there, unwelcome but with no other place to go.

He did not want to be a colonist, but he was. He profited from all the colonist advantages, indirectly at the expense of the natives. When his friends made fun of the local culture, he remained silent. Along with hundreds of thousands of others, he remained an alien who did not belong to that land.

This could be the portrait of a Ukrainian among the Russian-speaking colonists in Estonia. However, it was also my situation in French-colonized Morocco 1947–1954, and I can empathize with individual colonists in Estonia and their new quandaries after independence.[3] This parallel does not go over well with any audience in Estonia: Many Russians resent being compared to French colonists. Many Estonians object to my seeing any saving grace in colonists, and some bristle at being compared with Moroccans. Yet some parallels exist, though these do not put the colonists as a group on a par with the natives. The Moroccans and Estonians have in their respective countries rights that even second-generation colonists do not have, unless they make the utmost effort to blend into the culture.

The 600,000 non-Estonians in Estonia at the time of the 1989 census were a mixed and often transient population. Some 5 million people may have settled in Estonia during the occupation, but most left again. Of those who stayed, 125,000 had a non-Russian background—Ukrainian, Finnish, and so on. Of the 475,000 Russians, up to 100,000 were preoccupation Estonian citizens (or at least one of their parents was), and about one-half of them knew some Estonian. Close to 400,000 were Russian colonists in the literal sense. Some came as war refugees or as nonvoluntary labor. Thereafter, many were attracted by generous job and housing offers made by Soviet authorities. They did not know Estonia wasn't another Russian province and did not care when they found out. They could get along with the Russian language alone. Some were encouraged to stay in Estonia after their Red Army service or retirement from the officers corps; these individuals often were quite conscious of their mission as a civilian garrison. Some rushed in from Russian villages to join their relatives upon hearing that stores in Pribaltika had more than one kind of sausage. The grapevine quickly told them they could arrive by train, break into nearly completed apartments their friends knew about, and risk no retribution—no local official would dare to remove them once they pronounced the magic curse: "You fascists!" This was rather fun.

Official information boosted the colonists' egos. Civilization supposedly had come to Estonia with Soviet rule. The colonists supposedly were invited by the native government to help the helpless Estonians. Their brethren had liberated Estonia from German fascists, and what one liberates one keeps. At the same time, all too many colonists considered all Estonians fascists who had collaborated with the Germans, used the German (Latin) alphabet, and tended their gardens with German-like diligence. Liberation of the Estonian soil would not be complete until the people who spoke a "human language" safely outnumbered the so-called "fascists."

Is this a caricature of colonist attitudes? Yes and no. It was conscious imperialism among active and retired officers and coarse disdain of the natives among unskilled labor. Not all colonists subscribed to such views, but few would care to object to the more outrageous expressions when voiced in private. And all of them profited from linguistic imperialism. A university professor who found refuge in Tartu from intellectual persecution in Russia later taught for a while in Finland. During his second year in Helsinki he lectured in Finnish, but during twenty years in Tartu he never learned Estonian. When I asked him why, he looked perplexed: "But in Finland I *had* to learn the language. In Estonia there was no such need." In 1990, suddenly, there was.

Reforms took the colonists by surprise. For a long time they did not even notice that the natives were restless. When opinion polls became possible, the colonists responded that ethnic relations were good at a time when Estonians said they were bad. Both sides were right: The Soviet-imposed interaction pattern was good for speakers of Russian and bad for Estonians. Then the world of the colonists collapsed. They felt betrayed by Gorbachev and even more so by Yeltsin. They felt Estonia had invited them and, after making use of their labor, now wanted to get rid of them.

For the colonists, having to master Estonian as a second language seemed indistinguishable from being forbidden to speak Russian or even being expelled, because they had no experience with any nondominating role. Even after independence, they would address me in the streets of Tallinn in Russian as if this were the only human language, gruffly turning away upon my *"Vabandage, ma ei saa aru* (Sorry, I do not understand). Do you speak English?" It would have made a world of difference had any of them begun a conversation, in either Estonian or Russian, with "Sorry, I do not speak Estonian," but this simple courtesy was beyond their comprehension. The worst aspect was that the imperial insolence was not intentional—it came naturally.

Gradually, awareness of changed conditions began seeping in. After independence, some imperialist leaders switched over to protecting minority privileges within the framework of the Republic of Estonia. To Estonians this looked insincere, but it made some rational sense and paralleled the strategy of Rhodesian colonist leader Ian Smith: Play a hard game while there still is a chance, but adopt a new game when the old one is lost. Some other colonists continued to exhibit Soviet symbols and even destroy the Estonian symbols.

Actually, the colonists' options were limited. A Russian reannexation of Estonia (or parts of it) was unlikely. At the other extreme, wholesale forced expulsion was out of the question, especially given the Western and Russian reactions. A massive voluntary repatriation was beyond Russia's ability, and reemigration to the West was also difficult. Most colonists were stuck in Estonia, whether they wanted this or not. The question was how rapidly they would become sufficiently bilingual to function under postcolonial conditions.

Croatia or Finland as a Model?

If the Estonians had tried to reestablish rapidly an essentially monoethnic state, as Estonia was in 1940, they would have been fully within their rights—and yet it was far beyond their capabilities.

For the Estonians, this was the only corner of the world where their language and culture could survive, and their presence in Estonia stretched back 5,000 years. Soviet Russification practices brought the Estonian language dangerously close to forced extinction. Not surprisingly, the Estonians wished to retreat from the brink and increase the Estonian component in their country's population. For the colonists, Estonia was a way station of the last few decades; their language and culture thrived elsewhere and did not depend for survival on Estonia. This was the national aspect. The individual aspect was that some of the colonists had lived in Estonia for most of their lifetime, and it was hard for them either to leave or learn Estonian in their older age.

Both aspects were real, and making light of either would not lead to just and reasonable solutions. The question was how the basic needs of the colonists could be integrated with the legitimate national needs of the Estonians. In 1991, for example, the struggle between Croats and the Serbian settlers in Croatia escalated into a full-scale Serbian attack on Croatia. Regardless of the outcome, this was not the best way to handle such situations. It was a warning to Estonians and the Russian colonists to avoid deceptively simple and clear extremist positions.[4]

A more positive example was supplied by neighboring Finland. Over the last 100 years, it had worked out a mutually satisfactory deal with its

Conflict between Estonians and Russian colonists over monuments. A large So-viet monument glorified a failed 1924 communist coup in Estonia. The Estonians added a small stone specifying that the coup was externally engineered by the USSR against a legitimate regime. This small stone was toppled and broken shortly after Estonia's resumption of independence. Photo Kalju Suur, 15 September 1991. Reprinted with permission.

age-old Swedish minority. The solution involved nearly complete biling-ualism on the part of the minority and elaborate protection of minority language rights on the part of the majority, all in the context of administra-tive decentralization. In the early 1990s, Estonians were quick to point out that the speakers of Swedish were an ancient population in Finland, whereas Russians in Estonia were newcomers, and that an overbearing minority of 30 percent could not be handled with the same methods used for a compliant minority of 6 percent. However, in 1880 the speakers of Swedish had been 14 percent of Finland's population, and they could be extremely overbearing toward the Finnish language. (Indeed, I was per-sonally the target of one such putdown as late as 1961.) Thus, the Finnish model had some validity.[5] What made this approach more difficult was its misuse by some colonists who based their claim for two official languages in Estonia on Finland's example, but distorted it into an argument against bilingualism.

It should be noted that as was true in Finland, the main issue in Estonia was language, not race (although some racism manifested itself among Estonians as well as the colonists). More specifically, the Estonian demand was for bilingualism on the part of the Russians, not prohibition of Russian. Yet some colonists demanded the right to remain monolingually Russian, oblivious to the fact that this imposed bilingualism solely on Estonians—as had been the case during the Soviet occupation.

Although the basic problem was the physical presence of the colonists in Estonia, the political struggle in late 1991 focused on a surrogate issue: citizenship. Both sides agreed on attaching exaggerated importance to it. Estonian radicals made headway against the moderate views of the Savisaar government with proposals that would prevent any post-1940 arrivals from obtaining citizenship before the constitutional referendum and elections expected in 1992. The radicals somehow seemed to expect the colonists to evaporate if only they were denied citizenship. In turn, many colonists seemed to think that only citizenship would guarantee equal access to jobs, property ownership, and even purchase of consumer goods. As a Canadian citizen residing in the United States, I often had cause to exhibit my "green card" (U.S. permanent immigration document) and explain my rights to Russians in Estonia, but they seemed unimpressed. Remarkably, even the most radical Estonians agreed that noncitizen residents could vote and be elected in local elections—a right I as a Canadian citizen do not have in California. This aspect of goodwill was not noticed in the frenzy over citizenship.

However restrictive or all-inclusive citizenship was made, it could not solve the underlying issues. On the one hand, how could the Estonians afford to have large numbers of citizens who could not speak even a hundred words of the country's language? And why should they be given citizenship? Poland did not give it to the German colonists Hitler sent to the Poznan area. On the other hand, how could the Estonians afford large numbers of noncitizen resident aliens either? How could they hold on to the border city of Narva if 80 percent of its inhabitants (and local voters) were noncitizens? In particular, if thousands of young colonists went to Russia to do their obligatory military service as Russian citizens and then returned to Estonia, a dangerous fifth column could be built up.

It would of course be the simplest solution, from the Estonian viewpoint, if the Russian colonists simply left, just as the Algerian French had when Algeria became independent. In 1945, Czechoslovakia even expelled the Sudeten Germans, who had lived in the area for many centuries. However, it was no longer 1945—Europe would not tolerate forcible expulsion. The Algerian precedent, too, fit Central Asia more than Estonia. The Algerian French *pieds noirs* had a relatively prosperous France to go to. In contrast, only a few tens of thousands of colonists from Estonia were likely to return to Russia's more miserable living conditions. Yeltsin and any subsequent governments in Russia were likely to make a determined effort to repatriate Russians because central Russia had become disastrously depopulated. If this void was not filled by returning Russians,

Central Asians might fill it under the new conditions of market economy. In this perspective, Moscow's victory over Kazan 400 years ago may not have been definitive. However, the limited material incentives the Russian governments could marshal were likely to draw more colonists back from the southeastern reaches of the empire than from Estonia.

Emigration of colonists toward the West was another possibility. In the short run, more Estonians than Russians were likely to leave Estonia in the western direction, given the Estonians' better command of English and Finnish. In the longer run, more Russians might leave because no ancestral ties bound them to Estonia. Indeed, the very same economic considerations that brought them to Estonia and discouraged their return home would induce them to proceed even further in the same geographic direction. Few Western countries were probably willing to receive them, but a few tens of thousands might succeed over several years.

Should the population stabilize around 2000, Estonia might be left with about 100,000 non-Russian colonists, some of whom might be Estonianized as easily as they tended to be Russianized under the colonial management; others could make use of cultural autonomy laws to distance themselves from the Russians. Close to 100,000 preoccupation Russian residents might expand their fluency in Estonian relatively easily. Around 300,000 Russian postoccupation colonists had few options but to remain in Estonia even if they disliked Estonian majority rule. On the average, they would be older and less active people, slow to learn Estonian, and a drain on social welfare, but they also would have a relatively low birthrate. Estonians would represent around 65 percent of the population.

Later, the percentage of Russians in the population of Estonia would decrease even further, and repatriation and reemigration would not be the only factors. The reproduction ratio of Estonians, below 1.00 in the first half of the century, was at least 1.04 after the 1960s; that of the non-Estonians was around 0.84.[6] Thus, in the absence of new immigration, Estonians would slowly increase their share in the population. Because colonists tended to be younger, their crude birthrate (per 1,000 population of any age) used to be higher, but after 1989 even the crude birthrate of Estonians exceeded that of non-Estonians.[7]

In the absence of new immigration and under conditions of independence, slow integration and assimilation of colonists would also be furthered because Estonian culture had its attractive aspects and people often feel a need to identify with the history of the country they live in. This was especially true of the offspring of mixed marriages, who numbered close to 100,000. Even under occupation conditions, about 60 percent of them opted for Estonian nationality in Tallinn.[8] An overwhelming majority of them were likely to do so under the conditions of independence, so that mixed marriages were going to work in the Estonians' favor. The combined result of emigration, differential birthrates, and assimilation could be an extensive re-Estonianization of Estonia over the next half century, provided that major ethnic clashes in the near future did not block integration.

The likelihood of a peaceful outcome was increased by Estonia's tradition of cultural autonomy for minorities. The draft laws discussed in fall 1991 continued the principles of those of 1925, assuring the minorities schooling and social interaction in their own language as well as use of minority language in public life in areas where ethnic minorities predominated. Incidentally, such tolerance would increase the rate of integration of non-Estonians; ethnic groups survive best in hostile surroundings that minimize intermarriage and interaction.

Fifty years hence the language issue might fade, and Russian might even become a second official language, as Swedish is in Finland. In the foreseeable future, however, Estonian has to remain the only official language, because the Russian colonization was such a very recent experience. (The Poles, for example, did not make German a second official language after World War II in areas of Poland where Hitler settled large numbers of German colonists.) Most important, many colonists in Estonia were as yet not ready for Finnish-type bilingualism, which implies that public servants and most members of the minority group know both languages. The issue of a second official language could be seriously discussed only when the former colonists would have become as bilingual as Estonians had been forced to be under Soviet occupation. By that time, the intrusion of English might have overshadowed the other language issues.

Did the Baltic Russians in the 1990s offer any analogies to the Baltic Germans in the past? By 1992, most Estonians had rather positive attitudes toward their former German overlords, something unthinkable to their grandfathers in the 1890s or even the 1930s. Could the Estonian views on the recent period of Russian domination also change over time? Contrasts with the German rule abounded: The Germans were a small upper class; the Russian colonists were numerous and predominantly blue-collar workers. The Christian creed imposed by the Germans had taken root and survived; the Marxist creed imposed by the Russians looked like a total failure in 1992. Even so, Estonian goodwill toward Baltic Germans did not sprout after the loss of German privileges around 1919 but only after their physical departure in 1939. Despite such differences, Estonian-Russian relations were likely to change as thoroughly over time as Estonian-German relations did, but the direction of the change was still uncertain.

SOCIAL PROBLEMS

The new media openness and Western contacts brought to light ever new problem areas created or neglected under the occupation. Only a few are mentioned here.

Positive attitudes toward work had been impaired, as mentioned earlier. Although morality is hard to measure and always looks better in retrospect, I would dare to claim that norms of honesty, correctness, and politeness in interpersonal dealings were also damaged under the occupation and were not comparable to those in the West. Once Soviet rules and police forces were discredited, this inherent loss of morality contributed to general lawlessness and increase in crime—and the colonists contributed more than their proportional share.

Some attitudes prevalent in Western Europe fifty years earlier but since overcome were so inculcated by the occupation that at times they are now mistaken for Estonian national tradition. Attitudes toward women are a marked example. I drew a gasp out of Tartu University law students in December 1990 when at the end of my lecture series I called for intellectual achievement among female students and concluded: "Men, I expect as much from you as from women." All too typical was an interview statement by a liberal editor: "I'd like to have a third child. With two girls one does not sail very far."[9]

The country was impoverished in terms of skills. Soviet megalomania had destroyed the small local workshops and factories and reduced the variety of skills taught in trade schools. Coastal people were forbidden to fish because of security paranoia, and the local maritime tradition may have been wrecked irretrievably.[10] In 1918 a local printer could supply coarse postal stamps to the fledgling republic, but in 1991 Estonia no longer could do it and had to print its stamps in Sweden, causing another outlay of scarce foreign currency.

Housing scarcity tied people down to a limited territory to a degree reminiscent of serfdom. Job openings in Tartu would be effectively unavailable to qualified people in Narva or Tallinn because they could not find shelter. Expansion of housing was a major precondition for establishing a countrywide labor market, but without a market economy, no building boom could start.

Different attitudes toward private property contributed to tensions between Estonians and colonists. "If a German sees his neighbor has a nice house, he will work hard to have the same. If a Russian sees his neighbor has a nice house, he will burn it down."[11] *The Los Angeles Times* attributed this quote to entrepreneur Alexander Ponamorov of Khabarovsk, Russian Far East, but many an Estonian could also offer specific examples of being accused by Russians of excessive German diligence. As he gave me a ride

Historical costs to send a letter in Estonia: (Top row) seven tsarist kopeks in 1900; fifteen German "Upper East" pfennigs in summer 1918; one Estonian mark in 1920 (note lack of perforation); ten Estonian sents in 1930 that bear the Estonian coat of arms; (middle row) ten Estonian sents and a portrait of Päts from 1936 on; thirty Soviet kopeks in 1941 (here with a German printover); twelve German Ostland pfennigs in 1943; four Soviet kopeks in 1976. The bottom row shows two Soviet commemorative stamps featuring Estonian motifs such as folk costumes in 1961 and Tartu University in 1982. The final stamp is 2.00 in unspecified currency, for foreign air mail, in the Republic of Estonia, October 1991. Photo by author.

on 12 September 1991, Supreme Council member Rein Tamme (b. 1940) told me he had just returned from his cottage where for the second year in a row potatoes had been dug up. "Last year I caught them digging and patiently explained why I who had planted the potatoes should be entitled to harvest them. They listened politely, then asked: 'Can we go on digging now?' They have the mentality of primitive gatherers," he concluded in sorrow rather than anger, and I thought of the movie *The Gods Must Be Crazy,* in which a hunter cannot understand a cattleman's anger at his hunting down a cow. I do not generalize to all Russians, but it was a recurrent feature among the colonists.

Ecology was another casualty of Soviet occupation, with Soviet military bases among the worst offenders. The danger existed that urgent economic needs might tempt the Estonian government and local officials to allow unsound practices to continue on a supposedly temporary basis.

The list could continue indefinitely, but one might as well stop with these examples. Improvements were bound to be gradual and imperceptible. Still, Estonia was likely to muddle through.

FOREIGN AND MILITARY RELATIONS

As the Soviet Union was formally terminated and Gorbachev resigned in December 1991, Estonia remained a country with large numbers of uninvited foreign troops on its soil: at least 40,000, and 150,000 when family members were included—the actual figures still remained secret even from the Estonian government. It might take several years for the occupation troops, now presumably under Russian command, to withdraw. Given the large number of military families, this issue interacted with the ethnic. The immediate goal in late 1991 was to get rid of Soviet special forces and have the regular army move out of Tallinn and various nature preserves. Even some special forces, such as prison and border guards, were not scheduled to move until mid-1992, simply because Estonia needed time to train its own substitutes. Meanwhile, ex-Soviet troops in Estonia would continue to present a potential threat, given the unsettled conditions in the Turko-Slavic "Commondearth" and the resulting volatility of the military.

Long-term Russian naval bases in Estonia could lead to heated internal debates and protracted external negotiations. Because Russian troops would remain in the country during such negotiations, the Estonian government would be under pressure to agree to the lease of some bases as a way to get the foreign troops out of the rest of the country; yet it could also be accused of treason if it yielded any bases. However, changes in international relations might make Russia lose interest in bases in Estonia, costly and isolated as they were—remember that the USSR voluntarily gave up Porkkala, Finland, in the mid-1950s.

In foreign policy, the Baltic states would most likely maintain a neutral stance, as long as Sweden and Finland did. If Russian bases remained in Estonia, its neutrality would inevitably be imperfect, but trying to balance it by military commitments in the Western direction could only complicate matters and delay Russian disengagement from Estonia. However, if a blatantly nationalist and expansionist dictatorship were to be established in Russia, then Estonia might seek security through Western alliances.

On 12 September 1991, the Estonian Supreme Council expressly declared invalid the border changes between Estonia and Russia that were decided in Moscow in summer 1944 and approved by the puppet Supreme Soviet of the Estonian SSR in January 1945. At issue were 2,300 square kilometers east of Narva River and in southeastern Estonia. While establishing its claim, Estonia indicated that the matter would have to be resolved through negotiations with Russia. If poorly handled under domestic pressure from national radicals, the border issue could chill Eastern relations.

Cooperation among the three Baltic states was likely to receive more lip service than action. When problems were pressing, there would be little time to consult with neighbors. By the time immediate crises were overcome, the different solutions espoused by the three states would be even more difficult to reconcile. On 24 September 1991, the Baltic states agreed to form a customs union, but they still envisaged introduction of separate national currencies rather than replacement of the Soviet ruble by a common Baltic currency. Obviously, their large eastern neighbor could play them off against each other in trade relations, especially regarding agricultural products and transit through Baltic ports, because the profiles of the three countries were fairly similar in these respects. Cooperation among the three states could be enhanced if Western aid were made contingent on it.

In the long run, Baltic cooperation or lack of it could become a moot issue when these countries joined the European Community. From a later vantage point, the Benelux phase of cooperation in the Low Countries was desirable but not crucial.

DOMESTIC POLITICS

The Constitutional Assembly that first met on 13 September 1991 came up with a draft constitution in December 1991 to be submitted to popular referendum. A parliamentary regime was proposed, but it was strongly denounced by proponents of presidentialism who visibly banked on Arnold Rüütel as the man to run Estonia. Meanwhile, the Supreme Council had to review the electoral laws and settle the thorny issue of citizenship and voting rights. At the very earliest, new elections could be expected in summer 1992. If all went well, the election of a new parliament would mark the end of both the Supreme Council and the Estonian Congress, thus ending the era during which two separate bodies claimed parliamentary prerogatives.

Savisaar's People's Center Party and its centrist allies (Social Democrats, Rural Center Party, and maybe some moderate Russian group) might do well in these elections, but economic hardships and ethnic emotions could shift the balance to both extremes: Estonian national radicals and Russian reactionaries. If extremism prevailed, government formation might become quite difficult. If the option of Estonian citizenship were denied to a majority of the colonists through overly stringent residence and language requirements, colonist secession attempts in the northeast might resurface. In fact, even the most liberal offers of citizenship might not defuse the issue if imperialist forces regained power in Russia. One way or another, ethnic issues were bound to loom large in Estonian domestic politics and entail appreciable input, if not sheer interference, from abroad.

A breakdown of democracy could not be discounted, given that the institutions were new and democratic culture was perforce shallow. On the one hand, Estonia showed remarkable tolerance and maturity in the years leading to restoration of independence, but economic difficulties, ethnic frictions, and presidentialist ambitions could still undermine democracy. On the other hand, dictatorship was bound to cut off most Western aid, a loss the country could ill afford—and this might serve as a strong deterrent to possible authoritarian games by anyone.

In the long run, social issues were likely to crystallize into three "issue dimensions": the poor versus the wealthy, Estonians versus Russians, and city versus countryside. Accordingly, four major parties might emerge: center-left (possibly the Social Democrats), center-right (possibly the People's Center), a Russian party, and a smaller rural one. If ethnic relations worsened, the Russian party could become disloyal to the regime and the country, or it could split into moderate and disloyal factions. Also, a pseudo-rightist populist party could do well on a diet of Estonian nationalist rhetoric. The number of minor parties would depend on electoral laws adopted, and random events and the character of individual leaders could affect the developments. It was hard to envisage any future for the Communist Party, under whatever new label, but several of its individual leaders were capable of making a comeback in some form or other.

ESTONIA LOOKS TO THE FUTURE

I began this book with a discussion of Estonia's role in the world, and it is now time to return to this broad perspective. In the 1990s, Estonia's foremost task will be internal reconstruction. Estonia likely will become a member of the European Community at about the same time as Poland. Regardless of whether all or part of Russia follows suit or remains outside the European Community, trade and other relations with Russia will remain at least as important for Estonia as they have been for Finland. One cannot escape geography.

Estonia will probably continue in its role of laboratory for methods of peaceful political struggle and cultural autonomy for minorities. It also could become a link between Eastern and Western Europe. With the emancipation in the East, the center of gravity of the European subcontinent would shift back from the Atlantic toward what traditionally has been called Central Europe: not only Germany but also Czecho-Slovakia, Hungary, and Poland. Hence, Estonia would assume a more central position and might become an important bridge in the new downtown of Europe.

In the United Nations context, Estonia might supply leadership and articulation to the common interests of the smaller member states. Its size, degree of development, and experience would make such involvement a natural role for Estonia if it dares to play it. Estonia would also be likely to turn a sympathetic ear to the cultural strivings (as distinct from political) of nonindependent native peoples throughout the world, especially the struggling Finnic peoples in the northeastern corner of Europe: Mordvins, Maris, Udmurts, and Komis. As for contributions to world culture by individual Estonians, success will depend on escape from mental provincialism. The difference between Athens and Boeotia was not in size but in intellectual daring in the broadest sense.

As the heavy shield of the last imperial ice age receded, around 1990, Estonia was partly submerged. Relieved of its burden, Estonia began to rise. It still does, slowly changing into connecting peninsulas what used to be isolated islands on ancient mental maps.

NOTES

1. Rein Taagepera, "Introduction to the *JBS* Focused Issue on Baltic Futures—Getting the Discussion Started," *Journal of Baltic Studies* 17:3 (Fall 1986), 173–178.

2. Rein Taagepera, "Ethnic Relations in Estonia," *Journal of Baltic Studies* 23:2 (Summer 1992), 121–132.

3. Rein Taagepera, "Ma olin migrant" [I was a migrant], *Edasi*, 6 July 1989.

4. Rein Taagepera, "Õigus minna Horvaatia teed" [The right to go down the Croatian path], *Rahva Hääl*, 1 December 1991.

5. Rein Taagepera, "Homme ma nägin Eestimaad" [Tomorrow I saw Estonia], *Postimees*, 21 February 1991. In Russian, "Zavtra ia uvidel Estoniiu," *Politika* (Tallinn), no. 5 (May 1991), 59–61.

6. Rein Taagepera, "Baltic Population Changes 1950–1980," *Journal of Baltic Studies* 12:1 (Spring 1981), 35–57, especially table 6. This slightly higher fertility rate of Estonians later continued. In the 1989 census, the ratio of the number of people zero to 19 years old to that of those 20 to 39 years old was as high as 1.13 for Estonians and only 0.84 for non-Estonians; see Juhan Teder, "Meie ei sure välja niikuinii" [We shall not become extinct anyway], *Eesti Ekspress*, 6 September 1991, 3. If such a trend continued, in the absence of immigration, emigration, or assimilation, the number of non-Estonians would drop by one-half within 87 years; the number of Estonians would increase by 70 percent. By 2076, there would be 1.7 million Estonians and 0.3 million non-Estonians, and Estonia would be 85 percent Estonian. Needless to say,

232 of AN INTERDEPENDENT WORLD
232 ■ INDEPENDENCE IN AN INTERDEPENDENT WORLD

such extrapolations have an enormous margin of error. But the alarmist claim of national radicals that the Estonians would be outnumbered in births by non-Estonians was contrary to the evidence available.

7. Ene Tiit, "Eesti perest ja eesti rahva püsimajäämisest" [On the Estonian family and the survival of the Estonian people], *Postimees,* 4 May 1991, 2. In 1989 and 1990, the Estonians were 61.5 percent of the country's population but accounted for 65 percent of the births. In earlier years, the situation was the reverse, not because of the Estonians' lower fertility but because many of the most recent immigrants were of child-bearing age.

8. Ludmila Terentjeva, "How Do Youths from Bi-National Families Determine Their Nationality?" *Bulletin of Baltic Studies* 1:4 (December 1970), 5–11, translated from *Zinātne un tehnika* (Riga), no. 8 (August 1970), by Gundar J. King.

9. Interview with Mart Kadastik, in Ene Hion, *Kes on kes Eesti poliitikas* [Who is who in Estonian politics] (Tallinn: Olion, 1990), 75. The need to involve women in business and politics is stressed in Ardo Hansson, "Kus on eesti ärinaised?" [Where are the Estonian businesswomen?], *Eesti Ekspress,* 26 July 1991, 6.

10. Michael A. Hiltzik, "Freed of Moscow, Balts Return to the Sea," *Los Angeles Times,* 17 October 1991, A12.

11. Charles P. Wallace, "Used Car Wheeler-Dealers and 'Commodity Brokers' Strike It Rich," *Los Angeles Times,* 17 October 1991, A12.

· Appendix ·
Basic Data
and Chronology

EESTI VABARIIK (REPUBLIC OF ESTONIA)

Independence Day: 24 February 1918.
State language: Estonian.
National colors: blue, black, and white (arranged horizontally in the flag).
Capital city: Tallinn.
Main religions: Lutheran, Orthodox, Baptist.
Average life expectancy (1986–1987): women 75.1 years, men 66.4.

Area (1 square kilometer = 0.38 square mile):
    Tartu Peace Treaty borders—47,500 square kilometers.
    Estonian SSR borders—45,200 square kilometers.
    Transferred from ESSR to Russian SFSR in 1945—2,300 square kilometers.

Population within ESSR borders, 1989 census: 1,566,000.
Ethnic group percentages: Estonians 61.5; Russians 30.3; Ukrainians 3.1; others 5.1.
Percent urban: 71.6.

Estonian share (in percent) of the population (within ESSR borders):

1939:	92
1945:	94
1959:	74.6
1970:	68.2
1979:	64.7
1989:	61.5

Birth rate (per 1,000 population): Estonians 15, others 13 (1990).
Death rate: Estonians about 13, others about 7 (1990).

Population (1990) and percent Estonian (1989, shown in parentheses) in
largest cities:

Tallinn	484,000 (47)
Tartu	115,000 (72)
Narva	82,000 (4)
Kohtla-Järve	77,000 (23)
Pärnu	54,000 (72)

CHRONOLOGY

B.C.

9,000	Ice recedes from Estonia.
7,500	First human settlements: Kunda culture.
3,500	Comb-ceramic culture, probably Finno-Ugrian.
2,000	Boat-ax culture, probably Baltic.
500	Shift from stone to iron.

A.D.

1208–1227	German (and Danish) conquest.
1219	Tallinn formally founded by the Danes.
1343–1345	Last major uprising of Estonians.
1346	Denmark sells northern Estonia to the Teutonic Order.
1535	First printed book in Estonian.
1558–1583	Livonian Wars.
1561	Swedes in northern Estonia, Poles in southern Estonia.
1629	Poland yields southern Estonia to Sweden.
1632	Foundation of Tartu University.
1645	Denmark yields Saaremaa. Swedish rule throughout Estonia.
1700–1721	Great Northern War.
1710	Effective Russian rule in Estonia.
1739	Full Bible published in Estonian.
1740–1790	Peak of serfdom.
1816	Emancipation of serfs in Estland.
1819	Emancipation of serfs in Livland.
1821–1825	First Estonian-language newspaper.

1857	First durable weekly newspaper.
1857	Publication of *Kalevipoeg* (national epic) begins.
1866	Elected rural township councils begin.
1869	First nationwide song festival.
1888–1894	Peak of Russification.
1891	First Estonian daily: *Postimees*.
1904	Estonian-Russian bloc wins Tallinn city elections.
1905	All-Estonian Congress. First Estonian political party.
1913	Estonia opera theater built.
1917	*April:* Russian Provisional Government agrees to Estonian autonomy.
	28 November: Maapäev assembly proclaims sovereignty.
1918	*24 February:* Salvation Committee proclaims Estonia's independence.
	March–November: German occupation.
	22 November: Soviet attack starts war of independence.
1919	*23 June:* German intervention defeated by Estonians and Latvians.
1920	*2 February:* Estonian-Soviet Tartu Peace Treaty.
1922	Estonia becomes member of the League of Nations.
1925	Cultural autonomy law.
1934	Päts seizes power.
1938	Semifree parliamentary elections.
1939	*23 August:* Molotov-Ribbentrop Pact.
	18 September: Estonia yields military bases to USSR.
1940	*16 June:* Soviet ultimatum for entry of Soviet troops.
	18 June: Soviet occupation completed.
	21 June: fake revolution; puppet "People's Government."
	14–15 July: choiceless "elections."
	6 August: annexation by the USSR.
1941	*14 June:* 6,640 people deported.
	July–August: German conquest of Estonia.
1944	*July–October:* Soviet conquest of Estonia.
	18 September: Estonian Provisional Government installed.
	22 September: Soviet army seizes Tallinn from Estonians.
1945	*January:* border areas separated from Estonia.
1949	*March:* at least 20,000 deported.
1950–1952	Purge of native communists and cultural elite.
1957–1965	Regional economic councils; limited economic autonomy.
1972	Memo to United Nations by underground Estonian Democratic Movement.
1979	"Baltic charter" by Lithuanian, Latvian, Estonian dissidents.

1987	*Spring:* mass protests against phosphorite mining.
	23 August: Hirvepark demonstration; formation of MRP-AEG.
	26 September: Four-Man Proposal of economic autonomy.
	12 December: Estonian Heritage Society founded.
1988	*1–2 April:* creative unions leaders criticize CPE chief.
	13 April: initiation of Popular Front of Estonia.
	14 April: first major public display of national colors, by EHS.
	16 June: Väljas becomes CPE first secretary.
	23 June: ESSR Supreme Soviet legalizes national colors.
	19 July: founding of colonist Intermovement.
	20 August: founding of Estonian National Independence Party.
	11 September: The Song of Estonia; a record 250,000 attend.
	October: release of last political prisoner.
	16 November: Declaration about sovereignty of the ESSR.
1989	*18 January:* language law: Estonian declared state language.
	24 February: formation of citizens committees begins.
	26 March: PFE carries the elections to the USSR Congress.
	23 August: the Baltic Chain of one to two million people.
	11 November: General Committee of Citizens Committees elected.
	10 December: local elections.
1990	*January:* abortive start of Baltic economic autonomy.
	24 February: elections of the Estonian Congress.
	11 March: Lithuania declares independence; USSR objects.
	11–12 March: Estonian Congress elects Estonian Committee.
	18 March: elections of the ESSR Supreme Soviet.
	30 March: Supreme Soviet abolishes ESSR, becomes Supreme Council of Estonia "in transition" toward independence.
	3 April: Savisaar becomes prime minister.
	8 May: Republic of Estonia symbolism restored.
	15 May: colonist attempt to seize Toompea fails.
	12 October: Savisaar received by U.S. President Bush.
	22 October: economic border established with unarmed guards.
1991	*12 January:* Estonia and the Russian SFSR recognize each other's sovereignty.
	13 January: Soviet attack in Vilnius results in bloodshed.
	14 January: Yeltsin in Tallinn, signs mutual recognition of sovereignty with all three Baltic states.

3 March: referendum on independence; 78 percent say yes.

18 July: Estonian border guards forced to retreat from Narva.

19 August: reactionary coup in Moscow.

20 August: resolution on immediate independence of Estonia.

21 August: Latvia declares independence.

22 August: Iceland recognizes Estonia and Latvia.

23 August: Denmark and Norway recognize Baltic states.

24 August: Yeltsin urges the world to recognize Estonia.

29 August: Sweden opens embassy in Tallinn.

2 September: United States recognizes Baltic governments.

6 September: USSR accepts Baltic independence.

13 September: first meeting of Estonia's Constitutional Assembly.

17 September: Baltic states become members of the United Nations.

1 October: first Estonian postal stamps since 1940.

14 October: Estonia joins UNESCO.

16 October: Baltic states join the Council of Security and Disarmament in Europe.

References and Bibliography

BOOKS AND ARTICLES

This section includes an extensive list of books and research articles published since 1982. Earlier work is listed only selectively; see more thorough bibliographies in Raun (1991a) and, for post-1940, Misiunas and Taagepera (1983).

Ahmann, Rolf. 1989. "The German Treaties with Estonia and Latvia of 7 June 1939—Bargaining Ploy or an Alternative for German-Soviet Understanding?" *Journal of Baltic Studies* 20:4 (Winter), 337–364.

Anderson, Edgar. 1988. "How Narva, Petseri, and Abrene Came to Be in the RSFSR." *Journal of Baltic Studies* 19:3 (Fall), 197–214.

Arens, Olavi. 1982. "Soviets in Estonia, 1917/1918." In Ezergailis, Andrew, and Pistohlkors, Gert von, eds. *Die baltischen Provinzen Russlands zwischen den Revolutionen von 1905 und 1917*, 295–314. Köln: Böhlau.

Arjakas, Küllo. 1988. "Ühe riigi sünnist" [About the birth of a state]. *Vikerkaar*, no. 2 (February), 61–68.

Ashby, Arved. 1987. "An Introduction to Eduard Tubin (1905–1982) and His Symphonies." *Journal of Baltic Studies* 18:1 (Spring), 21–44.

Aun, Karl. 1953. "The Cultural Autonomy of National Minorities in Estonia." *Yearbook of the Estonian Learned Society in America* 1, 26–41. New York: ELSA, irregular series.

———. 1985. *The Political Refugees: A History of the Estonians in Canada.* Toronto: McClelland and Stuart.

Barnowe, J. Thad; King, Gundar; and Berniker, Eli. 1992. "Personal Values and Economic Transition in the Baltic States." *Journal of Baltic Studies* 23:2 (Summer), 179–190.

Bohnet, Armin, and Penkaitis, Norbert. 1988. "A Comparison of Living Standards and Consumption Patterns Between the RSFSR and the Baltic Republics." *Journal of Baltic Studies* 19:1 (Spring), 33–48.

Brundage, James A., ed. and trans. 1961. *The Chronicle of Henry of Livonia.* Madison: University of Wisconsin Press.

Bungs, Dzintra. 1988. "Joint Political Initiatives by Estonians, Latvians, and Lithuanians as Reflected in Samizdat Materials 1969–1987." *Journal of Baltic Studies* 19: 3 (Fall), 267–271.

Chambon, Henry de. 1936. *La République d'Estonie.* Paris: Editions de la Revue Parlementaire.

———. 1946. *La tragédie des nations baltiques.* Paris: Editions de la Revue Parlementaire.

Christiansen, Eric. 1980. *The Northern Crusades: The Baltic and Catholic Frontier, 1100–1525.* Minneapolis: University of Minnesota Press.

Clemens, Walter C., Jr. 1991. *Baltic Independence and Russian Empire.* New York: St. Martin's.

Dallin, Alexander. 1957. *German Rule in Russia, 1941–1945: A Study in Occupation Policies.* London: Macmillan.

Dassanovsky-Harris, Robert von. 1987. "The Philosophy and Fate of Baltic Self-Determination." *East European Quarterly* 20:4 (January), 493–504.

Dellenbrant, Jan Åke. 1987. "The Integration of the Baltic Republics into the Soviet Union." *Journal of Baltic Studies* 18:3 (Fall), 235–252.

———. 1991. "The Emergence of Multipartism in the Baltic States." In Berglund, S., and Dellenbrant, Jan Åke, eds., *The New Democracies in Eastern Europe: Party Systems and Political Cleavages.* Cheltenham: Edward Elgar.

Dreifelds, Juris. 1988. "Social Inequalities in the Baltic: The Case of Occupational Hierarchy and Upward Mobility." *Journal of Baltic Studies* 19:1 (Spring), 67–88.

Eesti NSV ajalugu [History of the Estonian SSR], 3 vols. 1971. Tallinn: Eesti Riiklik Kirjastus.

EMOR. 1991. *Toimetised I: Eesti avalik arvamus 1990 poliitikast ja majandusest* [Publications I: Estonian public opinion 1990 on politics and economy], Anneli Sihvart, ed. Tallinn: EMOR (Estonian Market and Opinion Research Center). This research group was the major such enterprise in Estonia.

Estonian Geographical Society (EGS). 1984. *Estonia: Nature, Man, Economy.* Tallinn: EGS.

———. 1988. *Estonia: Geographical Researches.* Tallinn: EGS.

Estonian National History Committee. 1968. *Estonian War of Independence, 1918–1920.* New York: Eesti Vabadusvõitlejate Liit.

Ezergailis, Andrew, and Pistohlkors, Gert von, eds. 1982. *Die baltischen Provinzen Russlands zwischen den Revolutionen von 1905 und 1917.* Köln: Böhlau.

Forgus, Silvia. 1992. "Soviet Subversive Activities in Independent Estonia (1918–1940)." *Journal of Baltic Studies* 23:1 (Spring), 29–46.

Gerner, Kristian. 1986. "Between Sweden and Russia: The Baltic Rimland." *Journal of Baltic Studies* 17:3 (Fall), 194–206.

Ginsburgs, George. 1990. "The Citizenship of the Baltic States." *Journal of Baltic Studies* 21:1 (Spring), 3–26.

Grazin, Igor. 1991. "On the Influence of Baltic Policy on the Process of Democratization in the USSR—The Ethical Aspect." *Lituanus* 37:2 (Summer 1991), 78–81.

Gregory, Paul. 1987. "Assessing Baltic Living Standards Using Objective and Subjective Measures: Evidence from the Soviet Interview Project." *Journal of Baltic Studies* 18:4 (Winter), 367–374.

Guertner, Gary L. 1985. "Nuclear Strategy in the Nordic Region." *Journal of Baltic Studies* 16:1 (Spring), 6–17.

Hajdú, Péter. 1976. *Ancient Cultures of the Uralian People*. Budapest: Corvina.

Haltzel, Michael H. 1981. "The Baltic Germans." In Thaden, Edward C., et al. *Russification in the Baltic Provinces and Finland, 1855–1914*, 111–204. Princeton, N.J.: Princeton University Press.

Herranen, Timo, and Myllyntaus, Timo. 1984. "Effects of the First World War on the Engineering Industries of Estonia and Finland." *Scandinavian Economic History Review*, vol. 32, 121–142.

Hiden, John. 1987. *The Baltic States and Weimar Ostpolitik*. Cambridge: University Press.

————. 1988. "From War to Peace: Britain, Germany, and the Baltic States, 1918–1921." *Journal of Baltic Studies* 19:4 (Winter), 371–382.

Hiden, John, and Loit, Aleksander, eds. 1988. *The Baltic in International Relations Between the Two World Wars*. Studia Baltica Stockholmiensia, no. 3. Stockholm: Almqvist & Wiksell International.

Hilkes, Peter. 1987. "The Estonian SSR as an Example of Soviet School Reform in the 1980s." *Journal of Baltic Studies* 18:4 (Winter), 349–366.

Hinkkanen-Lievonen, Merja-Liisa. 1983. "Exploited by Britain? The Problems of British Financial Presence in the Baltic States After the First World War." *Journal of Baltic Studies* 14:4 (Winter), 328–329.

————. 1984. *British Trade and Enterprise in the Baltic States, 1919–1925*. Studia Historica, no. 14. Helsinki: Suomen Historiallinen Seura.

————. 1986. "Britain as Germany's Commercial Rival in the Baltic States, 1919–1939." In Recker, Marie-Luise, ed., *Von der Konkurrenz zur Rivalität*, 15–49. Stuttgart: Steiner-Wiesbaden.

Hough, William J.H. III. 1985. "The Annexation of the Baltic States and Its Effect on the Development of Law Prohibiting Forcible Seizure of Territory." *New York Law School Journal of International and Comparative Law* 6:2 (Winter), 301–533.

Ilves, Toomas. 1991. "Reaction: The Intermovement in Estonia." In Trapans, Arveds, ed., *Toward Independence: The Baltic Popular Movements*, Boulder, Colo.: Westview.

Ivask, Ivar. 1989. "At Home in Language and Poetry: Travel Impressions of Estonia, Latvia, Lithuania, and Russia, Autumn 1988." *World Literature Today*, vol. 63, 391–405.

Jaanits, Lembit; Laul, S.; Lõugas, V.; and Tõnisson, E. 1982. *Eesti esiajalugu* [Prehistory of Estonia]. Tallinn: Eesti Raamat.

Jaanus, Maire. 1989. "Viivi Luik: War and Peace; Body and Genotext in Her Novel *Seitsmes Rahukevad*." *Journal of Baltic Studies* 20:3 (Fall), 265–282.

Jackson, J. Hampden. 1948. *Estonia*. 2d ed. London: Allen & Unwin.

Järvesoo, Elmar. 1987. "The Role of Tartu University and Riga Polytechnic Institute in Introducing Rational Agriculture into the Baltic Provinces and Russia." In Pistohlkors, Gert von; Raun, Toivo U.; and Kaegbein, Paul, eds., *Die Universitäten Dorpat/Tartu, Riga und Wilna/Vilnius 1579–1979. Beiträge zur ihrer Geschichte und ihrer Wirkung im Grenzbereich zwischen Westen und Ost*, 197–215. Köln-Wien: Böhlau.

Järvi, Neeme. 1987. "On Leaving Estonia." *Baltic Forum* 4:1 (Spring), 6–17.

Johnston, Hank. 1992a. "The Comparative Study of Nationalism: Six Pivotal Themes from the Baltic States." *Journal of Baltic Studies* 23:2 (Summer), 95–104.

———. 1992b. "Religion and Nationalist Subcultures in the Baltics." *Journal of Baltic Studies* 23:2 (Summer), 133–148.

Kaelas, Aleksander. 1958. *Das sowjetisch besetzte Estland.* Stockholm: Estonian National Fund.

Kahk, Juhan. 1982. *Peasant and Lord in the Process of Transition from Feudalism to Capitalism in the Baltics.* Tallinn: Eesti Raamat.

———. 1990. "The Mechanization of Agriculture in Estonia from 1860 to 1880." *Journal of Baltic Studies* 21:4 (Winter), 335–346.

———. 1992. "The East European Agrarian Reforms of the Middle of the Nineteenth Century in a New Historical Perspective." *Journal of Baltic Studies* 23:1 (Spring), 23–28.

Kaplan, Cynthia S. 1992a. "Estonia: A Plural Society on the Road to Independence." In Taras, Raymond, and Bremmer, Ian, eds., *Fraternal Illusions: Nations and Politics in the USSR.* Cambridge and New York: Cambridge University Press, in press.

———. 1992b. "New Forms of Political Participation." In Miller, Arthur; Reisinger, William; and Hesli, Vicki, eds., *The New Soviet Citizen: Public Opinion and Politics in the Gorbachev Era.* Boulder, Colo.: Westview, in press.

———. 1992c. "Elections in Estonia." In Slider, Darrell, ed., *Elections and Political Change in the Soviet Republics.* Durham: Duke University Press, in press.

Kaskla, Edgar. 1992. "Five Nationalisms: Estonian Nationalism in Comparative Perspective." *Journal of Baltic Studies* 23:2 (Summer), 167–178.

Kiin, Sirje; Ruutsoo, Rein; and Tarand, Andres. 1990. *40 Kirja lugu* [The story of the letter of forty]. Tallinn: Olion.

Kionka, Riina. 1990. "The Congress of Estonia: Day One." Radio Free Europe commentary, 12 March.

———. 1991. "Are the Baltic Laws Discriminatory?" *Report on the USSR* (Radio Liberty), 12 April, 21–24.

Kitching, Laurence P.A. 1988. "In the Spirit of Independence: Jaan Kaplinski's *Vercingetorix ütles*—Classical Sources and Metaphorical Interpretations." *Journal of Baltic Studies* 19:4 (Winter), 335–350.

Kochavi, Arieh J. 1991. "Britain, the Soviet Union, and the Question of the Baltic States in 1943." *Journal of Baltic Studies* 22:2 (Summer), 173–182.

Kross, Jaan. 1983. *The Rock from the Sky.* Moscow: Raduga.

Kruus, Hans. 1932. *Grundriss der Geschichte des estnischen Volkes.* Tartu: Akadeemiline Kooperatiiv.

———. 1935. *Histoire de l'Estonie.* Paris: Payot.

Kukk, Hilja. 1981. "The Failure of Iudenich's Northwestern Army in 1919: A Dissenting Russian View." *Journal of Baltic Studies* 12:4 (Winter), 362–383.

Küng, Andres. 1980. *A Dream of Freedom: Four Decades of National Survival Versus Russian Imperialism in Estonia, Latvia, and Lithuania, 1940–1980.* Cardiff, Wales: Boreas.

Kurman, Georg. 1968. *The Development of Written Estonian*. Indiana University Publications, Uralic and Altaic Series, no. 90. The Hague: Mouton.

Kurrik, Juhan. 1985. *Ilomaile: Anthology of Estonian Folksongs with Translations and Commentary*. Toronto: Maarjamaa.

Laitin, David. 1992. "Language Normalization in Estonia and Catalonia." *Journal of Baltic Studies* 23:2 (Summer), 149–166.

Levits, Egil. 1981. "Die demographische Situation in der UdSSR und in den baltischen Staaten unter besonderer Berücksichtigung von nationalen und sprachsoziologischen Aspekten." *Acta Baltica*, vol. 21, 18–142.

Liivak, Arno. 1987. "Soviet Responses to Western Nonrecognition of Baltic Annexation." *Journal of Baltic Studies* 18:4 (Winter), 329–348.

Lijphart, Arend. 1984. *Democracies: Patterns of Majoritarian and Consensus Government in Twenty-One Countries*. New Haven: Yale University Press.

Loeber, Dietrich A.; Vardys, V. Stanley; and Kitching, Laurence P.A., eds. 1990. *Regional Identity Under Soviet Rule: The Case of the Baltic States*. Hackettstown, N.J.: Association for the Advancement of Baltic Studies and Institute for the Study of Law, Politics, and Society of Socialist States, University of Kiel.

Loit, Aleksander. 1975. *Kampen om feodalräntan: Reduktionen och domänpolitiken i Estland, 1655–1710* [Struggle over feudal rent: The reduction and demesne policy in Estland, 1655–1710]. Vol. 1. Studia Historica Upsaliensia, no. 71. Uppsala.

———. ed. 1985. *National Movements in the Baltic Countries During the 19th Century*. Studia Baltica Stockholmiensia, no. 2. Stockholm: Almqvist & Wiksell International.

Mägi, Artur. 1967. *Das Staatsleben Estlands während seiner Selbständigkeit*. Stockholm: Almqvist & Wiksell.

Mägi, Arvo. 1968. *Estonian Literature*. Stockholm: Baltic Humanitarian Association.

Mark, Karin. 1970. *Zur Herkunft der finnisch-ugrischen Völker vom Standpunkt der Anthropologie*. Tallinn: Eesti Raamat.

Martinson, Helle. 1992. "The Development of Chemical Science in Estonia from 1945 to the Present." *Journal of Baltic Studies* 22:3 (Fall), 233–240.

McEvedy, Colin, and Jones, Richard. 1978. *Atlas of World Population History*. Harmondsworth, England: Penguin.

McHale, Vincent E. 1986. "The Party Systems of the Baltic States: A Comparative European Perspective." *Journal of Baltic Studies* 17:4 (Winter), 295–312.

Meissner, Boris. 1956. *Die Sowjetunion, die Baltischen Staaten und das Völkerrecht*. Köln: Verlag für Wissenschaft und Politik.

———. 1987. "The Change in the Social Structure of Estonia." *Journal of Baltic Studies* 18:3 (Fall), 301–322.

———. ed. 1990. *Die baltischen Nationen: Estland, Lettland, Litauen*. Köln: Markus Verlag.

Merkel, Garlieb. 1797. *Die Letten vorzüglich in Liefland am Ende des philosophischen Jahrhunderts*. Leipzig: Heinrich Gräff.

Miljan, Toivo. 1989. "The Proposal to Establish Economic Autonomy in Estonia." *Journal of Baltic Studies* 20:2 (Summer), 149–164.

———. 1991. "Democratization in Estonia." *Lituanus* 37:2 (Summer), 82–88.

Milosz, Czeslaw. 1984. "The Lesson of the Baltics." *Baltic Forum* 1:1, 1–23.

Misiunas, Romuald J., and Taagepera, Rein. 1983. *The Baltic States: Years of Dependence, 1940–1980.* London: Hurst; and Berkeley: University of California Press.

———. 1989. "The Baltic States: Years of Dependence, 1980–1986." *Journal of Baltic Studies* 20:1 (Spring), 65–88.

———. 1993, in press. *The Baltic States: Years of Dependence, 1940–1990.* Berkeley: University of California Press; and London: Hurst.

Moora, Harri, and Ligi, Herbert. 1970. *Wirtschaft und Gesellschaftsordnung der Völker des Baltikums zu Anfang des 13. Jahrhunderts.* Tallinn: Eesti Raamat.

Motyl, Alexander J. 1987. *Will the Non-Russians Rebel? State, Ethnicity, and Stability in the USSR.* Ithaca, N.Y.: Cornell University Press.

Myllyniemi, Seppo. 1973. *Die Neuordnung der baltischen Länder, 1941–1944.* Historiallisia Tutkimuksia, no. 90. Helsinki: Suomen Historiallinen Seura.

Niitemaa, Vilho, and Hovi, Kalervo. 1991. *Baltian historia* [Baltic history]. Helsinki: Tammi.

Nirk, Endel. 1987. *Estonian Literature.* Tallinn: Perioodika. First ed. 1970.

Nørgaard, Ole. 1992. "The Political Economy of Transition in Post-Socialist Systems: The Case of the Baltic States." *Scandinavian Political Studies,* vol. 15, 41–60.

Oras, Ants. 1948. *Baltic Eclipse.* London: Victor Gollancz.

Paalberg, Harry. 1989. "On the Origins of Soviet Economic Mechanisms and the Need for Radical Reform—An Essay." *Journal of Baltic Studies* 22:2 (Summer), 191–195.

Pachmus, Temira. 1985. "Russian Culture in the Baltic States and Finland, 1920–1940." *Journal of Baltic Studies* 16:4 (Winter), 383–402.

Page, Stanley. 1970. *The Formation of the Baltic States.* New York: Howard Fertig. First published in 1959.

Palm, Thomas. 1989. "Perestroika in Estonia: The Cooperatives." *Journal of Baltic Studies* 20:2 (Summer), 127–148.

Parming, Tönu. 1975. *The Collapse of Liberal Democracy and the Rise of Authoritarianism in Estonia.* London: Sage.

———. 1983. "The Electoral Achievements of the Communist Party in Estonia, 1920–1940." *Slavic Review,* vol. 42, 426–447.

Parming, Tönu, and Järvesoo, Elmar, eds. 1978. *A Case Study of a Soviet Republic: The Estonian SSR.* Boulder, Colo.: Westview.

Paulson, Ivar. 1971. *The Old Estonian Folk Religion.* Indiana University Publications, Uralic and Altaic Series, no. 108. The Hague: Mouton.

Peters, Rita. 1983. "Problems of Baltic Diplomacy in the League of Nations." *Journal of Baltic Studies* 14:2 (Summer), 128–149.

Petri, Johan C. 1802. *Ehstland und die Ehsten oder historisch-geographisch-statistisches Gemälde von Ehsteland.* 3 vols. Gotha: n.p.

Philips, Peter. 1986. "A Soviet Estonian Soldier in Afghanistan." *Central Asian Survey* 5:1, 100–115.

Pillau, Endel, comp. 1989. *Eestimaa kuum suvi 1988* [Estonia's hot summer of 1988]. Tallinn: Olion.

Pistohlkors, Gert von. 1978. *Ritterschaftliche Reformpolitik zwischen Russifizierung und Revolution.* Göttinger Bausteine zur Geschichtswissenschaft, no. 48. Göttingen: Musterschmidt.

Pistohlkors, Gert von; Raun, Toivo U.; and Kaegbein, Paul, eds. 1987. *Die Universitäten Dorpat/Tartu, Riga und Wilna/Vilnius 1579–1979. Beiträge zur ihrer Geschichte und ihrer Wirkung im Grenzbereich zwischen Westen und Ost.* Köln-Wien: Böhlau.

Popovsky, Mark. 1986. "My Estonia." *Baltic Forum* 3:2 (Fall), 25–44.

Raidla, Peeter. 1991. *Liidu kütkeist on raske vabaneda: Poliitikakuud aastail 1987–1991* [It's hard to free oneself from the shackles of the Union: Month-by-month politics in 1987–1991]. Tallinn: Rekrea.

Rakowska-Harmstone, Teresa. 1986. "Baltic Nationalism and the Soviet Armed Forces." *Journal of Baltic Studies* 17:3 (Fall), 179–193.

Ränk, Gustav. 1976. *Old Estonia: The People and the Culture.* Bloomington: Indiana University Press.

Ratnieks, Henry. 1984. "Soviet Hydrocarbon Exports and the Baltics." *Journal of Baltic Studies* 15:4 (Winter), 282–302.

Rauch, Georg von. 1974. *The Baltic States: The Years of Independence, 1917–1940.* Berkeley: University of California Press.

Raun, Toivo U. 1981. "The Estonians." In Thaden, Edward C., et al., *Russification in the Baltic Provinces and Finland, 1855–1914,* 287–354. Princeton, N.J.: Princeton University Press.

———. 1982. "Estonian Social and Political Thought, 1905–February 1917." In Ezergailis, Andrew, and Pistohlkors, Gert von, eds., *Die baltischen Provinzen Russlands zwischen den Revolutionen von 1905 und 1917,* 59–72. Köln: Böhlau.

———. 1984a. "The Estonians and the Russian Empire, 1905–1917." *Journal of Baltic Studies* 15:2 (Summer), 130–140.

———. 1984b. "The Revolution of 1905 in the Baltic Provinces and Finland." *Slavic Review,* vol. 43, 453–467.

———. 1985a. "Language Development and Policy in Estonia." In Kreindler, Isabelle T., ed., *Sociolinguistic Perspectives on Soviet National Languages: Their Past, Present, and Future.* Contributions to the Sociology of Language, no. 40, 13–35. Berlin: Mouton de Gruyter.

———. 1985b. "The Role of Journalism in the Estonian National Awakening." In Loit, Aleksander, ed., *National Movements in the Baltic Countries During the 19th Century.* Studia Baltica Stockholmiensia, no. 2, 389–401. Stockholm: Almqvist & Wiksell International.

———. 1986a. "The Latvian and Estonian National Movements, 1860–1914." *Slavonic and East European Review,* vol. 64, 66–80.

———. 1986b. "Estonian Emigration Within the Russian Empire, 1860–1917." *Journal of Baltic Studies* 17:4 (Winter), 350–363.

———. 1987a. "Finland and Estonia: Cultural and Political Relations, 1917–1940." *Journal of Baltic Studies* 18:1 (Spring), 5–20.

———. 1987b. "The Role of Tartu University in Estonian Society and Culture, 1860–1914." In Pistohlkors, Gert von; Raun, Toivo U.; and Kaegbein, Paul, eds., *Die Universitäten Dorpat/Tartu, Riga und Wilna/Vilnius 1579–1979. Beiträge zur ihrer Geschichte und ihrer Wirkung im Grenzbereich zwischen Westen und Ost,* 123–142. Köln-Wien: Böhlau.

———. 1991a. *Estonia and the Estonians.* Stanford, Calif.: Hoover. First ed. 1987.

_____. 1991b. "The Re-Establishment of Estonian Independence." *Journal of Baltic Studies* 22:3 (Fall), 251–258.

_____. 1991c. "The Petseri Region of the Republic of Estonia." *Jahrbücher für Geschichte Osteuropas*, vol. 39, 514–532.

Raun, Toivo U., and Plakans, Andrejs. 1990. "The Estonian and Latvian National Movements: An Assessment of Miroslav Hroch's Model." *Journal of Baltic Studies* 21:2 (Summer), 131–144.

Rebas, Hain. 1988. "Baltic Regionalism??" *Journal of Baltic Studies* 19:2 (Summer), 101–116.

Rei, August. 1970. *The Drama of the Baltic Peoples.* 2d ed. Stockholm: Vaba Eesti.

Ruus, Jurij, and Usackas, Vygaudas. 1991. "The Transition to Polyarchy in Lithuania and Estonia." *Journal of Baltic Studies* 22:1 (Spring), 77–86.

Saagpakk, Paul F. 1982. *Estonian-English Dictionary.* New Haven: Yale University Press.

Salo, Vello, comp. 1989. *Population Losses in Estonia, June 1940–August 1941.* Scarborough, Canada: Maarjamaa.

Segal, Zvi. 1988. "Jewish Minorities in the Baltic Republics in the Postwar Years." *Journal of Baltic Studies* 19:1 (Spring), 60–66.

Shafir, Gershon. 1992. "Relative Overdevelopment and Alternative Paths of Nationalism: A Comparative Study of Catalonia and the Baltic Republics." *Journal of Baltic Studies* 23:2 (Summer), 105–120.

Shipler, David K. 1989. "A Reporter at Large: Symbols of Sovereignty." *New Yorker,* 18 September, 52–99.

Shtromas, Alexander. 1984. "Political and Legal Aspects of the Soviet Occupation and Incorporation of the Baltic States." *Baltic Forum* 1:1 (Fall), 24–38.

_____. 1985. "Soviet Occupation of the Baltic States and Their Incorporation in the U.S.S.R." *East European Quarterly* 19:3 (September), 289–304.

_____. 1986a. "Prospects for Restoring the Baltic States' Independence: A View on the Prerequisites and Possibilities of Their Realization." *Journal of Baltic Studies* 17:3 (Fall), 256–279.

_____. 1986b. *The Soviet Method of Conquest of the Baltic States: Lessons for the West.* Washington, D.C.: Washington Institute for Values in Public Policy.

Shultz, George P. 1990. "What I'd Tell Mikhail Sergeyevich." *Wall Street Journal,* 9 April.

Siilivask, Karl, ed. 1985. *History of Tartu University, 1632–1982.* Tallinn: Perioodika.

Šilbajoris, Rimvydas. 1989. "Some Recent Baltic Poets: The Civic Duty to Be Yourself." *Journal of Baltic Studies* 20:3 (Fall), 243–258.

Sinilind, Sirje [Juhan-Kristjan Talve]. 1984. *Estonia in the Prison of Nations.* Stockholm: Estonian Information Centre.

Soom, Arnold. 1954. *Der Herrenhof in Estland im 17. Jahrhundert.* Lund: Eesti Teaduslik Selts Rootsis.

Taagepera, Mare. 1983. "Ecological Problems in Estonia." *Journal of Baltic Studies* 14:4 (Winter), 307–314.

_____. 1989. "The Ecological and Political Problems of Phosphorite Mining in Estonia." *Journal of Baltic Studies* 22:2 (Summer), 165–174.

Taagepera, Rein. 1982. "Size and Ethnicity of Estonian Towns and Rural Districts, 1922–1979." *Journal of Baltic Studies* 13:2 (Summer), 105–127.

_____. 1983. "De-Choicing of Elections: July 1940 in Estonia." *Journal of Baltic Studies* 14:3 (Fall), 215–246.

_____. 1984a. *Softening Without Liberalization in the Soviet Union: The Case of Jüri Kukk.* Lanham, Md.: University Press of America.

_____. 1984b. "Lithuania, Latvia, and Estonia 1940–1980: Similarities and Differences." *Baltic Forum* 1:1 (Fall), 39–52.

_____. 1985. "Inclusion of the Baltic Republics in the Nordic Nuclear-Free Zone." *Journal of Baltic Studies* 16:1 (Spring), 33–51.

_____. 1986a. "Citizens' Peace Movement in the Soviet Baltic Republics." *Journal of Peace Research* 23:2, 183–192.

_____. 1986b. "One of the Twenty Million: A Soviet Estonian WWII Army Diary." Tenth Conference on Baltic Studies, University of Wisconsin, Madison, 29–31 May.

_____. 1987a. "Casualties of Soviet Estonian Army Units in WWII." Baltic Studies Conference in Scandinavia, University of Stockholm, 3–6 June.

_____. 1987b. "History Has Started to Move." *aabs Newsletter* 4:2 (August), 1–3.

_____. 1987c. "Who Assimilates Whom?—The World and the Baltic Region." *Journal of Baltic Studies* 18:3 (Fall), 269–282.

_____. 1988. "Estonia Under Gorbachev: Stalinists, Autonomists, and Nationalists." *Occasional Papers on Baltic Political Action* (Baltic Appeal to the United Nations), no. 2/3 (September), 2–15.

_____. 1989a. "Estonia in September 1988: Stalinists, Centrists, and Restorationists." *Journal of Baltic Studies* 20:2 (Summer), 175–190.

_____. 1989b. "How Empires End: Is the Soviet Union to Become a Commonwealth?" *Homeland,* 12–26 July.

_____. 1989c. "On Goodneighborly Relations of Estonia and the Soviet Union." *Homeland,* 30 August.

_____. 1989d. "Discrimination Against Estonians, 1939–1989." *Homeland,* 13–27 September.

_____. 1989e. "Estonia's Road to Independence." *Problems of Communism* 38:6 (November-December), 11–26.

_____. 1989f. "The Chain and the Course." *aabs Newsletter* 13:4 (December), 10.

_____. 1990a. "A Brash Nation Awaits Do-It-Yourself Election." *Los Angeles Times,* 22 February, B11.

_____. 1990b. "In 1776, George III Made Unbearable Demands." *Los Angeles Times,* 12 April, B9.

_____. 1990c. "A Note on the March 1989 Elections in Estonia." *Soviet Studies* 42:2 (April), 329–339.

_____. 1990d. "The Baltic States." *Electoral Studies* 9:4 (December), 303–311.

_____. 1991. "Building Democracy in Estonia." *PS: Political Science and Politics* (American Political Science Association) 24:3 (September), 478–481.

_____. 1992. "Ethnic Relations in Estonia." *Journal of Baltic Studies* 23:2 (Summer), 121–132.

Taagepera, Rein, and Shugart, Matthew S. 1989. *Seats and Votes: The Effects and Determinants of Electoral Systems.* New Haven: Yale University Press.

Thaden, Edward C. 1984. "Finland and the Baltic Provinces: Elite Roles and Social and Economic Conditions and Structures." *Journal of Baltic Studies* 15:2/3 (Summer/Fall), 216–227.

––––––. 1985. "Baltic National Movements During the Nineteenth Century." *Journal of Baltic Studies* 16:4 (Winter), 411–421.

Thaden, Edward C., et al. 1981. *Russification in the Baltic Provinces and Finland, 1855–1914.* Princeton, N.J.: Princeton University Press.

Thomson, Clare. 1992. *The Singing Revolution: A Political Journey Through the Baltic States.* London: Michael.

Trapans, Arveds, ed. 1991. *Toward Independence: The Baltic Popular Movements.* Boulder, Colo.: Westview.

Treiman, Jaak. 1990. "The Soviet Secession Law Is a Sham." *Wall Street Journal* (European edition), 3 July.

Uibopuu, Henn-Jüri. 1988. "The USSR's Basic Legislation: Legislative Authority of the Baltic Republics." *Journal of Baltic Studies* 19:2 (Summer), 117–128.

Urban, William. 1975. *The Baltic Crusade.* Dekalb: Northern Illinois University Press.

––––––. 1981. *The Livonian Crusade.* Washington, D.C.: University Press of America.

Uustalu, Evald. 1952. *The History of Estonian People.* London: Boreas.

––––––. 1977. *For Freedom Only: The Story of Estonian Volunteers in the Finnish War of 1940–1944.* Toronto: Northern Publications.

Valgemäe, Mardi. 1989. "The Thermopoetics of Hando Runnel." *Journal of Baltic Studies* 20:3 (Fall), 259–264.

Vardys, V. Stanley. 1981. "Human Rights Issues in Estonia, Latvia, and Lithuania." *Journal of Baltic Studies* 12:3 (Fall), 275–298.

––––––. 1987. "The Role of the Churches in the Maintenance of Regional and National Identity in the Baltic Republics." *Journal of Baltic Studies* 18:3 (Fall), 287–300.

Vardys, V. Stanley, and Misiunas, Romuald J., eds. 1981. *The Baltic States in Peace and War, 1917–1945.* University Park: Pennsylvania State University Press.

Vesilind, Priit. 1990. "The Baltic Nations." *National Geographic* 178:5 (November), 2–27.

Viires, Ants. 1986. "Discovering Estonian Folk Art at the Beginning of the 20th Century." *Journal of Baltic Studies* 17:2 (Summer), 79–97.

––––––. 1991. "The Development of Estonian Ethnography During the 20th Century," *Journal of Baltic Studies* 22:2 (Summer), 123–132.

Vuorela, Toivo. 1964. *The Finno-Ugric Peoples,* trans. John Atkinson. Indiana University Publications. Uralic and Altaic Series, no. 39. The Hague: Mouton.

Westing, Arthur H. 1988. "The Greening of Estonia." *Environmental Conservation* 15:4 (Winter), 299–302.

JOURNALS AND NEWSPAPERS

This section includes only periodicals mentioned in chapter notes and published in Estonia or elsewhere in Estonian or specifically dealing with the Baltic states. Many Estonian periodicals were renamed around 1990, abandoning Soviet titles and often returning to pre-occupation ones.

aabs Newsletter, quarterly, New Jersey, Association for the Advancement of Baltic Studies, 1976–.

Baltic Events, bimonthly newsletter, Rein Taagepera (University of California, Irvine) and Juris Dreifelds (Brock University, Canada), 1972–1975. Former title (1967–1972): *Estonian Events.*

Baltic Forum, biannual, New York, 1984–1989.

Baltic Independent, weekly, Tallinn, 1991–. Former titles (1985–July 1990): *Homeland,* a supplement to *Kodumaa,* and (August 1990–June 1991); *Estonian Independent.*

Bulletin of Baltic Studies—see *Journal of Baltic Studies.*

Edasi [Forward]—see *Postimees.*

Eesti Aeg [Estonian times], weekly, Tallinn, 1991–.

Eesti Ekspress [Estonian express], weekly, Tallinn, 1989–.

Eesti Loodus [Estonian nature], monthly, Tallinn, 1958–.

Estonian Events—see *Baltic Events.*

Estonian Independent—see *Baltic Independent.*

Estoniia, daily, Tallinn, in Russian, September 1991–. Former title (1940–1941 and 1944–1991): *Sovetskaia Estoniia.*

Homeland—see *Baltic Independent.*

Journal of Baltic Studies, quarterly, New Jersey, Association for the Advancement of Baltic Studies, 1971–. Former title (1970–1971): *Bulletin of Baltic Studies.*

Kodumaa [Homeland], weekly, Tallinn, 1958–.

Lisandusi mõtete ja uudiste vabale levikule Eestis [Contributions to unimpeded circulation of ideas and news in Estonia], irregular, underground, Estonia, 1978–1986. Issue numbers 1–19 (1978–1984) have been reprinted in Sweden (Stockholm: Relief Centre for Estonian Prisoners of Conscience in the USSR, 1984–1986).

Lituanus, quarterly, Chicago, 1954–.

Looming [Creation], monthly, Tallinn, 1923–1941 and 1945–.

Nationalities Papers, semiannual, United States, Association for the Study of Nationalities of the USSR and Eastern Europe, 1973–.

Noorte Hääl [Voice of the youth]—see *Päevaleht.*

Õhtuleht [Evening paper], daily, Tallinn, 1944–.

Päevaleht [Daily paper], daily, Tallinn, 1905–1940 and 1990–. Former title (1940–1941 and 1944–January 1990): *Noorte Hääl.*

Postimees [The courier], daily, Tartu, 1886–1940, 1941–1944, 1945–1948, and 1991–. Former titles (1940–1941): *Tartu Kommunist;* (1944) *Uus Postimees* [The New Courier]; and (1948–December 1990) *Edasi.*

Raduga [Rainbow]—see *Vikerkaar.*

Rahva Hääl [The people's voice], daily, Tallinn, 1940–1941 and 1944–.

Reede [Friday]—see *Sirp*.

Sirp [Sickle], weekly, Tallinn, 1991–. Former titles (1940–1941 and 1944–1989): *Sirp ja Vasar* and (1990) *Reede*.

Sirp ja Vasar [Hammer and sickle]—see *Sirp*.

Sovetskaia Estoniia—see *Estoniia*.

Vaba Eestlane [Free Estonian], twice weekly, Toronto, Canada, 1951–.

Vikerkaar [Rainbow], monthly, Tallinn, 1986–. Russian edition, *Raduga*.

DOCUMENT AND DATA COLLECTIONS

Baltic Assembly, Tallinn, May 13–14, 1989. Tallinn: Valgus, 1989.

Baltic Chronology: Estonia, Latvia, Lithuania 1989. New York: BATUN (Baltic Appeal to the United Nations).

Baltic Chronology: Estonia, Latvia, Lithuania 1990. New York: BATUN.

Baltic Chronology: Estonia, Latvia, Lithuania 1991, monthly issues. New York: BATUN.

The Baltic States: A Reference Book. Tallinn/Riga/Vilnius: Estonian, Latvian, and Lithuanian Encyclopedia Publishers, 1991.

Diskussioonid IME-projekti üle [Discussions about the economic self-management project]. Liina Tõnisson and Erik Terk, comps. Tallinn, 1991. Reprints of press articles, September 1987–February 1988.

Documents from Estonia: Articles, Speeches, Resolutions, Letters, Editorials, Interviews Concerning Recent Developments, from April 1986 to March 1989. Michael Tarm and Mari-Ann Rikken, eds. New York: Estonian American National Council, 1989.

Documents from Estonia: Articles, Speeches, Resolutions, Letters, Editorials, Interviews Concerning Recent Developments, vol. II. Michael Tarm and Mari-Ann Rikken, eds. New York: Estonian American National Council, 1990.

Documents from Estonia on the Violations of Human Rights. Stockholm: Estonian Information Centre, 1977.

Eesti Komitee ja juhatuse materjalid [Materials of the Estonian Committee and its board]. Tallinn, 1991.

Eesti NSV üheteistkümnenda koosseisu erakorraline kaheksas istungjärk 16. novembril 1988—Stenogramm [The extraordinary eighth session of the eleventh Supreme Soviet of the Estonian SSR, 16 November 1988—stenograph]. Tallinn: Eesti Raamat, 1989.

Narodnyi kongress: Sbornik materialov kongressa Narodnogo Fronta Estonii, 1–2 oktiabria 1988 g. [People's Congress: collection of materials of the Congress of the Popular Front of Estonia, 1–2 October 1988]. Tallinn: Perioodika, 1989. Also in Estonian. For a shorter English version, see *The Popular Front of Estonia*.

Nazi-Soviet Conspiracy and the Baltic States: Diplomatic Documents and Other Evidence. August Rei, ed. London: Boreas, 1948.

Nazi-Soviet Relations, 1939–1941: Documents from the Archives of the German Foreign Office. Raymond J. Sontag and James S. Beddie, eds. Washington, D.C.: U.S. Department of State, 1948.

1940 god v Estonii: Dokumenty i materialy [The year 1940 in Estonia: Documents and materials]. Arno Köörna et al., comps. Tallinn: Olion, 1989.

The Popular Front of Estonia: Charter, General Programme, Resolutions, Manifesto, adopted at the Congress of the Popular Front of Estonia on October 2, 1988. Tallinn: Perioodika, 1989.

Restoration of the Independence of the Republic of Estonia: Selection of Legal Acts (1988–1991). Advig Kiris, comp. Tallinn: Estonian Institute for Information, 1991.

"Samizdat Documents from the Period 1969–1987." Dzintra Bungs, comp. *Journal of Baltic Studies* 19:3 (Fall 1988), 272–299.

The Soviet-German Secret Agreements of 1939 and 1941 in Retrospect: A Selection of Materials. Dietrich André Loeber, ed. Hamburg, 1989.

Third Interim Report of the Select Committee on Communist Aggression. 83rd Congress, 2d Session. Washington, 1954. Reprinted as *The Baltic States: A Study of Their Origin and National Development; Their Seizure and Incorporation into the USSR.* Buffalo, N.Y.: International Military Law and History Reprint Series, vol. 4, 1972.

World War II and Soviet Occupation in Estonia: A Damages Report. Juhan Kahk, ed. Tallinn: Perioodika, 1991.

· About the Book and Author ·

After breaking free from the Bolsheviks in 1918, Estonia enjoyed independence until 1940 when the country was subsumed by the Soviet Union. Not until 1991 was Estonia able to make its next successful bid for sovereignty. In this book, Rein Taagepera traces the evolution of Estonia from prehistory to the present, when a radical turn of events in the former Soviet Union once again altered the destiny of this Baltic nation.

The author explores in depth the remarkable changes in Estonia since 1980, framing his analysis within the larger picture of the Soviet Union and its demise. He also examines the issue of ethnic tensions between Estonians and Russian colonists and speculates on how unrest will affect the future of the country. Throughout his analysis, the author weaves in such key questions as: Why did Sovietization fail? How did Estonia's quest for autonomy affect Soviet dissolution? What role will the country play on the global stage? What will Estonia's future hold?

Rein Taagepera is professor of social science at the University of California–Irvine and was a member of Estonia's 1991 Constitutional Assembly. Dr. Taagepera was born in 1933 in Tartu, Estonia, and left the country with his family in 1944. He specializes in the analysis of electoral systems worldwide and in 1992 was the founding dean of a new School of Social Sciences at Tartu University and a presidential candidate in Estonian elections.

· Index ·

255